(85)OK

LEGACY OF CLASSICAL DANCES IN INDIA

LEGACY OF CLASSICAL DANCES IN INDIA

USHA MEHTA

CYBER TECH PUBLICATIONS
4264/3, Ansari Road, Daryaganj, New Delhi-110002 (India)
Ph.: 011-23244078, 011-43559448 Fax: 011-23280028
E-Mail: cyberpublicationsdelhi@yahoo.com
Website: www.cybertechpublications.com

LEGACY OF CLASSICAL DANCES IN INDIA

USHA MEHTA

First Edition 2011

Published by :

G.S. Rawat for **Cyber Tech Publications**

4264/3, Ansari Road, Daryaganj, New Delhi-110002 (India)

Ph.: 011-23244078, 011-43559448 Fax: 011-23280028

E-Mail: cyberpublicationsdelhi@yahoo.com

Website: www.cybertechpublications.com

Printed at: Asian Offset Printers, Delhi-53

Contents

Preface

The twenty-first century, such a neat division into mutually exclusive territories no longer holds; nor indeed, as this book demonstrates, were such strict demarcations ever wholly operative in dance research. Some branches of ethnography, in the Eastern European and Scandinavian disciplines of ethnology, ethnography, and folk life studies, explicitly aimed to document dances from the past by seeking out older ways of life to record for posterity. From the middle of the twentieth century, some historians of dance, influenced by Western European and North American practices of oral history, for example, similarly found sources among the living about dancing that was no longer performed. In pursuing dance research, it has not always been easy, nor necessarily desirable, to ignore the potential benefits to be gained by combining synchronic and diachronic perspectives.

Both ethnography and history may be found interrelated in studies of dance that, for their theoretical and methodological frameworks, are located in anthropology, ethnology, cultural studies, social and cultural history, performance studies, sociology, ethnomusicology, and folklore studies. There are also the hybrid disciplines that clearly indicate their focus on dance, as in dance anthropology, dance ethnology, and ethno-choreology. As a comparatively new subject within academia, dance studies in general draws upon established disciplinary frameworks in which ethnographic and historical methods have already taken on distinctive hues that may not always be immediately evident to the dance researcher's eye. Very often the precise meaning of ethnography and history when applied within a particular discipline may be the result of certain intellectual traditions and geographical circumstances. There is, for example, no consensus about the meaning of the term "ethnography," even within its home disciplinary bases of the social sciences.

—Author

1

Dance, History and Ethnography

FRAMEWORKS, SOURCES, AND IDENTITIES OF PAST AND PRESENT

Ethnography and history, as methodologies through which dance may be researched, suggest contrasting spheres of space and time. For the dance ethnographer, her or his usual territory is that of the field, where source materials are created through the researcher's systematic description of the transient actions and words of people dancing in the present. For the dance historian, the familiar realm is the archive, where extant sources, often fragmentary and sparse, have been created by people other than the researcher, who now employs their surviving artifacts as testimony to the dancing of the past. Stereotypically, the dance ethnographer investigates the customary dance practices of an aggregate of people, such as an ethnic or cultural group. The dance historian more frequently focuses on individuals or perhaps a dance company, often seeking evidence of innovative rather than consensual activity.

In the twenty-first century, such a neat division into mutually exclusive territories no longer holds; nor indeed, as this book demonstrates, were such strict demarcations ever wholly operative in dance research. Some branches of ethnography, in the Eastern European and Scandinavian disciplines of ethnology, ethnography, and folk life studies, explicitly aimed to document dances from the past by seeking out older ways of life to record for posterity. From the middle of the twentieth century, some historians of dance, influenced by Western European and North American practices of oral history, for example, similarly found sources among the living about dancing that was no longer performed. In pursuing dance research, it has not always been easy, nor necessarily desirable, to ignore the potential benefits to be gained by combining synchronic and diachronic perspectives.

Both ethnography and history may be found interrelated in studies of dance that, for their theoretical and methodological frameworks, are located in anthropology, ethnology, cultural studies, social and cultural history, performance studies, sociology, ethnomusicology, and folklore studies. There are also the hybrid disciplines that clearly indicate their focus on dance, as in dance anthropology, dance ethnology, and ethno-choreology. As a comparatively new subject within academia, dance studies in general draws upon established disciplinary frameworks in which ethnographic and historical methods have already taken on distinctive hues that may not always be immediately evident to the dance researcher's eye. Very often the precise meaning of ethnography and history when applied within a particular discipline may be the result of certain intellectual traditions and geographical circumstances. There is, for example, no consensus about the meaning of the term "ethnography," even within its home disciplinary bases of the social sciences. It is beyond the scope of this introductory chapter to explore the detailed and diverse terrain of disciplinary legacies, differences, and correspondences in their application to dance. But some background to the older traditions of dance ethnography and dance history, together with some reflections on past and present sources and identities of dance, are presented here as a frame through which the essays that constitute this book may be viewed.

DISCIPLINARY FRAMEWORKS AND QUESTIONS OF CONTEXT

The terms "ethnography" and "history" share the characteristics of referring simultaneously to their practice and to their end result. In most West European and North American practice, ethnography is a methodology that deals with the present and typically concludes in a book known as an ethnographic monograph or ethnography. History—or, more properly, the historical method—similarly signals a methodology but investigates the past to produce a history, also most often in book form. The practice of dance history and the production of dance histories were established features of mainstream dance scholarship for much of the twentieth century.

For most of that period, mainstream dance scholarship in North America concentrated on dance as an art form. This was certainly the case during the late 1960s when dancer and anthropologist Joann Kea-liinohomoku wrote her seminal article on ballet as an ethnic form of dance. Research that addressed consensual meanings and the socio-cultural contextualization of dance was regarded as the sole concern of anthropologists. Anthropologists, unlike most dance scholars, predominantly studied supposedly oral, homogenous societies that were positioned as "other" to so-called civilized and literate white European and North American society. Oral cultures were believed to possess no history since there were often no literary records to study their pasts. In any case anthropologists sought to understand the present of cultures as holistic systems, an aim for which the methodology of ethnography— documenting and explaining the present—was essential. Culture, in the broad anthropological sense of a discrete systematic totality of socially transmitted beliefs, values, institutions, and practices, became a hugely influential concept across academia in the later twentieth century, even if debate raged over its usefulness as an analytical construct both within and outside its home discipline.

In the 1960s, though, for most dance scholars, the term "culture" had quite another meaning. Culture was instead understood as synonymous with "high" art. This meaning, as elucidated by Victorian literary critic Matthew Arnold, equated culture with "the best which has been thought and said." Such a definition positioned popular or vernacular artistic expression in opposition, so that the category of culture as "high" accorded with the preferred arts of the aristocracy and bourgeoisie. Artifacts and practices eligible for the designation of "culture," furthermore, were evaluated by Eurocentric criteria for the label of "art." This socially hierarchical and evolutionist conception of culture continued to hold sway in the middle of the twentieth century, and most dance scholars were not unusual in professing it. In line with other arts and humanities subjects, those forms and practices deemed by society to possess high aesthetic value were granted primacy as sources for academic investigation. Accordingly, dance forms other than ballet and modern dance were ranked lower in this order of aesthetic values and received less attention.

Those scholars interested in the arts of non-Western cultures, or in forms and practices other than those regarded as high culture, sought theoretical perspectives and methodologies that aimed to circumvent Eurocentric and evolutionist bias. Their work owed much to the outlook of the human sciences, particularly to the discipline of anthropology. In these studies, following classical anthropology, the focus was upon contemporary manifestations of movement in societies that had been colonized and where the retrieval of history was not a priority. Classically trained anthropologists preferred to designate the field of study as that of culturally codified human movement systems. They thus highlighted the fact that the concept of dance was not necessarily universal and underscored anthropological concern with indigenous conceptualizations of dance and related phenomena.

Anthropological thinking had a shaping influence on the discipline of dance ethnology in the dance department at the University of California, Los Angeles (UCLA). Unlike studies of dance conducted from within departments of anthropology, here there was greater use of literature from the European disciplines of ethnology, ethnography, and folk life studies. In European ethnographic studies of dance, it was not necessary to question what conceptually constituted dance, since the object of inquiry was the dance of one's own culture. Another characteristic of European ethnographic study was the status of the past and its continuing relevance to the present.

In Eastern Europe, much of the research on dance was carried out within the long established and government-funded institutes of ethnology and ethnography, where the folk paradigm continues to dominate. In North America and Western Europe, the concept of "the people" or "the folk" has been subject to considerable critique since the second half of the twentieth century, even where the disciplines of folklore studies and folk life studies have been maintained within the university sector. In this academic context, the early-twentieth-century conceptualizations and practices of anthropology and folk studies have been the subject of political interrogation, especially with respect to their construction in and contribution to the maintenance of power inequalities.

If the ongoing legacies of colonialism have been the source of much debate in classical anthropology, in folk studies the major dispute has concerned political affiliations with nationalism. Through this examination, the concept of the folk has been revealed as an ideological construct whereby rural communities and their older practices were perceived by the intelligentsia as survivals from an ancient, pure culture.

This "folk culture" had become a resource for asserting specific ethnic and ultimately national identity and was principally constructed in opposition to European high culture. With respect to dance categorization, cosmopolitan genres such as ballet were positioned as comparatively recent, individually and consciously created sophisticated art forms, in contrast to primitive, simple "natural" folk dances that arose as a collective spontaneous expression of a people's spirit. The songs, dances, poetry, costume, dialect, and so on of the peasantry were collected as relics of antiquity since such expressive forms were believed to be dying out in the advance of modernity. The process and motivation behind this form of cultural rescue archaeology shared similar aims to that of nineteenth-century anthropological activities, and both shared an evolutionist perspective. It was deemed essential to collect the signs of primitive and folk cultures for posterity, before they became contaminated by modern civilization and disappeared in the wake of urbanization and industrialization.

Given the significance of history in nation building and in articulating ancient ethnic identities, a diachronic perspective has been an integral part of folk studies for most of its existence. The political significance of history has ensured a continuous emphasis on selecting dance forms with long histories of performance tied to place or ethnicity. Largely as a result of the political situation when much pioneering work on dance was carried out in Eastern Europe during the Cold War years of 1945–89, the dominant attention was not so much on issues of socio-cultural context but on the dance forms themselves.

The past has been granted a differing status in classical forms of anthropology and folk studies, having been viewed as irrelevant to scholarly exegeses of cultural practices in the former and pivotal to those of the latter. As suggested above, however, this broad characterization does not reveal the nuances and exceptions in approach that came increasingly to the fore from the 1970s onward. In the extensive literature in anthropology that does engage with historical perspectives are a number of works on dance such as those by Adrienne Kaeppler, Cynthia Novack, Sally Ann Ness, and Zoila S. Mendoza. In late-twentieth-century writings, proper attention to colonialist legacies has necessitated engagement with the past, not in a naive replacement of the colonizer's histories with those of the colonized, but in a critical recognition of their mutually constitutive nature.17 Within the broad frame of folk studies, as pursued in North America, Britain, and Scandinavia in particular, challenges to nationalist legacies in the scholarship have resulted in critiques of dance scholarship and practice that have arisen from examination of historical records, both written and oral.

Beyond these more established paradigms of anthropology and folk studies, ethnographic and historical perspectives on dance have been utilized within the fields of cultural studies, performance studies, and sociology. A clear indication of growing interest in ethnographic perspectives on dance is the specialized designation of "dance ethnography." The application of this label emerged more purposefully from the New York school of performance studies during the 1990s to indicate a specific focus on dance as embodied cultural knowledge. Exploration of this premise is realized through methodological and theoretical approaches, drawn from feminism and postmodern anthropology to address the distinctive nature of an ethnographic practice that is "necessarily grounded in the body and the body's experience." Elsewhere, as in my own usage of the term, the term "dance ethnography" has been employed as an umbrella term to embrace a variety of intellectual traditions and theoretical positions.

There has been considerable cross-fertilization between disciplines that have traditionally used ethnographic and historical perspectives in the study of dance and increasingly so, following both the fall of the Berlin Wall in 1989 and the earlier shift toward dismantling disciplinary boundaries in the arts and humanities in the late twentieth century. Nonetheless, all terms and methodologies have legacies, and it must be remembered that the selection of disciplinary context is fundamental to both methodological procedures and analytical outcomes. The choice of social context through which to investigate dance emerges from the choice of disciplinary context. The social context, however defined, whether as the anthropological understanding of "culture" or as ethnic group in the concept of "the folk," provides both frame and resources for interpretation. The problem with all contexts, of course, is that they are "constructed for specific purposes and thus always negotiable, which makes futile any attempts at defining contexts substantively." This means that it is imperative for researchers and readers to make public the circumstances of their choice and to identify as far as possible ensuing implications for their interpretation of dance.

ETHNOGRAPHY AND HISTORY: METHODOLOGIES AND SOURCES FOR DANCE

The differing contexts of "culture" and "folk," in whatever guise they are utilized as an interpretive framework, lead to differing practices in the methodology of ethnography and in the delineation of the field. Typically, ethnography in classical anthropology has entailed long periods of a year or more living within the selected society, which traditionally has been far from the researcher's normal country of residence. The focus continues to be on the present. In folk studies, in contrast, the researcher tends to work within her or his own country and undertakes more restricted field trips.

This latter style is generally characteristic of ethnographic work undertaken in sociology, a discipline in which ethnography has been practiced since the early twentieth century. British sociologist Helen Thomas characterizes ethnography as an in-depth study of a culture, institution and context over a sustained period of time, which is usually longer for anthropologists than sociologists. Ethnographic research employs a range of methods and techniques such as participant-observation, interviews, filed [*sic* field] notes, audio and visual recordings and, in the case of dance, movement analysis. The aims of ethnography, the (far/near) relation between representation and reality and the observer and the observed, are subject to debate and largely depend on the theoretical, political and/or methodological stance of the individual researcher.

One thing is clear: ethnography is not a set of methods to collect data. Nor is it value-free description. In anthropology and sociology, the aims of ethnography are to analyze and interpret the perspectives and evaluative concerns of insiders; it is not to impose judgments, explicit or implicit, that are derived from the researcher's own cultural position. In this approach, the fieldwork is normally conducted by an individual. In Eastern European ethnography, the aims have been to observe, document, and analyze the cultural forms as manifestations of past and present ethnic identities. More typically here, the research is conducted by a team composed of specialists in different cultural forms, such as music, song, and costume.

Aside from distinctions relating to intellectual traditions across differing continents, over the twentieth century and into the twenty-first, ethnography has been utilized in a myriad of ways across a diverse range of disciplines. Within the narrower band of the social sciences as formulated in Western Europe and North America, it "escapes ready summary definitions. . . . [and] has become a site of debate and contestation within and across disciplinary boundaries." Ethnography's exact interpretation and application have never been uniform in anthropology, sociology, and folk studies, but within these contexts ethnography has at least a common history of initial development within the positivist paradigms of the early twentieth century. It was believed that if the fieldwork had been conducted properly in the first place with sufficient scholarly precision and objectivity, the results could be replicated on subsequent visits and by other equally proficient ethnographers. This "scientific method" underpins the ethnography practiced in much of Eastern Europe, where the very term of "ethnography" also signals a disciplinary framework that remains very much rooted within positivist sensibilities. The aim to document traditional rural culture for posterity relies upon belief in a past that can be systematically and objectively recorded.

In the wake of postmodernism, these once cherished certainties, believed to be indicative of true scientific method, have broken down in the practice of ethnography across much of Western Europe and North America. The post-positivist climate has led to recognition that however much rigor the ethnographer exercises, the field does not have a static existence in "reality"; results cannot be replicated. So, too, the once strict division between "insider informant" and "outsider researcher," positioned as such in the name of objective scholarship, has also undergone considerable criticism in the post-positivist climate. The notion of the field as a site of inquiry has itself been subject to much debate, being recognized as just as much a construction of historical, so-ciocultural, and personal circumstance as the data discovered within it. Despite the crises surrounding ethnography in Western Europe and North America, the methodology has emerged, having undergone the fires of intense criticism, still recognizable as a distinctive practice, if perhaps differently forged than earlier in the twentieth century.

Such epistemological concerns have equally swept across the study of the past. The impact of post-positivist "new history" on dance historiography has enjoyed greater prominence in mainstream dance scholarship than that of reflexive ethnography, largely as a result of dance academia's traditions of scholarly interest. Increasing engagement with ideas that the past can only be known through the present, that it is particularized and subject to manipulation, has opened up new territories for research and debate. In the new history, there can be no one "true" account of a historical event, as recognition of multiple perspectives reveals the complexities underlying what was once selected and interpreted as singular fact; for "when it comes to the historical record, there are no grounds to be found in the record itself for preferring one way of construing its meaning rather than another."

Not only does the researcher shape the field of inquiry that is determined as the past or the present, but historical or ethnographic sources are inevitably part of that shifting process. Recognition of and engagement with issues and dilemmas raised by post-positivism, however, should not necessarily lead to anarchical clouds of unknowing in the pursuit of ethnographic and historical methodologies in studying dance. Nor should they ever be an excuse for not following precise scholarly procedures of critical evaluation and reflection upon source materials, whether they have been garnered in the past or present.

EVALUATING PAST AND PRESENT SOURCES FOR DANCE

In moving from the present to the past in research into dance as cultural practice, the investigator has a number of source materials at her or his disposal, including personally recorded ethnographic field notes or those written by previous researchers; taped interviews; traditional historical sources such as journal entries, diaries, and letters; iconographic material such as paintings and photographs; audiovisual records of film and videotape; and personal memory in both its traditionally understood meaning as a product of "mind" and as an embodied manifestation.

Traditionally, written evidence has been deemed the province of historians; the oral, that of anthropologists and folklorists. The oral traditions of so-called folk and primitive cultures were judged through European literate eyes to be poor history and therefore rarely admissible as factual evidence. Since the mid-twentieth century, however, the discipline of history has largely rejected the former hierarchical relationship between oral and written testimonies. Historians accept that the written is not necessarily any more reliable than the oral, both being situational records of perceived realities. Furthermore, within the disciplines of anthropology, folk studies, and history, there has been increased recognition that in the construction of histories, both written and oral, the interaction and interreliance of evidence stemming from both types of material is often richly complex. To an extent, of course, ethnography is always history, in that the events recorded have already passed in time. But the ethnographer usually has the benefit of moving people to observe, imitate, and hopefully interact with when pursuing an investigation; not so the researcher of the past, the historian, who must locate and interpret sources that bear witness to the transient nature of dance.

In the majority of dance scholarship, both past and present, most of the documentation has been made by those external to the dancing itself, even if witnessed at source. Both anthropology and history as disciplines owe their existence to textualizing practices. The ethnographer commits her or his observations to a variety of texts, both written and visual, before drawing upon them to create the written monograph. The historian, as dance scholar and anthropologist Georgiana Gore observes, normally uses the records of other people. She points out that both anthropologist and historian require the legitimating "presence of the author."

This is a vital process of validation in both ethnographic and historical methodology, although the motivation and positioning of the author should always be subject to questioning. In distinguishing between first- and second-hand testimonies, "the source which in history is considered primary . . . would be generally considered secondary in anthropology." An anthropologist or folklorist is the author of the written field notes, the taker of the photograph, the maker of the film, the notator of the dances, or the recorder of the interview. A historian's primary sources, on the other hand, have always been constructed by somebody else. Yet a further distinction occurs between the anthropologist and the folklorist in their written documentation. The folklorist's field notes have always been written for public consumption; she or he creates records as historical documents, in the sure knowledge of their future use in the archive. There has always been an intended audience. Not so the traditional anthropologist whose field notes and journals have typically been private documents.

Traditional textual sources of the past frequently prove fragmentary, scattered, and sparse. In contrast, sources of the present may appear to offer a clear route to the lost past. Individual oral testimony has a long and rich history of being fruitfully mined in folk studies to recover past practices in dance. But testimonies articulated in language, whether in oral or written form, are not the only sources in the present. When conceived as a repository of cultural meanings both past and present, the moving body may be a source to be observed and documented from the outside.

Traces of the past may be discovered in the ways in which people execute particular movements and use their bodies; but caution needs to be exercised. Researchers of today do not possess the same bodies as those constituted in different material and symbolic circumstances of particular pasts. When attempting to uncover cultural values of the past in present dance forms, other source materials need to be consulted in elucidating this archaeology of the body. The physical biography of the individual dancer may not always be the same as the idealized cultural notions of the dancer's body—age, injury, and health may transform earlier practices, and as a living, moving source, the body may not always replicate with exactitude the moves of the past. Treating "the body" as a text to be read carries inherent dangers of objectification and Cartesian dualities of inner/outer meaning. But new strategies have arisen in a seemingly phenomenologically driven approach to understanding the moving body from an ethnographic perspective.

In ethnographic descriptions of dancing in the present, it has become a favored technique since the 1990s to use the researcher's body as a means of access to information. Cultural embodiment is explored through the researcher's participation in and reflection upon the dancing. Movement competence in the cultural forms on the part of the researcher has always been an essential strategy of dance scholarship since at least the 1950s, but as Sally Ann Ness makes clear, the later mode of participation as a research tactic is of a different order. One obvious difference to the objectified ethnographic descriptions of the earlier inquiries has been the foregrounding of participation. The researcher's own movement experiences become part of the means of comparative analysis.

Such an approach is not without its epistemological dangers, as anthropologist and semasiologist Brenda Farnell has argued. Nonetheless, the "I" persona as a source, dancing and reflecting on sensation and meaning, has produced a significant extension and alternative to earlier objective modes of analysis. In this endeavor, the methodology of embodied practice in late-twentieth-century ethnography, despite obvious analogies, is not, according to Ness, phenomenological in its inquiry, since the aim is to gain, rather than to "bracket out" cultural understanding. In these examinations of the dancing self as culturally embodied, the individual's potential location in relation to the parameters and associated values of time and space operates within a largely consensual framework of meaning. The performance and representation of self in such studies, though, is not reduced to that of static and "perfect replicants of some cultural template." Instead, the process affords opportunity to explore embodied cultural knowledge as temporally and spatially dynamic, situational in its meaning, and creative in the interstices of personal and communal histories that reach across experiences of researcher and researched. Such departures of inquiry are often inextricably, though not exclusively, linked with issues of identity.

CONSTRUCTING IDENTITIES THROUGH DANCE: MYTHIC PASTS AND CULTURAL MEMORY

Postmodern scholarship has challenged notions of identity as being singular and essential in character, treating the performance of identity as historical and sociocultural. Since the 1980s, a considerable literature has viewed dance performance through the lenses of gender, race, ethnicity, nation, and age, all of which have diachronic trajectories to explore; "any activity or practice, the agents who engage in them and the patients who are their subjects, are themselves partly a consequence of, but are not fully determined by, past practices and activities." Whether we construe the contexts of past(s) as culture, national heritage, tradition, local history, or oral history, affiliation to the particular construct and its use in the present often serves the needs and aspirations of personal and communal identities. The use of dance as a symbolic political strategy in shaping a future society was particularly evident in the often integrated aims of research and reconstruction in the institutes and state dance ensembles of Cold War Eastern Europe. This formula for collecting, selecting, and constructing once participatory dances for staged display has been pursued elsewhere in the world to various ends.

The use of a dance form to evoke former or authentic contexts of performance may often be encountered in the public domain. Performances of traditional dances in international festivals and in tourist displays owe much to a twin embracing of the powers of nostalgia and exoticism. Audience and performers are locked in a mutually constitutive framework of interpretation and appreciation in which they, the modern, gaze at dance, the tradition. In this respect dance is emblematic of another culture, or another past that the audience cannot access through normal travel. As such, the act of dancing has become a piece of repertoire, an object of aesthetic appreciation, and a symbol of a way of life. In such stagings, in a manner analogous to that of a traditional museum exhibition, the audiences' lack of access to the dances' former histories precludes them from recognizing their own positioning or from understanding the lived experience of its earlier dancers. The historicity of the past is denied to the audience since all that is represented to them is a piece of theater with no ethnographic context. Often this is presented nonetheless as an authentic representation of another culture or a since vanished piece of history.

Critical literature on concepts of "cultural heritage" and "invented traditions" by historians David Lowenthal and Eric Hobsbawm has influenced considerable interrogation of how the past is represented in the present. The move to debunk what has popularly been regarded as authentic history and traditions of origin has been particularly visible in studies of dance with professed ancient histories. Much discussed examples are the Indian genre of bharata natyam and the English morris, both of which appear in this book.

Such analyses have certainly been useful correctives to an uncritical acceptance or failure to engage with mythic histories. Interrogations of "invented traditions" demonstrate that formerly unchallenged conceptualizations and performances of the past may have functional purposes for particular groups or agents in terms of power relations. The performance of memory, whatever the political discourse within which it is constructed, may also be considered through other analytical perspectives.

Anthropologist Paul Connerton's distinction between incorporation and inscription as modes of documentation offer important signposts to the study of cultural memory as embodied performance in which the practices of ethnography and history may be aligned.45 His characterization follows classic divisions between bodily, ultimately transient modes of transmission (incorporation) and those of traditional textual practices that use language or visual delineation to fix the moment (inscription).

Elsewhere I have suggested that "in traditional forms of danced display . . . longevity of human memory is publicly enacted, demonstrating the ethereality of human existence and the continuity of human experience, as successive generations re-present the dancing."46 Not that exact replication is a necessary condition in every ethnographic community, and even then, as noted above, human bodies are never stable over time. Yet they may be perceived to be stable in some instances and viewed as an authentic conduit to a past and continuing performance identity. As one English dancer explained to me:

It's something that, you know, has been handed down and handed down and it's all been handed down by word of mouth and practical help in learning the steps. It's not something you can just go and pick a book up, read about, go and do it. Impossible. In such instances, the human body is both recipient and manifestation of a local history that claims authenticity through its mode of transmission. The quotation above is ultimately embedded in earlier dichotomies of tradition and modernity that were operative in the folk paradigm to designate primitive or folk cultures from the civilized. But nonetheless the significance of so-called tradition to modern life is not to be simply dismissed by dance scholars as redundant regurgitation of old evolutionist theory circulating within ethnographic communities. In constructing narratives of continuity in dance, dancers themselves often draw upon such theory, self-consciously or not, to situate themselves within a temporal framework that may differentiate their identities in opposition to those dancers with perhaps younger histories of performance.

But the embodiment of the past in performance form may serve more concrete territorial needs. During the 1990s, tensions between contrastive cultural understanding of the role and significance of embodied documentation was highlighted in court cases concerning Australian aboriginal lands. The presentation of traditional performance as evidence to claim territorial rights was rejected as inadmissible evidence. Yet such means of performance, as Connerton has discussed, help to bind people to their own history. Cultural memory as performance operates to construct and consolidate identities even if that cultural memory may be at odds with personal memory. Multiple voices of memory, however, tend to be quieter in such events where the performance is a recurrent public enactment. The performance of memory in collective terms consolidates an agreed interpretation of what happened or what is valued.

The inclusion and positioning of voices within ethnographic and historical texts has undergone considerable discussion since the advent of postmodernism. The new benefits and drawbacks to understanding have been variously assessed—at worst, as evidence of a cultural relativism that evades material and moral responsibilities; at best, as a positive means of giving voice to the repressed, marginalized, or ignored. Authentic representation of experience has been a driving factor in this scholarship, bringing to prominence the native ethnographer and historian. Interrelated questions of authentic identity and knowledge in speaking, writing, and dancing continue to circulate in ethnographic and historical studies of dance. In some respects, the "I" persona and the practice of placing the author's dancing body at the center of reflexive inquiry is a further symptom of the drive toward authenticity of representation. Ironically, of course, the concept of authenticity in contingent areas of ethnographic and historical practice is, at the same time, subject to intense critical scrutiny. While applauding and embracing the long-awaited integration of individual embodied histories and the experiential, it remains necessary to guard against naive belief in the body and in the native researcher as sources of "natural" unmediated knowledge. Attempts to question and to understand the often complex and circuitous relationships between past and present are then inseparably constituted in present discourse and biography. Yet such recognition inspires dance scholars to acquire greater knowledge and insight of their own values in relation to those of others, whether past or present. Extreme positions in predicating the past as an extension of the present need to be critically examined, for if we argue, as J. D. Peel does, that "conceptions of the past are facts of the present," and that "the content of such conceptions of the past . . . may well be largely or entirely the product of particular present interests," then we are led "to the logical absurdity of unhinging the present from the past completely"

Dancing pasts across several presents—for example, as an African Caribbean performing the quadrille in London or a Caucasian swinging in California—necessitate acts of selection, omission, exclusion, transformation, and creation in the embodied production of cultural memory. And the study of dance as representative practice requires the skills and perspectives of history and ethnography, not only to explore legacies of colonialism and nationalism, but also to interrogate the continuing impact of globalization and the politics of identity articulation. Through reflexive and dialogic strategies, synthesizing synchronic and diachronic perspectives, we can exercise our cultural and political choices purposefully toward a more informed and imaginative future for dance and its scholarship.

2

Dances and Dancing in Tonga

ANTHROPOLOGICAL AND HISTORICAL DISCOURSES

The study of dances as historical *and* cultural discourses can be an illuminating anthropological project. The combination, however, diverges from typical anthropological research and analyses where these two approaches are usually separated. Classic ethnographic research was based on extended fieldwork that attempted to present a picture and synchronic analysis of a contemporary society and usually resulted in a detailed account of the "ethnographic present." In contrast, late-nineteenth-century "armchair anthropologists" studied written accounts and theorized about diffusion or migration in the long ago. More recently, historians have researched historical records for societies usually reserved for the anthropological gaze. The twain did meet during the second half of the twentieth century when some anthropologists, such as Fernand Braudel and Marshall Sahlins, began to focus their attention on history and embarked on studies of "structures in the long run."

Even though many anthropologists have felt that structure and history are opposing concepts, they have used history in their studies— especially the long view of history as taken from archaeology and oral history with its contributions to the study of myth and genealogy.

Because of the problematic heritage of evolutionism and diffusionism, however, anthropologists have generally shied away from history and especially from grandiose schemes. Those, such as Marshall Sahlins, who have attempted to bridge the gap between the structural/functional emphasis on synchrony and the historian's emphasis on di-achrony, have carried out long-term fieldwork in contemporary societies and combed libraries and archives to place them in a historical perspective. Sahlins has demonstrated the possibilities and significance of combining structural analysis, history, event, and action in his structures in the long run and has concluded that "the historical process unfolds as a continuous and reciprocal movement between the practice of the structure and the structure of the practice."

As a student in the 1960s, I became drawn to the vibrancy and importance of dance performances while carrying out anthropological fieldwork in Tonga. Why was dance so important? Who were the patrons, composers, performers, and audiences? How did these dances come to their present complexity? What could dance tell me about society? Over the years I have often focused my attention on dance (or on its broader application as "structured movement systems") and its relationships to social structure, authority, gender, and art, as well as more theoretical concepts such as the analogy of dance with language, style, and aesthetics. I have also, nonetheless, found it necessary to place these concepts into historical perspectives. Here I explore this combination of some historical and cultural aspects of dance.

That dance can be a form of historical and cultural discourse is not common in the study and analysis of dance; historically anthropologists have not often focused on dance, except for its use in ritual.3 Dances are surface manifestations or exemplars of movement languages that convey information, just as speech sequences are surface manifestations of spoken languages. The analogy is a convenient one, but it is always necessary to point out that what movement and speech communicate may be similar *or* quite different. If discourse is "communication of thought" usually through conversation (as the dictionary tells us), how can bodies converse and convey history? And how can history help us to understand dance and other structured movement systems in the present?

The term "history" evokes the idea of a linear knowledge of what happened in the past that has been recorded in writing. But even in the best of times, written history records only select "moments" when someone happened to write down what she or he saw or was told. When we attempt to look at the history or historical processes of dance outside of the Euro-American traditions, we find that only occasionally did someone commit to writing information about dance performances. But history does not just depend on what was written down by outsiders or insiders. In this chapter, I pursue an anthropological approach to dance history and ethnography in the Kingdom of Tonga in the south Pacific that does not depend only on accounts that were written down, but rather on a variety of discourses derived from oral history, ethnohistory, ethnography, and movement itself. Dancing and its history are not just "out there" in some positivistic sense; it is the framing and interpretation of dancing that makes history for the present.

HISTORY, POLITICS, ORATORY, DANCE, AND AESTHETICS IN TONGA

Ethnographic fieldwork often elicits a series of puzzles—puzzles that cannot be solved by the ethnographer without the use of historical sources and the dialectical engagement of the ethnographer with the ethnographer's mentors and hosts. My mentors and hosts in Tonga and their ancestors have been literate for more than a century, but they do not have a tradition of writing down their impressions of dance performances or the meanings of the dances to their contemporary lives. Nor do they have a tradition of written dance criticism. Indeed, the most important aspects of a dance are the sung text that the movements accompany and the skill with which this text is conveyed. Although many dance song texts are written down, their *interpretation* is in the oral tradition, and there are specialists who are skilled in such interpretation. These specialists became my mentors, and this chapter is the result of interaction with these dance specialists and interpreters of historic and contemporary events.

Because of the lack of written critical analyses of how specific works influence later works, dance historians often deny to non-Western productions the status of "works of art"; here I demonstrate that historic Tongan dances are known and do influence later works, and that they embed an aesthetic system that is widely recognized. Tongan dance is essentially an extension of the "oratorical voice." Oratory is the most important art form in Tonga; through oratory emotions are expressed and reciprocated. The job of the orator is to make people laugh and cry, by metaphorical (and sometimes direct) references to personified, yet abstract, objects of sympathy. To Tongans, oratory is a "high art," and dances that express the texts, with their oratorical power, are, in the words of Sherry Ortner, a "key elaborating symbol, extensively and systematically formulating relationships between a wide range of diverse cultural elements."

The oratorical art is central to social activity— constructing and imposing hierarchy and political potency. Through the oratorical voice fundamental cultural values are constructed and passed from generation to generation through the oral and written word. But *who* has the authority to project this oratorical voice and thereby to construct history for the present? Essentially, it was the aristocrats of the twentieth century, and especially Queen Salote (1900–65), who objectified history into written form and codified the thinking of the nation to revere certain genealogical lines and their intermixture. It was the *selection* of historical and cultural information by those with the authority to do so that gave political potency to the status quo. Although the present powerful genealogical lines can be traced to the mythological charter of Tongan society and history and have the philosophical force of Mikhail Bakhtin's "epic," a study of oratory reveals how the past, present, and future can be shaped for political ends.5 The concepts are embedded in the deep-seated Polynesian philosophy by which contested, or uncontested, genealogical links and historic events are brought to bear on contemporary authority and power.

Written poetic texts, the people who perform them in time and space, and the movements themselves are interpreted and explained in the oral tradition, thereby imposing knowledge about social order through an aesthetic medium that results in the shared values of the society.6 Historic events, like Bakhtin's epics, have analogies in myth and can impose order on contemporary life. To Tongans, dance performances—like rituals—communicate messages that, for the most part, are already known. How social and political order are constructed from these messages is ever evolving depending on the contexts in which they are used for political action—an example of Sahlins's historical process unfolding "between the practice of the structure and the structure of the practice."

HISTORIC DANCE MOMENTS IN TONGA

Since the first European descriptions of dance performances in Tonga made during the third voyage of Captain James Cook in 1777, observers have been fascinated by the coordinated performances of huge groups of men and/or women dancing in honor of the chiefs and visitors. The eightieth birthday of King Taufa'ahau Tupou IV, on 4 July 1998, was marked with dancing by large groups of villagers and whole islands. In the intervening two centuries after Cook's voyages, all important events (except funerals) have featured dance performances, and some of these events have been described in the literature. These descriptions can be considered sources for a history of Tongan dance. Instead of confining myself to the paradigm of linear written history, however, I want to enlarge our historical purview to suggest that dance history does not depend on accounts that were written down—usually by outsiders—but on a wider variety of historical sources that includes written history, oral history and cultural memory, ethnohistory, and ethnographic research. Even with this variety of sources, sometimes we know only about specific "moments." Moments, however, can be extended to represent a particular stage in something's development, or a stage in a course of events. As constructed here, a "moment" is essentially a historiographic abstraction, which can vary from a single written description of a specific performance to a period of years with intensive observations and numerous written sources.

I focus here on four moments in the history of Tongan dance and the importance of historical and ethnographic sources in our understanding of the transformations of the dance genre now known as *laka-laka,* the embodiment of history par excellence. It is the interpretation of these moments that makes "history" for the present—not only for the study of dance, but for the study of Tongan history. The first "moment" was a visit of the British explorer Captain James Cook to Tonga at the end of the eighteenth century and the descriptions and illustrations that resulted from the journal entries and drawings made in situ and their subsequent publication. This written and visual "history" (along with other eighteenth- and early-nineteenth-century written accounts and drawings by outsiders) is equally revealing about the outsiders and their points of view as it is about the dances. A second "moment" was the last third of the nineteenth century when the dances witnessed by Cook were transformed into the dance form now known as *lakalaka.* This moment combines oral history, accounts written by outsiders, and illustrations in the new medium of photography, as interpreted in the context of my own ethnographic research. It is an example of "ethnohistory."

A third "moment" encompasses my continuing research on the *lakalaka* performing genre from 1964 until the present in which the method is the classic ethnographic participant-observation. Finally, the fourth "moment" took place in July 1998 when elements of *lakalaka* were transformed once again, and during which I just happened to be an observer. The first two moments are based on written historical accounts and on Tongan interpretations of written accounts and oral history. The third and fourth moments are based on my own ethnographic research as a participant-observer. This included talking to the composers, performers, patrons, and audience members, taking part in dance performances, and, with Tongan help, interpreting contemporary accounts from local newspapers and magazines, as well as photographs made by Tongans. Much of this ethnography has now become history. From this variety of accounts we see how language and points of view color what we see and do not see, and what knowledge is necessary to understand and interpret historic and contemporary accounts and illustrations.

SOME PREHISTORY AND HISTORY

Millennia ago, peoples from Asia and Southeast Asia began moving into Oceania, bringing with them musical, movement, literary, and theatrical ideas and concepts that evolved and became codified into "dances." These dances and the systems of knowledge in which they were embedded changed over time, owing to restyling from within and the influences of intercultural contact and later migrations. During the late eighteenth century and the first part of the nineteenth century, Europeans began to travel to the Pacific and to write about and illustrate what they experienced. Eighteenth-century voyages of exploration were organized primarily by England, France, Holland, and Spain. The best early descriptions of dance were recorded by individuals who traveled with Captain Cook, especially in some areas of Polynesia. The published results of these encounters record descriptions of music, movement, and costume as seen from the outside. Though sketchy, early eyewitness accounts are invaluable sources when used in conjunction with later reports from missionaries, whalers, traders, tourists, beachcombers, anthropologists, and indigenous peoples.

An Eighteenth-Century Moment

An important historic moment is the first recorded description of a Tongan dance called *me'elaufola*. Performances of *me'elaufola* were described in Cook's journals during his visit in 1777 and were illustrated by the official artist on the voyage, John Webber. Webber made drawings of two large group dances, and professional engravers reworked these drawings into finished engravings. The two engravings depict "A Night Dance by Men in Hapaee" and "A Night Dance by Women in Hapaee." Descriptions of the dances became part of the official published version of the journal of the voyage. A description of the women's dance illustrates how we can learn about dance history from movement itself. Cook notes:

The concert having continued about a quarter of an hour, twenty women entered the circle. Most of them had, upon their heads, garlands of crimson flowers of the China rose, or others; and many of them had ornamented their persons with leaves of trees, cut with a great deal of nicety about the edges. They made a circle round the chorus, turning their faces toward it, and began singing a soft air, to which responses were made by the chorus in the same tone; and these were repeated alternately. All this while, the women accompanied their song with several very graceful motions of their hands toward their faces, and in other directions[,] at the same time, making constantly a step forward, and then back again, with one foot, while the other was fixed. They then turned their faces to the assembly, sung some time, and retreated slowly in a body, to that part of the circle which was opposite the hut where the principal spectators sat. After this, one of them advanced from each side, meeting and passing each other in the front, and continuing their progress round till they came to the rest. On which two advanced from each side, two of whom also passed each other, and returned as the former; but the other two remained, and to these came one from each side, by intervals, till the whole number had again formed a circle about the chorus.

Their manner of dancing was now changed to a quicker measure, in which they made a kind of half turn by leaping, and clapping their hands, and snapping their fingers, repeating some words in conjunction with the chorus. Toward the end, as the quickness of the music increased, their gestures and attitudes were varied with wonderful vigour and dexterity; and some of their motions, perhaps, would, with us, be reckoned rather indecent; though this part of the performance, most probably, was not meant to convey any wanton ideas, but merely to display the astonishing variety of their movements.

The engraving based on Webber's drawing shows two groups of women, one on each side of the musicians. I have described elsewhere how this excellent description and illustration can be interpreted as an important arm-movement motif still used today and how the drawing suggests that Webber had actually distilled the essence of the most important arm motif for women used in the *me'elaufola* dance genre.

Webber's illustration of a men's dance shows a similar understanding of the arm movements. Again, there is a written description from Cook's journal:

To this grand female ballet, succeeded one performed by fifteen men. Some of them were old; but their age seemed to have abated little of their agility or ardour for the dance. They were disposed in a sort of circle, divided at the front, with their faces not turned out toward the assembly, nor inward to the chorus; but one half of their circle faced forward as they had advanced, and the other half in a contrary direction. They, sometimes, sung slowly, in concert with the chorus; and while thus employed, they also made several very fine motions with their hands, but different from those made by the women, at the same time inclining the body to either side alternately, by raising one leg, which was stretched outward and resting on the other, the arm of the same side being also stretched fully upward. At other times, they recited sentences in a musical tone, which were answered by the chorus; and, at intervals, increased the motions of the feet, which however, were never varied. At the end, the rapidity of the music, and of the dancing, increased so much, that it was scarcely possible to distinguish the different movements; though one might suppose the actors were now almost tired, as their performance had lasted near half an hour.

Webber's drawing of this or a similar performance again shows his understanding of the importance of the arm movements and has captured the essence of the most important arm movement motif for men—that is, with extended arms *(laufola)* the lower arm is rotated to alternate the palm facing from forward to back or from up to down. I have elsewhere drawn attention to how the engraver of this drawing has misinterpreted Webber's original drawing of the arm movements. These descriptions and illustrations have captured and conveyed the important movements and the differences between men's and women's movements in Tonga. The moment constitutes a historic base for all subsequent moments in Tongan dance. Webber's illustrations correspond to the journal description that "some of the gestures were so expressive, that it might be said they spoke the language that accompanied them, if we allow that there is any connection between motion and sound."

A Nineteenth-Century Moment

Before the next "moment" occurred, Protestant missionaries arrived in Tonga and forbid dancing for their converts in the mistaken idea that dances were about religion and the gods, and were licentious and heathen. The Tongans, however, turned out to be much more clever than the missionaries. A historic moment in the late nineteenth century, recorded primarily in oral tradition, occurred when Tuku'aho (1858–97), the high chief of the village of Tatakamotonga, one of the Protestant villages, held a competition for the development of a new dance form. It is said that this competition was won by Fuapau of the northern island of Vava'u.

The composers/choreographers *(punake)* of the time were familiar primarily with the *me'elaufola* described above and other traditional dances such as *me'utu'upaki* (a men's standing dance performed with small paddles) and *fa'ahiula* (a women's dance with complex arm movements), and they essentially transformed remnants of the old dance forms into a "new dance" that became known as *lakalaka.* Chief Tuku'aho worked in conjunction with a *punake* from his own village, Fineasi Malukava, to further develop the *lakalaka* and train the performers. "Malukava" became an inherited title, appointed by the king.

A grandson of Malukava (Tevita Kavaefiafi) became the titleholder during the mid-twentieth century. This Malukava told me, "the *me'elaufola* was a form of *lakalaka* before the modern *lakalaka,* done by all women in which they stood and slowly performed *laufola* [outstretched arm movements]."15 Although oral traditions do not record exactly what year this new dance was created, it is thought to have been in the late 1870s or early 1880s. By the mid-1880s, *lakalaka* became popular and spread throughout Tonga. In a description from 1885, the British vice-consul, Henry Francis Symonds, described a *laka-laka* performance in Neiafu on the northern Tongan island of Vava'u and its background:

The Lakalaka is a dance that preserves some of the old forms of Ton-gan dancing united with what the Wesleyan missionaries have introduced as their idea of the proper way for natives to amuse themselves. The old dances, like all the old Tongan customs, were long ago prohibited by the Missionaries, apparently for no earthly reason than because they belonged to the days before the people were Wesleyans. . . . When Mr. Moulton assumed the direction of the Mission affairs (in 1881) being an educated man, he perceived the mistake that had been made, and consequently allowed them further latitude than they had hitherto been given, and the result is one of the prettiest and most graceful dances I have ever seen. . . . [T]he subjects embrace every conceivable thing; legends and war songs, descriptions of scenery, and tales of Foreign lands, and last but not least, love.

Basil Thomson, visiting Tonga in 1900, noted that those *lakalaka* "that become popular may endure for many years. *Langa fale kakala* (Build a house of flowers), for example, . . . is as popular a favourite now as it was when I was in Mua in 1886." Photographs of *lakalaka* performances are known from the nineteenth century. On this occasion "there was a grand *laka-laka* (dancing) competition between the young men and women of Mu'a, Fua'amotu, Houma, and Hihifo. The Mu'a dancers . . . won the first prize." Unfortunately, we do not know who did the judging, but the Mu'a dancers were those from the village of Tatakamotonga and were trained under the original dance master Malukava (Fineasi).

As noted above, the arm movements of *me'elaufola* appear to be the same kinds of movements now used in *lakalaka.* There are two major categories of arm movements *(haka)* recognized by Tongans. *Haka nonou* refers to movements in which the upper arms are held close to the body and are characteristic of certain movement motifs, used especially by women. The other category, *laufola,* describes movements in which the upper arms are extended forward and away from the body. The term *me'elaufola* described the eighteenth-century dance form: *me'e* (dance) in which arm movements were *laufola,* extended. *Laufola* arm movements also became characteristic of the nineteenth-century form. The new name, *lakalaka,* is a word that means to walk quickly, "to step it out." Whereas the term *me'elaufola* described the arm movements, *la-kalaka* describes the leg movements.

I have argued elsewhere that *lakalaka* is a nineteenth-century evolved form of the pre-European *me'elaufola,* retaining the structural, vocal, and movement characteristics of the old form even though it has lost the instrumental accompaniment (of bamboo stamping tubes and struck idio-phones. The vocal polyphony appears to be an evolved form of the traditional six-part polyphony, and although the pitch intervals may have changed, the structure has not. In addition to retaining the arm and leg movements characteristic of *me'elaufola, lakalaka* incorporates changes in floor plan as dancers move from place to place on the dancing ground (also described in Cook's journals) and has developed the polyphonic and polykinetic prototypes found in early forms. From the similar, but separate, choreographies for men and women in *me'elaufola,* it was only a small step to simultaneously perform separate choreographies for men and women that became characteristic of *lakalaka,* in which the graceful movements of the women contrast with the more virile movements of the men illustrating the separate but interdependent roles of men and women in Tongan rank and social structure. *Lakalaka* did not simply incorporate the old forms but transformed them into something new. This transformation was carried out in accordance with the aesthetic principle on which Tongan poetry, music, and dance is based, *heliaki* (indirectness).

Heliaki means to say one thing but mean another, never stating something directly, but making reference by allusion and metaphor. For example, when referring to an individual, he or she is never named but is referred to as a bird, flower, wind, or place. Deeds are never detailed, but are referred to only indirectly. The transformation of *me'elaufola* into *lakalaka* was in itself a kind of *heliaki.*

An Ethnographic Moment

What I will consider an ethnographic moment is the time of my own participant-observation research on Tongan dance, beginning in 1964 and still continuing. By the middle of the twentieth century, *lakalaka* had become the most important performing genre, with *heliaki* becoming more and more complex, especially in *lakalaka* composed by such luminaries as King Tupou II, Queen Salote Tupou III, Fakatava, Ve'ehala, and a few others. Queen Salote's *lakalaka* are the best known and over the years have been revived, restaged, and repeated as examples of the classical tradition of Tongan dance and as identity markers for members of the villages for which she composed them. By the 1950s the transformation was complete; *lakalaka* were based on the style and structure promulgated by Queen Salote, with their basis in *heliaki.*

The structure of a *lakalaka* is based on formal speechmaking, having three sections:

(1) an introductory *fakatapu,* which acknowledges the important family lines of the chiefs relevant to the occasion;

(2) the main *lakalaka* section, which conveys the theme, information about the occasion, genealogies of relevant people, history, or mythology of the village performing, and other relevant information; and

(3) the *tatau*, a closing counterpart to the introductory *fakatapu*, in which the performers say goodbye and again defer to the chiefs.

One stanza may be a *tau*, a verse that expresses the essence of the performance, during which the performers do their very best to compel the audience to pay strict attention. This formal structure forms the outline of the composition. The overall design, and thus the meaning of any specific composition, need not be apparent until the end of the performance, however. The meaning is revealed as each verse, through verbal and visual allusions, builds on those that went before, mediated through the aesthetic principle of *heliaki*.

The performers of *lakalaka* are both men and women, often two hundred or more, arranged in two or more rows facing the audience. The men stand on the right side (from the observer's point of view), the women stand on the left. Men and women perform different movements that are consistent with the Tongan view of what is suitable and appropriate for their sex. Women's movements are soft and graceful; men's movements are strong and virile. Leg movements are minimal, especially for women, who move only a few steps from side to side and forward and back. Men may take larger steps, bend, turn, and sometimes strike or lay on the ground. Arm movements allude to the words of the poetry—which are often allusions to a deeper meaning—creating double abstractions much admired in Tongan performing arts.

The poetry of a *lakalaka* is a series of concepts and references rather than a complete story and is usually composed for performance by a specific group at a specific event. Poetic allusions are often to mythology and genealogy—usually in a quite roundabout or indirect way—which illustrates the Tongan ideal of *heliaki*. Although many of the allusions are understood by everyone, others are understood only by other poets, and the desire is often to take old allusions and transform them into something new. In order to understand the poetic transformations, one must "work from one's own knowledge," which has been gained through the study of genealogy, mythology, and history. It is necessary to listen to every word and watch every movement. Many of the references are common knowledge, but the association must be made instantaneously in order to go on to an understanding of the next allusion.

The poetry is performed as a sung speech with choreographed movements, which in figurative language and allusive movements elevate the monarch and chiefs, paying them the highest possible respect and dignity. At the same time, the poetry also honors the performers and their villages. The texts become frames for interpreting history and the politics of prestige and power and encode knowledge about social order through an aesthetic medium that results in the shared values of the society. Metaphorical associations are made to specific places, residences (or former residences), trees, flowers and flower constructions, birds, winds, and *mdtanga* (historic monuments or places associated with individuals of the past and present) as well as to the Christian god from whom they gained status as Christian aristocrats. The texts can be read in many ways, but especially as historical narratives relevant to contemporary politics.

The classic performance event for *lakalaka* is at a *kdtoanga,* a public festivity or celebration. Large-scale government *kdtoanga* are rare, but smaller *kdtoanga* occur nearly every year and seem to have become more frequent. During the reign of Queen Salote (1918-65) there were seven important *kdtoanga.* After Queen Salote's death in 1965 the next *kdtoanga* was the coronation of Tupou IV in July 1967. The last important *kdtoanga* of the twentieth century was the eightieth birthday celebration of Tupou IV in 1998.

Experiencing a *kdtoanga* places the importance of performance and presentation into perspective and confirms the perpetuation of tradition in modern life. The presentations/performances described by Cook and others—such as J. H. Labillardière, D. Alejandro Malaspina, William Mariner, Basil C. Thomson, E. E. V. Collocott, Edward Wins-low Gifford, Eric B. Shumway, Larry Shumway, Richard Moyle, 'I Futa Helu, and myself—during the past two hundred years have continued to encompass some of the most important social and political events in modern Tonga.

Kdtoanga comprises several important performance activities including the mixing and drinking of *kava* (made from the infusion of a pepper plant called *kavd*), the presentation of food and valuables, and the presentation of sung speeches with choreographed movements, primarily *lakalaka* that embed traditional rites and speeches and thereby confirm the importance of tradition in modern life. Ideally, a large segment of the men and women of each area of the kingdom perform, thereby involving every family in traditional allegiance. The central performers are the sons and daughters of the king, nobles, and chiefs who learn the rites and history of the lineage and villages they represent by enacting them and commenting on the event.

The complex verbal and visual performances of *lakalaka* display the social organization of the villages and the hierarchical structure of the kingdom embedded in metaphorical poetry delivered in an aesthetically charged atmosphere. The composition of these three-dimensional forms is done by specialists, and to learn and perform them requires a substantial investment of time and energy by the many performers and teachers. Researching a *katoanga* lies in obtaining and comprehending the poetry of as many examples of *lakalaka* as possible, understanding how the movements project these sung speeches into visual form, analyzing the variations of the melodic contours and voice parts during as many practices and performances as possible, getting aesthetic evaluations during and after various performances, and placing the *katoanga* into its total social context.

Understanding such a complex event can only be attempted by immersion and in-depth research in a limited number of venues during the *pre-katoanga* period, during the *katoanga* itself, and during *post-katoanga* evaluations. That is, long-term, in-depth ethnographic research is necessary for understanding "an ethnographic moment." My involvement in this ethnographic moment consisted of more than four years of fieldwork in Tonga as a participant-observer. In addition to interviewing hundreds of Tongans—ranging from Queen Salote and members of the aristocracy to composers/choreographers to dancers and audience members—I took part in the *lakalaka* of the village of Ha'ateiho for the coronation of King Tupou in 1967.

There were weeks and weeks of daily practices (with much personal interaction with other participants), a performance for the approval of the ceremonial attendants (when we were photographed by the *National Geographic* in our practice costumes24), the grand performance for the coronation, and numerous other performances in the following days (including one for the visiting Duke and Duchess of Kent, who represented the British monarch). Without such personal involvement, my description of this third moment would only have been as incomplete as the above descriptions of the first and second moments.

To experience a *kdtoanga* is to be transported back in time to the rituals associated with propitiation of the descendant of the sky god Tanga-loa, the sacred Tu'i Tonga, or supreme ruler, whose function was to see to the continued fertility of the land and people. Continued fertility necessitated the offering of "first fruits" during an annual presentation of large quantities *of kava,* staple root crops, pigs, other foods, women's valuables *(koloa)* of mats and barkcloth, as well as music and dance performances. First fruits and women were sent to the supreme ruler, not only from all the Tongan islands, but also from a larger region over which Tonga held influence—Samoa, 'Uvea, Futuna, and other areas. Performances were also brought to honor and entertain the Tu'i Tonga, the people, and the performers. A new composition might be presented to the Tu'i Tonga in this extended "first fruits" category. Performances with new movements and musical settings were also brought from the far-flung territories of the Tongan Empire; some were added to the repertoire, and some were eventually Tonganized.

Kdtoanga today continue these traditions in the court of the Tupou dynasty and include most of the same ingredients. The king's birthday celebrations and the annual agricultural show are contemporary expressions of the giving of first fruits and valuables to the king, who gives them a Christian blessing. They are then redistributed and used in his court. Dances are first performed with the food and valuables before they are publicly performed—usually during the public days of the *kdtoanga* and the days leading up to it. Sons and daughters of the king and chiefs are often the central performers—they will be the next generation of chiefs and parents of future generations of chiefs.

In the court of the sacred Tu'i Tonga, the presentations and performances included the *me'elaufola* described above and *tau'a'alo* (work songs) in conjunction with food presentation. In 1800 the missionary George Vason described such a ceremony; approaching the Tu'i Tonga "in regular rotations, in a slow, solemn pace, with a kind of monotonous song, and upon their bended knees, [they] presented the first production of their *abbees* [gardens].... When the ceremony of the first fruits of their fields is completed, they usually have a dance." The bestowing of titles was (and remains) an important event. Investiture of titles takes place during a ritual in which *kava* is mixed and served with great ceremony.

The manner of presentation of *kava,* food, valuables, and performances was, and still is, as important as the objects themselves—as Vason noted, "the manner of doing it rendered the present doubly valuable." All of the niceties and etiquette continue today. In the court of the Tu'i Kanokupolu, of which King Taufa'ahau Tupou IV is the twenty-second ruler, food and valuables are presented and counted in a most ceremonious manner, and the final offering is a music and/or dance performance—the most highly regarded are *lakalaka.*

A Moment of Change in 1998

This brings us to a historic moment when a *lakalaka* was transformed from *heliaki* in performance into a biographical "history." In the first week of July 1998 was a large-scale celebration in honor of the eightieth birthday of King Taufa'ahau Tupou IV. Although there have been several large-scale celebrations in recent years, this was the largest since the king's coronation in 1967, and much of it was planned and implemented by the king's only daughter, Princess Pilolevu (b. 1951). The princess is especially interested in the cultural life of Tonga and especially in dance. She performed as the principal dancer in the 1967 *k ¯atoanga* for her father's coronation and in several *lakalaka* for her father's village Kanokupolu since that time. She has always had the benefit of someone to explain to her the complex *heliaki* of the poetry and movements.

She is concerned, however, that because of the difficult *heliaki,* people of her generation and younger cannot understand the poetry. Thus, in 1998 she initiated the beginning of what may become another transformation in Tongan dance. This transformation included changes in the makeup of the performing group, changes in placement of the dancers, and especially changes in the literary content of the poetry. *Lakalaka* are traditionally performed by a single village that is the estate of a noble, or a few closely affiliated villages—either located near one another, or villages from different areas of Tonga that are the estates of the same noble.

Princess Pilolevu's husband, Ma'ulupekotofa, had recently been appointed governor of Vava'u, the northern area of Tonga. He was not yet a titleholder because his father, Baron Tuita, was still alive. The great island of Vava'u is made up of a large number of villages, including several that are the estates of important nobles, including the brothers of the princess. Princess Pilolevu thought it would be marvelous if all the Vava'u villages would perform together in a huge *lakalaka,* which would create a spectacular effect, and she asked them to perform in a grand new *lakalaka* composed for the event. This proposition was widely accepted by the village leaders and the villagers, and more than five hundred decided to participate.28 Never before had villages of this variety performed together for a *lakalaka* for a government *katoanga* and with such a large number of dancers.

The second transformation that took place during this moment was the choice and placement of the important dancers. The principal dancer, *vahenga,* is classically the daughter of the village noble. For example, the noble of the village of Kanokupolu is the king, and in recent decades Princess Pilolevu, as daughter of the noble/king, was *vahenga*. In the 1998 *lakalaka* of Vava'u, instead of the daughter of a village noble, Lupepau'u Tuita, the daughter of the governor (and Princess Pilolevu), was *vahenga*. But where would Princess Pilolevu stand? She is the daughter of the king and not simply the daughter of a Vava'u estate owner. She was the organizer of the *lakalaka* and is one of the most famous and respected dancers in the country. The people of Vava'u wanted to honor her. She chose to dance in the tenth place (from the center) on the ladies' side. Her husband, Governor Ma'ulu-pekotofa, chose to dance in the tenth place on the men's side. From this time forward, it is likely that the tenth place will be considered a place of honor. The most radical change, however, was in the composition of the poetry. Although at least one new piece had already been created in traditional *heliaki* style by a composer for a Vava'u village, Princess Pilolevu wanted a different one and requested a little-known composer to attempt a new style. This was Mele Suipi Latu, the granddaughter of Fa-katava, the famous composer from the area. Mele was requested to read a newly published biography of King Tupou and to create a *lakalaka* with little or no *heliaki*—that is, to speak directly, to tell the king's story so that everyone could understand it. She did, resulting in an extremely interesting new composition. Although the overall structure remained the same, *heliaki* (indirectness) was not incorporated into the text. The king's ancestors were named, and their deeds were described. The king's accomplishments were enumerated chronologically. His academic degrees and royal orders were listed, and his government positions were elaborated.

In spite of rain during part of its performance, the *lakalaka* was a resounding success. Everyone loved it; they could understand the poetry; they enjoyed the visual impact of five hundred dancers, who even displayed signs printed with the king's degrees and royal orders; and they knelt and sat on the ground in order to convey poetic meaning visually. *Heliaki* had been transformed into poetically sung biography. New movement motifs were invented to convey the King's successes in the sports of pole vaulting and shotput.

Even with these changes, *heliaki* was not completely abandoned. Before the performance, each dancer placed a six-pound can of corned beef at the front of the performing space ostensibly as a gift to the court to help feed the visitors. The *heliaki* was not overlooked by the many knowledgeable audience members, who remembered comic allusions to a farmer from Leimatu'a village in Vava'u who attempted to plant corned beef hoping it would grow like vegetables. Also enlightening was a newspaper photo caption of the dancers. The English caption was "Vava'u dancers enjoying a relaxing moment before performance" while the Tongan version, with traditional *heliaki*, noted that the dancers came from "Lolo 'a Halaevalu," the metaphorical name of the water in Vava'u harbor that is so calm it appears to be oil. Tongan speakers were expected to understand the metaphor, whereas English speakers had to be told that the dancers were from Vava'u.

Evaluating the Moment

What are we to make of these historic moments when changes were intentionally made by persons of authority—Chief Tuku'aho, Queen Salote, and Princess Pilolevu?

Each performance is only a *parole* or act (to use Ferdinand de Saussure's terms)—one instance or surface manifestation of the underlying system, that is, the deep structure, or *langue*— and in order to understand this, it is necessary to know the "structures of the *longue durée*."

In this examination of what can be discerned about a specific genre of Tongan dance over two centuries, we are able to see the historical process unfolding "as a continuous and reciprocal movement between the practice of the structure and the structure of the practice." Each *parole* is a "performance" for which viewers need "competence" to understand—competence that has changed during the past two hundred years. Each instance (1770s, 1880s, mid-twentieth century, 1998) that manifested in the moment of a "dance system of knowledge" is only a small part of the system of sociocultural knowledge, which requires another level of competence. As levels of competence within a society in traditional forms change, the sociocultural context responds.

The transformation of *me'elaufola* into *lakalaka* was a response to the outside influence of Protestant missionaries, and although the musical content of the dance changed, the dance movements and the values associated with poetry probably remained much the same (the level of competence among composers, performers, and viewers had not changed). The changes that elaborated *heliaki* into a complex aesthetic, promulgated by Queen Salote and her contemporaries, was evolutionary. Indirectness had always been there, but from the 1930s to the 1960s it became more elaborated and systematized (the level of competence increased). The 1998 series of changes from within could have a more profound influence in the transformation of literary artistic style (the level of competence was thought to have diminished). On the other hand, the future may show that this was only a temporary change for a specific occasion that entered the historic stream of events simply because someone was there who chose to write about it.

History and Ethnography

It remains to suggest that a historical perspective in conjunction with ethnographic research has enlarged our understanding of what Tongan *lakalaka* can reveal about politics, power, poetry, music, movement, and aesthetics. As Sahlins has reminded us, when people of different cultures come in contact, events may convey quite different meanings to each group, and the reaction to the event is shaped by their different understandings of the occasion, which, in turn, may affect and transform basic structures of the society. Events are interpreted through the "structures of significance" that the people of a culture have derived from history. By examining historic and ethnographic records of specific events and actions as well as oral traditions about them in Tonga, we can see that reactions to dance events were sometimes shaped by different intercultural understandings, such as the misunderstanding of the Protestant missionaries of the *me'elaufola*. Christianization affected and modified dance traditions along with religious and political structures that were transformed by outside contact—thus the origin of the *laka-laka*. For Queen Salote, *lakalaka* gave her the opportunity to speak publicly on matters important to the nation, such as political independence and the retention of cultural traditions and aesthetics—matters that she promulgated as structures of significance for the mid-twentieth century.

Tongan *lakalaka* are socially realized cultural constructions of history, embedded in the aesthetic system. As we have seen by examining four historic moments, the more detail we have about each moment, the more we learn about cultural discourses of the time. The first two moments were interpreted with the aid of written history and oral tradition, whereas the two later moments used written history, oral tradition, and long-term ethnographic research.

The study of Tongan *lakalaka* and its history reveals a great deal about poetry, aesthetics, and Tongan society. Cloaked in *heliaki, lakalaka* distill Tongan historical, social, and political values in an artistic medium of heroic form. The poetics of history, prestige, and power are artistic refinements of the Tongan elite and especially those who have the ability and authority to present their interpretations of history publicly. Since my anthropological studies of dance have always been informed by history, I can only agree with Sahlins: "Practice clearly has gone beyond the theoretical differences that are supposed to divide anthropology and history. Anthropologists rise from the abstract structure to the explication of the concrete event. Historians devalue the unique event in favor of underlying recurrent structures. And also paradoxically, anthropologists are as often diachronic in outlook as historians nowadays are synchronic."

3

Constructing a Classical Tradition

The Republic of Indonesia is politically and culturally dominated by the island of Java, which has reputedly enjoyed an unchanging history of court performance dating back hundreds of years. Subject to colonial rule, principally by the Dutch from the seventeenth to the early twentieth centuries, the Indonesian archipelago of several thousand islands has a complex history of invasion, rebellion, and division. In the middle of the eighteenth century, the Islamic kingdom of Mataram (1582–1749) in Central Java was divided into two principalities, each with their city and royal court: Yogyakarta and Surakarta, or Yogya and Solo, as the cities are popularly known today. When the independent nation-state of Indonesia was declared in 1945, the city and principality of Surakarta became absorbed into the province of Central Java, whereas Yogya-karta was preserved as a special province and city, with Sultan Hameng-kubuwana IX (1939–88) as its governor. Both royal courts of Yogyakarta and Surakarta support a distinctively styled performance tradition and rival one another in their claims to antiquity and cultural superiority. This chapter considers the historical claims for and present practice of the performance tradition of Yogyakarta from the perspective of a British social anthropologist.

Indonesia includes a wide diversity of histories and ethnic groups. During the New Order period (1966–98), President Suharto began to emphasize the development of a national culture based on regional traditions. Despite this emphasis on regional diversity, it was the history and values of the Javanese, the largest ethnic group, that were used to promote Indonesian nationhood. During this period the movement styles of court performance assumed significance in Indonesian educational policy, and Javanese court dance was transformed into the Indonesian classical tradition.

Continuity and longevity are emphasized in written histories of classical court dance in Java and in stories about the origins of the dances. Local historians play down processes of change and construct the dances as genres that are defined by essential and unchanging qualities.

My anthropological research into contemporary performances, on the other hand, revealed that in practice, rather than being fixed as discrete genres, dances varied over time according to the context.

Such fluidity made problematic any attempt to classify and secure the dances as belonging to wholly separate genres. Experience of this difficulty led me to look more closely at contemporary local histories of Javanese classical dance traditions and the historical sources upon which they were based. Might, indeed, such histories indicate more about present-day cultural policies and their future application than an explicit focus on the past might suggest?

A major problem encountered by any researcher is how to treat and to understand speculative mythic histories that have accrued to genres of performance. Such stories about the historical origins of the court's dance repertoire in fact formed part of the political rhetoric about Indonesian national identity and the place of Javanese culture within the modern state. I explore here some of the interpretive processes that produced the performance repertoire and its mythology in the sultan's court in the city and province of Yogyakarta. I consider, in particular, the elaborate and lengthy ceremonial dances known as the Bedhaya dance tradition, normally performed today by nine women. It is a performance tradition that has been especially associated with the power of the ruler in Java and, as such, has been particularly subject to mytho-historical constructions.

READING HISTORIES

Before my first period of research in Yogyakarta (1979–86), I prepared for fieldwork by reading across the disciplines everything I could about Javanese performance, especially the dances of the sultan's court, written in English, Dutch, French, and Indonesian. During fieldwork I continued to read published and unpublished studies, in Indonesian and Javanese, as well as dance manuscripts in many libraries, including those of the sultan's palace and the Institute of Indonesian Arts (then named ASTI, the Indonesian Academy of Performing Arts). My initial research aimed to discover the reality behind what had struck me as romanticized accounts by Western travelers and scholars that were colored by stereotypes of the Orient as representing ancient and authentic traditions redolent of primeval sacrality.

At that time the classic model of anthropological explanation, structural functionalism, had already been under radical criticism for its neglect of the historical dimensions of contemporary experience. Looking back, I was still under the impression that by being a participant-observer in Java I would see the total significance of dance without having recourse to the systematic methodologies of the historian.

In fact, I spent many long hours working in court libraries, but archival and manuscript work was marginal to the central methodologies I employed: these constituted learning embodied practices and working interpretively to establish an indigenous discourse of dance.

As well as dancing and talking to local people, I read writings by contemporary Indonesian historians and social and political scientists on performance and culture, which would contribute to my understanding of that discourse. In attempting to deconstruct the mystique produced by the writing of outsiders through these methods, however, I ended up being faced in these local authors' writings with local ideologies about dance that were as much part of mythologizing structures as outsider accounts had been.

I came to understand that modern Indonesian culture is a response to a perceived modernization that calls on the ideology of the traditional to act as a panacea to the negative face of change. A further characteristic of Indonesian culture is the separation of connected performance practices into discrete elements, each identified in past documentation and artifacts. Attributions of origin and the implementation of what has come to be viewed as traditional with regard to standards or styles, I realized, needed to be treated with caution. The common practice of fixing a name to a genre that drew on prior conventions and that was then subsequently presented as traditional underlined the fact that tradition is a process, not a thing.

Indeed, tradition should not necessarily be understood as referring to customs that are authentic, indigenous, and long established, although there may be particular instances, but rather as an ideology that attributes precedents to practices that may have recently been revived, recast, or reinvented, even if the label or contents refer back to a previous practice.

As Eric Hobsbawm and Terence Ranger famously pointed out in their study of tradition and the emergence of the nation-state, so-called traditions may often be comparatively recent inventions; the rhetoric of wholeness and authenticity associated with traditional practices are not so much matters of fact but rather political strategies associated with legitimization.

Making History

During Indonesia's New Order period, stories about the continuity of cultural traditions together with a projected long and stable political past became especially significant, with historians playing a key role in their construction. In attempting to understand local concepts of history and the significance of cultural traditions, the Western researcher has to come to terms with how the brute facts of Java's past—disruption, discontinuity, contingency, and adaptation to numerous cultural impacts, including Hinduism, Buddhism, Islam, Dutch colonization, postcolo-nial westernization, and now globalization—are treated in local written and oral historiography. These factors have been transformed into elegant cyclical patterns, with events imbued with a sense of inevitability based on allegorical connections with myths. An effect of these uses of history is to provide myths of origin for different dance forms to give legitimacy to the Central Javanese courts, a legitimacy that has now been absorbed by the Indonesian state.

Writing about the past in Java has long been understood to inform the political present, which is why writing history in Indonesia continues to be a powerful tool, and why particular historical interpretations have been favored. Writing history was also about writing the future. Even before and during the colonial period, Javanese historians became adept at re-presenting the past to represent the present, drawing on particular patterns and excluding others that did not support the orthodoxy.

Establishing the longevity of traditions contributes to the maintenance of the dominant culture as well as constructing a legitimate past. In his important study on how court literature became formalized and mytholo-gized as a political strategy in the establishment of the kingdom of Yogya-karta in 1755, the Dutch historian Merle Ricklefs observes that it "seems possible that this schematization then had a reciprocal effect upon political behavior, which tended to fit the pattern. Events had been rewritten to become tradition, and the tradition then molded events to fit itself." In a similar manner, the re-modeling of the diversity of performance practices as discrete and stable traditions was constructed through the attribution of mythic history and through the selective use of old records. The result was that well before the New Order period, the invented traditions had become naturalized and their constructedness forgotten.

This phenomenon is typical of the colonial and postcolonial situation, where history and culture may be collapsed into "cultural heritage." Such conceptual constructions deny local complexities and local modes of understanding the past. As

Nicholas Dirks observes, history in colonial situations is "a metaphor for the subtle relationships between power and knowledge, between culture and control." Colonialism creates both the conditions that make "culture" a conceptual necessity and the templates of practice that provide political cultural markers in any postcolonial reordering. Cultural manipulation is thus a response to the disruptions and the negation of local history brought about by colonization. When those in power talk about culture, their interest is not in the purportedly long-standing and enduring practices per se but rather in shifting these practices into new frameworks to address the needs of the present and the future.

In Indonesia, as in most postcolonial nations with a plural population, cultures are used for political purposes and are in turn constituted through those actions. The political dominance of Java means that the construction of Indonesian culture is both assisted and motivated by this (re)construction of history. If government policies during the New Order emphasized the development of a national culture based on regional traditions, the debates about Indonesian culture were crosscut by Javanese claims to be the true bearers of the ancient national heritage.

Much court performance in Java is, in fact, relatively modern. During the early nineteenth century, John Crawfurd, the British Resident (an official colonial post) in Yogyakarta, was struck by the lack of historical depth to court practices, noting that "[e]ven tradition does not pretend to an antiquity of above a few centuries." Such a statement reveals much about his preconceptions and expectations; yet historians in Java were also to be preoccupied with projecting an ancient past for court performances. The relative shallowness of the history of the Central Javanese courts and the fractured complexity of Indonesia have been compensated for with stories that trace lineages from ancient history, asserting in particular the influence of Indian culture over a thousand years ago.

The Hindu-Javanese period, so-called because powerful rulers in the island were influenced to varying degrees by religion, administration, and culture from India, originated with trade connections between the subcontinent and the Sriwijaya kingdom (ca. 400-ca. 1300). (The Buddhist kingdom of Sriwijaya was not established in Java, but in the city of Palembang on the island of Sumatra, but it is nonetheless regarded as the mother empire of the Indonesian archipelago.) These links continued through the first kingdom of Mataram (seventh to tenth centuries) until the end of the Majapahit kingdom (ca. 1222-1451).

The relation of performance and politics was already established during the

Hindu-Javanese period. Before the tenth century, drama was employed to demonstrate to the population the might of the government and the role of the king, and god-kings *(dewa-raja)* sponsored ceremonial dances and spectacles as offerings to deities and to honor and impress other human beings. That there were concrete links between the Indian subcontinent and Indonesian kingdoms is evidenced by inscribed charters as early as 840 that refer to mask plays with actors from as far away as Sri Lanka and Southern India. These charters also refer to other performances such as shadow plays and fighting dances.

Of particular interest is how these sources, together with other cultural products from the fifth to the fifteenth centuries, have been used to equate past performance practices with present ones. Specialists in Indonesian performance pay close attention to the poses of the carved dancing figures at Borobudur, the Buddhist temple, and at Prambanan, the Hindu temple, both built during the first Mataram kingdom. Parallels are drawn with the *Natyasastra,* the classical Sanskrit canon for performance, as evidence of a direct link between the performance traditions of India and Java. This connection remains speculative but is highly influential in the Indonesian histories of dance and also in Western scholarship.

Another important model for present national aspirations also dates from the late Hindu-Javanese period. This is the *Nagarakrtagama,* a court chronicle of events between 1359 and 1365 in the kingdom of Majapahit. Detailed descriptions of performances have undoubtedly been important for understanding what the court performance culture of Majapahit might have been like, but they are also employed to give meaning to the present-day court repertoire. Traits evident in these early descriptions are often presented as having been crystallized over time into a distinctive Yogyakartan tradition.

The kingdom of Majapahit was defeated by Java's first Islamic kingdom, Demak (ca. 1478-ca. 1550), which was itself defeated by the kingdom of Pajang (1568-82), which in turn was overcome by the second kingdom of Mataram (1582–1749). Although more information about performance is available for these centuries, the sources are fragmented, rarely contemporaneous, and heavily mythologized.

The second kingdom of Mataram has been significant in providing models of leadership for the twentieth-century Indonesian state, especially in the figure of Sultan Agung (1613–45), who, it is claimed by historians, "invented" the female ceremonial dance tradition of Be-dhaya. In the late seventeenth century, Rijklof Van Goens, the Dutch governor-general (1678–81), noted both the militaristic ethos of the court and its female dancers, features that were subsequently perceived as significant in tracing the lineage of the Bedhaya tradition as practiced in twentieth-century Yogyakarta.

In the same period, the Englishman Edmund Scot referred to a royal circumcision ceremony at which he saw duels with pikes, figures in masks, "tumbling tricks" by men and women, and other "prettie shews" that had been taught to the "Javans" by Chinese, Gujeratis, Turks, and other traders. This description of a culturally varied and carnavalesque event is interesting because such diversity in performances patronized by a ruler has been overlooked by recent historians. Instead, they define past repertoires according to contemporary ones and create origin stories for contemporary performance culture by tracing a single history for each dance tradition back to the Hindu-Javanese kingdom of Majapahit in order to represent the quintessence of Javanese culture in Yogyakarta.

COMPETITION AT THE CULTURAL HEARTLAND

Local distinctiveness in the performance traditions of Yogyakarta has been represented historically by the difference between the culture of the sultan's court in Yogyakarta and that of the *susuhunan* or *sunan* (the local term of respect for the ruler) in Surakarta. This distinction, evident even in the different titles for the rulers, dates back to the division of the kingdom in 1755, when Prince Mangkubumi rebelled against the accession of Pakubuwana III and established the separate court of Yogyakarta. Taking the name of Hamengkubuwana I, he became its first sultan and founded a dynasty that has continued to the present day. Two minor or junior courts associated with each of the principal royal courts were also established: the Mangkunegaran in Surakarta in 1757 and the Pakuala-man in Yogyakarta in 1813.

The split of Central Java into two royal courts produced duplication of a power base characterized as the center of the cosmos. As a result, legitimacy in historical interpretations about court practices needed to be determined. The competition between the traditions of Yogyakarta and Surakarta to represent Javanese culture might appear to the outside eye to be a competition between the performance of an identical set of cultural practices—however, the distinction is apparent to insiders. Yogyakarta's dance movement is described locally as controlled, disciplined, and authoritative, in contrast to Surakarta's softer, sensual, romantic style. In Yogyakarta, the contrast in style epitomizes differences that carry moral weight endorsed by history: the militaristic ethos is proudly associated with the revolt that led to Yogyakarta's foundation.

During the 1980s, there was a feeling of urgency about establishing a distinct

Yogyakartan dance style to sustain traditions and the sense of *naluri,* or traditional basis for identity. This was because since the 1960s the state academies in Indonesia had taught not only Yogyakarta-style performance, but also Surakarta-style, Balinese, West Javanese, and, by the late 1980s, other Javanese regional traditions. "Javanese dance" had become associated with the Surakarta style because Soekarno, the first president of Indonesia, had preferred it. Similarly, his successor, although born close to the city of Yogyakarta, had allied himself with the court traditions of Surakarta, through his wife's connections with the junior court of Mangkunegaran. Such affiliations intensified the debate about origins and authenticity, and the children, nephews, and nieces of Sultan Hamengkubuwana VIII (1921–39) and their children put considerable energy into distinguishing a Yogyakartan style in order to produce discrete forms of culture. As a well-known aristocrat and dancer put it, "Because I was born a Yogyakartan, I feel obliged to sustain my *naluri.* I don't use that word in a fanatical way, but in Surakarta, many are continuing their *naluri,* and if I support theirs as well, it means that the ones here will be lost."

THE CREATION OF YOGYAKARTA'S HEIRLOOMS

The attribution of legitimacy to cultural practices in Javano-Indonesian culture can be compared metaphorically to the process of an object or activity being designated as an heirloom. Practices and objects classed as heirlooms include oral traditions of knowledge, skill in all kinds of performance, weaponry, musical instruments, furniture, items of clothing, ritual prescriptions and relics, and books. Performances may be heirlooms in themselves; they may use objects that are heirlooms; or they may be inspired by texts that are heirlooms. Heirlooms have provided the Central Javanese courts with their power and continue to provide comparatively recent practices with historical depth. To ensure their power, though, all heirlooms require "feeding." In the case of the heirloom of the Javanese dagger, or *keris,* this maintenance is achieved through an annual "ritual" meal of oil and arsenic. In a less concrete but nonetheless equally essential fashion, all heirlooms, even in the form of oral and embodied traditions, need conversations and debates to feed them.

Oral traditions and, indeed, published writings keep such practices alive in the social memory and give them political substance. Thus, the principle of continuity is central to the heirlooms' status, but the possibility does exist that old heirlooms may be displaced by new heirlooms that are more intensely charged with identifications. This is a complex process that is assisted by argument, gossip, and interpretation. The eighteenth-century split presents a problem for the relative antiquity and power of the two court traditions of performance, which are explained in two stories. The first tells how Hamengkubuwana I (1749-92) of Yogyakarta personally created the new fighting dances and dance drama that are performed today.18 The second story relates how Paku-buwana III (1749-88) of Surakarta gave the old forms and objects to Yogyakarta so that he could create new and more powerful ones in his court.

This supports the frequent claim in Yogyakarta that it has the older, more authentic performance traditions reaching back to Sultan Agung and beyond, to the Majapahit kingdom. Both these stories, however, lack documentary evidence and do not take into account the considerable movement of people and ideas between the two courts for the first thirty years after the division. Polarization has since been crosscut by intermarriages and cultural exchanges, and also by the founding of the junior courts, each of which developed dance styles reflecting that of the senior courts of the rival principality. Apart from polarizing differences between the two court centers, stories about performance overlook likely changes within performance practices and the fact that more recent court practices are the result of a process of formalization. Nonetheless, the search for origins to endorse distinctiveness between the two courts through the ideology of heirlooms remains a compelling trait in Javanese historiography and oral tradition.

The precedence of the past to authenticate present practice through the selective interpretation of documentary evidence and through mythic history is particularly noteworthy in the elaborate and lengthy formal women's dance tradition known as Bedhaya.

Bedhaya and Women's Dance

Javanese has no generic word for "dance," and evidence for the historical relationships between different forms of Javanese court performance is extraordinarily complex. The attribution of a mythic past that serves present ideological interest is a further complicating factor. There is an extensive and tangled web of references and sources to explain the origins and antecedents for the performances of the court. The term "Bedhaya" may refer to the female dancers, the dance genre, and specific dances within the genre. Performed at both royal courts of Yogya-karta and Surakarta, Bedhaya is typically enacted by nine dancers, although there is a Bedhaya dance performed at Mangkunegaran, the junior court of the latter, which requires only seven dancers. Particularly revered are the Bedhaya Ketawang, performed annually in the palace of Surakarta on the anniversary of the ruler's accession, and the Bedhaya Semang, performed in the court of Yogyakarta. Srimpi is a related but less grandiose form of women's court performance, enacted by four women. The formalization of "women's dance" in the senior courts has followed the mythologizing pattern of the creation of heirlooms. As noted above, the Bedhaya tradition is said to have been created by Sultan Agung in the seventeenth-century kingdom of Mataram; yet Sultan Agung is a semi-mythical figure when judged by Western criteria of historicity. He is believed to have married the Queen of the South Sea, a goddess, with whom he lived at the bottom of the sea and who, it is said, inspired the Bedhaya Semang. This dance was performed in Yogya-karta for the birthdays of the sultan and of the crown prince until the reign of Hamengkubuwana VII (1877–1921). Significantly, it was always performed at the heart of the court in the Bangsal Kencana, the chief ceremonial hall of the sultan's palace, where the court heirlooms were stored. It ceased to be performed in 1914 for a number of reasons, not least of which was the fear of the goddess.

WOMEN'S DANCE AND NUMERICAL FORMALIZATION

Prior to 1918 (when the first school of training in Yogyakartan court performance was established), the Bedhaya with nine dancers was not allowed to be performed outside the Yogyakartan court unless the sultan gave special permission. It could, however, be enacted in Yogyakarta with seven dancers. The precise number of dancers to perform Bedhaya is perceived by Javanese and Indonesian historians to be an important factor in tracing the lineage of this courtly performance. They have sought out references to nine female dancers, performing at court prior to the establishment of the Yogyakartan sultanate, in the drive to establish antiquity and continuity for the Bedhaya tradition as danced in the twentieth century. The fixing of the number of dancers at nine correlates with the sacred connotations of the number nine both for Hindu-Buddhism and for Islam, and the number has been a key factor in making connections between present practices and past texts. Some origin myths link Bedhaya to the seven heavenly nymphs of Hinduism as in the Mangkunegaran version. The discrepancy of seven rather than the later nine dancers is explained by the claim that it was Sultan Agung who later increased the number. The contents of historical documents, however, do not necessarily support the prevalent assumption about contemporary performances and their past.

Evidence for the creation of Bedhaya by Sultan Agung is drawn from court manuscripts and for its appearance from the writings of Rijklof Van Goens, the Dutch governor-general who visited Sultan Agung's court in the seventeenth century. According to Van Goens, he witnessed ceremonial women's dancing, in which five to nineteen young dancing girls, dressed in green and red, black and green, white and red, and white and green, performed to the accompaniment of flutes and violins. When Van Goens's record was published in 1956, his description produced a problematic generic essentialization. His original text refers simply to "daer eerst Koninghs jonge dansmaechden" (the king's young dance maidens), but the Dutch scholar H. J. de Graaf provided the explanation of "de bedaya's" and decided that Van Goens's reference to nineteen was a clerical error for nine. Thus de Graaf interpreted what Van Goens saw in the mid-seventeenth century according to the conventions of the mid-twentieth-century female court performance of Bedhaya. This interpretation has since fed into Indonesian accounts of Bedhaya's historical origins as being from the time of Sultan Agung. It is highly unlikely that Van Goens saw anything as elaborate as the twentieth-century Bedhaya dance, which, I would argue, emerged as a result of later court formalization.

A particularly problematic interpretation concerns attempts to construct an enduring tradition of court performance culture from the earlier Majapahit kingdom of the thirteenth to fifteenth centuries. In his 1960s translation of the fourteenth-century court chronicle the *Nagarakṛtagama,* referred to above, the scholar Theodore Pigeaud explains the word *nawanatya,* used to describe the king's performance, as "the Nine Physiognomies." Pigeaud then links this to the nine dancers who perform the "sacral" Bedhaya Ketawang in front of the enthroned ruler at Surakarta. The scholar R. A. Kern's later interpretation of this word as "nine dances" rather than "nine dancers" has added a further complication.

Connections have also been postulated between the Bedhaya dancers and the *devadasi,* or sacred temple dancers of South India. Such claims now need to be reconsidered in the light of Stuart Robson's more recent translation of the *Nagarakrtagama* in which he transcribes *nawanatya* as "The Nine Principles of Drama," the title of a specific Sanskrit treatise. Robson emphasizes that the term refers not to the number of dancers, but to qualities of drama, such as farce *(hasya)* and pathos *(ka-runa)*. In this reading, then, the number "nine" has lost its supposed ancient link with the performances during the Hindu-Javanese Majapahit kingdom, but this has not yet been registered by dance historians in their interpretations of Bedhaya. Although there is evidence of Sanskritic aesthetics in Hinduized Javanese courts, there is no account of Bedhaya-like dances being performed.

Other textual evidence shows that the number of Bedhaya dancers in court performances has varied over time and according to context. Sultan Amangkurat IV (1719–26) gave his son costumes for seven dancers, and in June 1726 a Dutch official saw fourteen groups of seven dancers, followed by nine dancers of the king, and then another group of seven royal dancers. These accounts suggest that by 1726 nine and seven dancers had become signs of relative status in the Mataram court. Another source, however, claims that in 1755 the regent *(bupati)* of Ponorogo had seven groups of nine Bedhaya dancers. To confuse the matter, in the early nineteenth century, Thomas Stamford Raffles (lieutenant-governor of Java, 1811–16) saw eight Bedhaya dancers.28 It is then wiser not to assume that nine had become standard for court Bedhaya until some point during the nineteenth century, despite the claims of Indonesian and Javanese historians.

WOMEN'S DANCE AND CONTROLS ON FEMALE SEXUALITY

In addition to the search to correlate the present number of dancers in the Bedhaya tradition with examples from the past, there has been a similar effort to fix the gender of its performers as having been unchanged throughout history. At the *sunan*'s palace in Surakarta, Bedhaya dancers were a hereditary professional group of court dancers, whereas Srimpi dancers were often related to the ruler. My research indicates that it became conventional in the Yogyakarta court from probably the nineteenth century until 1922 for female dancers of Bedhaya to be the daughters of court officials who lived in the female quarters and often became unofficial wives of the ruler. As such, they were subject to more stringent rules of purity and protection than the Srimpi dancers, who were often the children and grandchildren of the Sultan. Between 1840 and 1914, Srimpi dances could also be performed by men at the Yogyakartan court. Indeed, until the start of Hamengkubuwana VIII's reign in 1921, both Bedhaya and Srimpi were performed either by women or by men in female dress.

Asserting historical continuity on the basis of gender is problematic, particularly when we consider terminological variation across time and space. The word "bedhaya" on the north coast of Java (Pasisir) means "taledhek," a woman who sings and dances. In the East Java towns of Prabalingga and Lumajan the word "bedajan" refers to a dance by a man dressed as a woman. Amid this confusion of gendering it may be of significance that in Cirebon, in West Java, the kingdom from which Sultan Agung took his wife and various cultural forms, "badhaya" refers to female dancers—a possible origin for the current Central Javanese court usage and even for Bedhaya itself ? These regional variations indicate that gender ascription of performance has been less predictable in the past and even now should not be taken as fixed.

It is evident that in the early twentieth century, the process of for-malization, including rules on the gender of participants in court performance, is related to changing patterns of control over female sexuality. Furthermore, it is aligned with the creation of a second opposition over and above that of the two courts of Surakarta and Yogyakarta. This second opposition concerns the idea of an "inside" Javanese court tradition that contrasts absolutely with an "outside" culture in order to serve as a model for a high classical Indonesian art dance tradition. Because of the emphasis on the court as a distinctive performance sphere separated from outside, it has been ideologically expedient to overlook another possible genealogy for women's court dance. This is the tradition of healing performance found throughout the Malay archipelago, such as *sanghyang* dances in Bali in which young girls possessed by deities perform to protect the community or cure epidemics, and *tayuban,* a kind of "village dancing party" and ritualized performance, still enacted today to the southeast of Yogyakarta, in which professional female singer-dancers *(taledhek, ledhek)* heal or protect babies and animals with face powder.

The *(ta)ledhek* also dance with men, a contrasting aspect to the women's court performances and one that has earned them a reputation of prostitution. The dancing is, however, a gift to the protective spirit in exchange for well-being. In the past, healing roles no doubt gave women status in the community—a status that would have been severely undermined, although not totally eradicated, much earlier by the coming of Islam in the fifteenth century.

The existence of historical records that reveal potentially close analogies between the present-day *tayuban* and former court performances is undoubtedly problematic for Indonesian historians. Certainly, the absence of male partners in Van Goens's account in the seventeenth-century court of Sultan Agung suggests that what he saw was not a *tayuban.* There is, however, an intriguing Javanese reference to a court performance that predates this influential description of women's ceremonial performance. Here, female dancing in the late sixteenth-century court of Senapati in the Pajang kingdom did take the form of a *tayuban* where professional dancers would dance with male guests and serve them drinks.35 There is even earlier evidence.

The *Nagarakrtagama* of the fourteenth-century Majapahit court describes a female performer, Juru i Angin, who makes jokes with another performer, sings, and dances humorously, and then serves drinks to the king. Robson has recently radically suggested that the eight noble *"tekes"* in the Majapahit *raket* play with whom the king jokes, sings, and dances are female, "his minor wives," and not male as previously claimed.36 Humor, eroticism, and alcohol have been excluded from female court performance in Yogyakarta but were clearly present in the 1300s. Whether or not such exclusions began in Sultan Agung's Islamicizing reign, when Hindu traditions were also preserved, must remain speculation. But it provides grist to the mythmaker's mill. The historical sources suggest that the changing status of women is marked by the appearance in the courts of a form of ceremonial dance that, unlike women's ceremonial temple dance in Bali, has no religious function independent of the royal cult of glory.

It is noteworthy that even in the nineteenth century female singers in the court included *taledhek*. Well-known singer-dancers used to be invited to train in Bedhaya inside the court or to dance in *tayubans* in the residences of princes and the prime minister, skillfully guiding their male partner through the dance. A *(ta)ledhek* could become a performer, inside the court, and Hamengkubuwana II even married one. Nyai Riya Larasati, one of Yogyakarta's most esteemed female singers, performed until 1942 as a singer-dancer in a princely residence, where she had learned to sing. She did not dance inside the court but only in the houses of nobles: in the court she only sang, and after independence she worked professionally for Indonesian Republic Radio.

In the New Order period, *tayuban* came to be seen as rowdy and erotic, epitomizing the culture of "outside" and undesirable female behavior, in contrast to polite feminine behavior, represented quintessentially in court performance and the culture of "inside." The pattern of Nyai Riya Larasati's career is symptomatic of the general move after Indonesian independence to control female performance and, indeed, in some respects reflects attempts to abolish dance as a professional activity outside the control of the court and its sanctioned training schools. The perception of the tradition of *tayuban* has been constructed to stand in opposition to that of court performance, which might, unlike the informal *tayuban*, be strictly controlled by men as "culture."

Healing dancers, rather than the conjectured Hindu *devadasi*-like models, as suggested by Th. B. Van Lelyveld in 1931, might seem feasible as a historical source for contemporary female court performers. By the twentieth century, however, such a genealogy had become unspeakable because of the formalization of the "inside" and the formal-ization of the "feminine" dance mode in the court as the only dance mode for women.

Formalization of court culture has involved a process of exclusion. The contemporary Yogyakartan view of feminine court dance excludes erotic, magical, and humorous elements, and recognizes the control by the sultan over female sexuality. In the days when the dancers provided sexual services for the sultan, of course, the restraint on sexuality was a matter of the power of ownership, rather than an aesthetic based on the exclusion of sexuality.

Unlike the commoditized performance of *ledhek*, who take money for their dancing, contemporary court dance as exemplary culture rests on a transcendental, nonmaterial ideology of honor as the basis for exchange, an ideology connected to the dissimulation or deflection of any physical expression of sexuality. Dance teachers, like the court choreographer B. R. Ayu Yudanegara, explain that sinuous and sensual as the Yogyakarta court's female movement traditionally has been, the quality of gentle refinement *(alus)* requires the strict exclusion of eroticism, flirtatiousness, and coyness. Female dancers are taught to control their gaze, lowering it to a point on the floor at a distance of not more than twice their height, to secure the aesthetic effect of sexual detachment. Subtle and oblique, this aesthetic rests on the absence of any overt signs of sexuality, in direct contrast with the "outside" performances of *ledhek*, which, I suggest, continue to be marked by the eroticism and sociality of the dance of the fourteenth-century performer Juru i Angin. The construction of a particular history has been achieved by a repression: these "outside" dancers were described by my informants as the polar opposite to what women's dance in the court, exemplified by Bedhaya (and Srimpi), should be like.

The gendering of court performance to express an essentialized and distinctive Yogyakartan court cultural aesthetic is also formulated in opposition to feminine performance in the *sunan*'s palace in Surakarta. In Yogyakarta, the Surakartan feminine dance style—the exposed shoulders, the arm movements revealing the armpit (concealed in Yogya-karta normally by a more modest costume and always by a lower position for the elbows) and the unlowered eyes—was denigrated for being unseemly. The dance was altogether too lively *(linca)*. Of course, both courts exercise strict control over female sexuality, though Surakarta court performance traditions in general have been less immured than those of Yogyakarta.

Female dance in Surakarta is not contrasted with the performance of *ledhek* outside the court, but is perceived as being on a continuum. What has been "purified" from the Yogyakartan court remains in the Surakarta courts. The immured dance, performed by *ledheks* to open *tayubans* in villages, forms part of the court repertoire, referred to by Yogyakarta diehards as the "Surakarta palace *tayuban*." K. R. T. Hardjanegara, a senior official of the *sunan*'s palace in Surakarta, suggested that these different court ideologies of female performance reflect the conditions under which the courts were founded. Surakarta is agrarian and maintains its links to rites of fertility, while Yogyakarta celebrates its origins in rebellion and military prowess. The heirlooms of Surakarta are related to farming, and court performance is associated with fertility and thanksgiving, expressed through themes of marriage and sexual union in Bedhaya Ketawang and in plays performed from the Pañji and Damarwulan story cycles. In Yogyakarta, on the other hand, military themes from the Mahabharata are the most popular, and love and marriage only come into the story as a result of abductions occurring in warfare.

To summarize, the modern gendering and genres of dance are the result of change and innovation, not repetition of fixed past practices. Long-standing traditions of cross-dressing in ritual performance have been replaced by fixed identifications between performers and forms, giving women more scope to perform, albeit within a strictly controlled ethos. The female court dancers are at once the opposite of *ledhek* and their purged incarnation. Women's court dance provides a model for Indonesian women's dance and has been articulated in terms of an opposition to village and professional performance, an opposition that is seen by people in Yogyakarta as being weakly maintained in Surakarta, and that thus articulates the second opposition, between Yogyakarta and Surakarta. What was once a control of sexuality and rights over reproduction by the sultan has been transformed into an indirect control of female sexuality, which is given generalized aesthetic exemplary value in the contemporary Javano-Indonesian culture.

A Skeptical Attitude

Performance histories in Indonesia have worked to naturalize contemporary practice with reference to the past, just as traditional Javanese historiography mythologized events to produce impressions of preordained order and continuity. In the case of female performance, the demarcation between "inside" and "outside," which contemporary Yog-yakartan commentators use to distinguish the practices of its court, has come about by a process of monopolization and formalization expressive of strict control. It is likely that Sultan Agung's dance maidens had more in common with *ledhek* than with contemporary Bedhaya dancers, but we will never know, unless some new manuscript evidence comes to light. This is why it is also the case that the significance of present practices gains weight and power from resonances with practices referred to in writings of the past. Bedhaya dances have been a particularly effective resource for enhancing the mystique of Javanese rulers and their courts, and the martial ethic in Yogyakarta has given rise to a modern aesthetic.

The uses of history and anthropology for dance research as illustrated in this account require a skeptical attitude because sources, which became fact by status or iteration, have to be interpreted from a different standpoint. During my fieldwork in the 1980s, Indonesian historians and intellectuals espoused strongly rationalistic scientific models of explanation in order to build a foundation of knowledge that would be appropriate for the development of the postcolonial state. The agenda among dance experts was to establish a positivist factual history—but as my research has revealed, this did not necessarily prevent the selective use and interpretation of documentary evidence by local and Western researchers. My example shows time and again how scholarly research by foreigners made points that have been taken up by Indonesian scholars—who themselves have read the works of foreign scholars and been trained by them.

The visibility of dance makes it particularly appropriate in the invention of tradition through a process in which appearances come to symbolize cultural reality. So dance has been and remains particularly susceptible to attracting discourses that contribute to that reality and inform how those embodied practices are perceived and valued. When the New Order ended in 1998, cultural politicians in the courts and ministries started to take stock of political and economic contingencies and are still waiting to see where things might go. As people begin to discuss more openly the stories and myths promoted during the New Order years, they are also wondering which ones it will be expedient to promote in the future, and from where the inspiration for those inventions of tradition will come.

Meanwhile, the analysis of historiography in Western theory has recognized increasingly the mythic fictional dimensions that have characterized the making of history and that remain present in contemporary practices, under the guise of a factual "modern" approach. As this chapter has demonstrated, my own attempt to get behind the representations of outsiders and insiders and to piece together another story to show dance as something other than that represented in the language of power—without beginning to slip back into the very mythologizing I was questioning—remains problematic, or maybe even impossible.

4

Utopia, Eutopia and E.U. Topia

Cultural performances may signal differing meanings according to changing political and symbolic economies. The use of dance, particularly folk dance, to project various images of nationalism and ethno-nationalism in Eastern Europe has a long history dating back to the nineteenth century. In this chapter, I consider symbolic representation and the play of memory in the performance of folklore ensembles in the former Yugoslavia, from the Second World War to the early years of the twenty-first century. This period witnessed a transition from a politically unified Communist state under General Tito to the country's violent collapse and virtual dismemberment in the civil wars of the 1990s. Throughout, and in the uneasy peace of the following decade, staged and seemingly spontaneous performances of folk dance took place, thus posing questions with regard to representations of nationalism and ethno-nationalism. Based on the conceit of utopia—a perfect and harmonious world—this chapter narrates the shifting meanings and tensions of such performances within three broadly delineated periods, in order to underline the relationship between the ideological goals and experienced realities of changing political economies and the memories and meanings these performances of folk dance held for their participants and local audiences.

BRIDGING HISTORY, SYMBOL, AND MEMORY: AN ETHNOGRAPHIC MOMENT CRYSTALLIZES

An interesting phenomenon occurred during live television coverage by Cable News Network (CNN) of the bombing of the capital of Belgrade by the North Atlantic Treaty Organization (NATO) during the Yugoslav war of the 1990s.1 Rather than engage in an indiscriminate bombing campaign that might have resulted in a politically unacceptable level of civilian casualties, NATO embarked instead on a deliberate air campaign aimed at destroying or disabling Belgrade's infrastructure. In fact, one of NATO's goals was to avoid casualties altogether. As a result, the Yugoslav government acted defensively to protect the city's infrastructure by surrounding it with people, thus hoping to dissuade NATO attacks. In Belgrade, this tactic focused on the city's bridges. Night after night civilians pinned paper targets onto their clothing and stood on the bridges of Belgrade.

One of those nights stands out in my memory. As the camera panned through the milling ranks of Belgraders, dressed for a cool night spent standing on a bridge, its gaze fell upon three young women dressed in the typical folk costume of Sumadija, a rural area in north central Serbia. Amid the drab browns and blacks of coats and jackets, these three young women, linked hand to elbow, stood out as they danced a traditional *kolo,* a dance form characterized by a circular or curvilinear pattern. Although the video clip was a short one, these young women were clearly good dancers, seemingly perfectly acquainted with the standardized choreography of the stage performance of this dance (body position and linkage, curved path, and so on), and the bystanders obviously approved of both their appearance and their performance. Since these young women were evidently not nineteenth-century rural women dancing together after church on Sunday, nor did they appear to have ridden in on the bus from Sumadija in order to defend the bridges of the capital, one might well ask just what were these young women doing there and what did they represent to those surrounding them? The answer to this question lies in an anthropological analysis of the role of folk dance performance in creating a type of social and cultural memory, contributing, in both a symbolic and actual sense, to the formation of modern nation-states and to what we might call one form of an "imagined community."

The relationship between dance and political economy has been explored by dance folklorist Anthony Shay in the Yugoslavian context and elsewhere. Using LADO (the Croatian professional folk dance company) as one example, he has examined some of these types of professional state-sponsored performance ensembles in their role as representations of the state. His historical and folkloristic perspective focuses on examples from anti-liberal, authoritarian states or those that have had fragile democracies. I propose that an alternative future research direction, from a more anthropological perspective, is to investigate the types of political economies that result in the creation of a state-sponsored, professional folklore ensemble. Such a line of questioning needs to be pursued along with an analysis of the processes by which some dances are selected for representation, while others are rejected. The ethnographic research that underpins my argument in this chapter uses a North American, cultural anthropological paradigm, which tends to emphasize the constructivist role of culture and its idealist, as opposed to materialist, nature. Specifically, the research is situated within that body of work through which North American scholars have viewed the expressive cultures of Eastern Europe. My work has largely focused on analyzing the relationship between folk dance performances and the political economies within which they are embedded and has been primarily centered on Bosnia-Herzegovina, the one non-ethnic-majority republic of former Yugoslavia.

Bosnia and Herzegovina, the symbolic and geographic center of the country, from which the Yugoslav state was formally constituted in 1942, was the only republic in which no one group was in the majority.6 The other five republics had eponymous ethnic majorities: Serbs were the majority in Serbia, Slovenes in Slovenia, Croatians in Croatia, Montenegrins in Montenegro, and Macedonians in Macedonia. In the post–Second World War Yugoslav federation, an additional two autonomous provinces, Kosovo and Vojvodina, which were formally incorporated within Serbia, held a majority of ethnic Albanians (in Kosovo) and a mixed population of Serbs, ethnic Hungarians, and other national minorities (in Vojvodina).

Thus, of the full republics in the post– Second World War Yugoslav federation, Bosnia's predominantly Muslim population was not of one ethnic group. Rather than being ethnic Turks left behind when the Ottoman Empire retreated, the Muslims were the descendants of Christians, Serbian Orthodox and Croatian Roman Catholics, whose ancestors had converted to Islam, if for no other reason than to avoid Ottoman taxes on non-Muslims. I have had many conversations over the years with native chauvinists attempting to "prove," often using ethnographic, cadastral (documents pertaining to taxation), or historical data, that Bosnian Muslims are "really" Serbs or Croats. It is because of the unique nature of the republic of Bosnia and Herzegovina within the Yugoslav polity that the attempt at the creation of a national memory was most important, most easily ascertainable, and had the greatest potential to succeed. I make the argument here that folk dance performance had, and still has, an important symbolic and actual role to play in the construction of national memory.

In Marcel Proust's classic novel *Remembrance of Things Past,* a madeleine pastry serves as an aid to memory in order to link the protagonist with his own past. Dance performances, specifically those of amateur and professional folklore ensembles in former Yugoslavia, played a similar part in helping to build three kinds of Yugoslav nation-state. The first relates to an imagined Yugoslav *utopian* past. Utopia signifies an idealized, romanticized society and is used here to represent the post-revolutionary stage of building state socialism, undertaken in accordance with the goals of Yugoslav policy and practice after the Second World War. The second kind of nation-state relates to a *eutopian* recent present. Here, *eutopia* refers to the actual conditions under the Yugoslav variant of state socialism, especially from about 1960 until the dissolution of the Yugoslav state in the early 1990s.

The third and final characterization I identify as *E.U.-topian*—an imagined post-Yugoslav European Union (E.U.) future. This designates the end of the Yugoslav experiment, seen clearly in retrospect as beginning with the death of Tito in 1980, accelerating along with the geopolitical repercussions of the fall of the Berlin Wall in 1989, and culminating in the 1992–95 Bosnian War and violent dismemberment of the country. The post-1989 events, including the eventual collapse of the Soviet Union, subsequently led to the demise of all the national variants of state socialism in Eastern Europe. In the Yugoslav case, the country itself disintegrated into separate nation-states, each of which now independently seeks ultimate accession to the imagined "paradise" of the European Union. In each of these periods—that is, the utopian, eutopian, and E.U.-topian— the performance of folk dance and the founding and organization of ensembles had, and has, an important role as a symbol for Yugoslav and post-Yugoslav society. The "topia" are not intended to represent discrete periods in the following discussion but act as heuristic devices to stimulate thought on the relation between performance as an aesthetic production and as political economy.

In a sense, group expressive behaviors, formalized and enshrined in public performances, have served as a sort of social memory in twentieth-century Yugoslavia. This social memory through public performance simultaneously interpreted the past, explained how the present should be, and projected a future. Particularly under Communist ideological direction, the past, present, and future were ideologically reinterpreted through national cultural policy, much as occurred elsewhere in Eastern Europe and the Soviet Union. The pre-Communist past was invoked in two ways: first, through the distorting lens of a sort of pernicious negative nostalgia directed at urban elites, and second, as a romanticized image of a bucolic rural life. Meanwhile, the present was conceptualized as progress toward the perfection of the future. These social memories created through folklore performance are in the mode of historian Eric Hobsbawm's "invented tradition" in that they "seek to inculcate certain values and norms of behavior by repetition, which automatically implies continuity with the past. In fact, where possible, they normally attempt to establish continuity with a suitable historic past."7 In the Yugoslav instance, dance and music performances, as manipulated by the state, tried also to establish a link with a socialist utopian future.

In the post–Second World War Yugoslavia of Tito, as in the 1920s and 1930s, cultural elites attempted to direct the creation of a supranational culture, a Yugoslav identity. From 1945 to roughly 1960, the Yugoslav government played a central role in the development and implementation of cultural policy. Slavic literary historian Andrew Wachtel points out that the separate national cultures were allowed to exist at what he felt was characterized as the "harmless level of folk culture."8 While this folk stratum may have been perceived as harmless in other Eastern European countries, I believe this was less so in the multinational Yugoslav polity, where nationalism and ethno-nationalism were ultimately able to appropriate symbols of folk culture, including dance and music.

A YUGOSLAV UTOPIA

Although attempts to create a Yugoslav utopia, or at least a common Yugoslav culture, date at least to the 1840s when the Romantic nationalism of the era spread to the Balkans, the Second World War marked a decisive break with previous attempts. From 1945 to the early 1960s, the creation of an ideologically driven socialist utopia was a goal of the state that was reflected in cultural policy. In this post–Second World War period, following the Marxist/Leninist model of national/state development, all significant cultural organizations and activities were subsumed under the rubric of the state. State agencies quickly utilized the model provided by the Soviet Union in which no activity was allowed to develop that might allow an alternate view of the state or an alternative base of power. This resulted in what social scientist and media critic Miklos Haraszti calls "directed culture" in which the state holds a monopoly on art and the official aesthetic. As encapsulated by the classic Stalinist formula, culture could be "nationalist in form" as long as it was "socialist in content."

Folk dances, with their ability to be appropriated and transformed for the stage, were significant cultural grist for this ideological mill. As a result, and with the emphasis on the importance of the urban proletariat, socialism often attempted to render ideologically harmless the more rural-oriented folklore through a process of fossilization, festivalization, and antiquarianization. These related terms, which I broadly adapt here from folklore-oriented studies, refer to reducing the variation in performance (fossilization), orienting those performances toward formally sanctioned and sometimes competitive events, separating audiences from performers (festivalization), and displacing referents in the performance backward in time/space (antiquarianization). Under the guise of preserving folklore, the former state of Yugoslavia decontextualized several of these group expressive behaviors, sanitizing them ideologically and transforming dance and music into passive entertainment for urban audiences.

A number of formal performance events, such as festivals and folk concerts, were established as venues for the performance of folklore, rather than for participation in folklore. At the International Folklore Festival in Zagreb, for example, "Plesite s nama" (Dance with Us) is presented as an opportunity for the audience and dancers of various groups to dance folk dances together on the outdoor stage. This participatory aspect, however, occurs only after the live television broadcast of the festival ceases. In the nonparticipatory events aimed at urban, national, or, indeed, international audiences, dance and music have become re-presentations of the ubiquitous and anonymous "folk." The models created for performance serve both as a social experience, that is, of integration in a common experience of performance for the performers, and as a form of public entertainment for audiences.

In developing a distinctive Yugoslav form of Communism, worker self-management (instituted in 1950) joined "the brotherhood and unity of the peoples of Yugoslavia" and the idea of worker self-management spread to the organization of amateur folklore groups, KUDs (Kulturno Umjetnicko Drustvo, or Cultural Art Societies). In the excitement of building socialism during this immediate postwar period, party cadres were instructed to encourage and assist in their formation. The first Five Year Plan for Education and Culture was enacted to direct and fund these activities. These amateur ensembles, some based on prewar groups, were sponsored by labor-affiliated organizations such as the Railway Workers (ZKUD), Workers (RKUD), and University/Academic (U/AKUD) groups. Amateur folklore ensembles had begun to appear in the republics of Yugoslavia by 1945, although political scientist and cultural theoretician Stevan Majstorovic states that during this period quantitative growth was not equaled by growth in quality.

By the late 1940s, professional folklore groups were founded on the model of the Moiseyev Ensemble in what was then the Soviet Union. Some, such as Croatia's LADO, were converted from amateur ensembles. Slovenia, Bosnia-Herzegovina, and Montenegro did not support the establishment of a professional ensemble, thus usually the best of the university-affiliated folklore groups acted in that role. In 1950, the first Smotra Jugoslavie (Gathering of Yugoslavia) was held in Belgrade, featuring groups from all over the country: eleven choirs, seven drama groups, seventeen folklore groups, fifteen ethnic art sections, and twenty-two individual singers and other performers. These large public gatherings later appeared in Zagreb, Croatia, as well as in other republics and continue today in Zagreb as the Medjunarodna Smotra Folklora (International Gathering of Folklore).

Typically, the amateur organizations were controlled by a board of directors, and their activities were divided into areas of interest and age group. A typical amateur folklore group would be made up of separate sections. Characteristically, these were a Pioniri (Pioneer) group for children, "B" and "C" groups that functioned primarily as training groups, and an "A" group that gave most of the public performances. These amateur folklore groups competed in public performances that were judged by visiting choreographers or other approved experts.

A standard requirement for a typical KUD was the performance of an all-Yugoslav program. This meant that a KUD (as opposed to village folklore groups, which could perform their local mono-ethnic or national material) had to be able to perform suites of dances and music from all six republics and the two autonomous provinces. Successful performance of the all-Yugoslav choreography could result in more funding being directed to that group through its sponsoring organization, as well as other benefits, such as being authorized to travel and to represent Yugoslavia in international folklore performances. As an informant remembers this period: "In some places, it was more important to have a good KUD than a factory, because everybody is happy to have a big KUD which can perform the all-Yugoslav program."

In many ways KUDs represented a recapitulation of the nineteenth-century nationalists' search for a symbolism based on peasant culture. A few KUDs (the minority) were categorized as *izvorni* KUDs (meaning from the spring or a pure source, that is, traditional) because they performed using traditional instruments and costuming and focused on the preservation and performance of one repertoire, while others (a majority) were *stilizatsia* KUDs (meaning stylized, that is, allowing the use of modern instruments and stage costumes) and performed a two-hour-long, pan-Yugoslav program. Village folklore ensembles, outside the urban-oriented state system, were encouraged to preserve and perform their own folklore, that is, of the nationality of their village.

Given that in the postwar era, villages all over the country were emptying out as young people moved to the city, this sometimes meant that obviously elderly people would be performing dances associated with youth. Village folklore groups were also strongly influenced by KUDs and professional ensembles. This is exemplified by an incident at a *smotra*, or festival, in Bosnia in which a local village ensemble wanted to be taught to perform the suite from Vranje in south Serbia that they had seen performed by KUDs, rather than their own village's traditional material.16 Ethnic minorities were encouraged to form KUDs of their own, focusing on their own ethno-national repertoire. A Hungarian KUD in Croatia, a Ukrainian KUD in Bosnia (Taras Sevchenko), and a Turkish KUD in Macedonia (Jeni Jol) were among this latter type. During ethnographic research in 1985, the complexity of types of folk dance performance that had arisen was clarified for me by eminent Bosnian choreographer Vaso Popovic. He outlined his view of the traditional-theatrical continuum of folk dance in Bosnia thus:

1. *Izvorni* (pure) folk dancing in the villages.

This would be the realm of traditional dances done in traditional contexts such as dancing *kolo* after church on Sunday.

2. *Izvorni* dances performed on stage by what he called *seoske grupe* (village groups).

I have to comment here that "pure" and "on stage" may not always be compatible. In another example from my fieldwork in Bosnia, a village dance group was highly resistant to such elementary stagecraft as modifying their dance so as to not have their backs to the audience. In a sense, they were resisting *scenska kultura* (stage culture). In the living memory of these villagers, this was simply not the way the dance was done.

3. *Izvorni* dance in the city.

Some urban KUD performances of this material were his example. In other words, urban performers had learned these dances in rehearsal, not in the village.

4. Stylized *izvorni* dances in urban KUDs.

An example is Popovic's own *Ozrenske Igre* (Dances from Ozren), a choreographed suite of dances from the mountains of north central Bosnia, performed by KUD Veselin Maslesa of Banja Luka.

In 1999, I witnessed a perfect example of this at the Second International Folklore Festival in Sarajevo. A group from a dance academy in Tirana, Albania, performed a typical Albanian suite of a type familiar to Yugoslavs from suites of dances representing Kosovo. Everything from the dancers' pointing feet to the women's short skirts to the athletic and balletic movement accentuated the fact that this suite of dances was a confection of a stage-oriented choreographer.

5. High style—what Popovic called *balet,* that is, ballet and modern dance.

I would include in this category some *estrada,* or popular folk dances, that is, those intended as stage entertainments of the type seen on Yugoslav television variety programs.

Popovic's first category represented traditionally contextualized dances. The second represented those dances recontextualized by their traditional performers. The third and fourth represent *izvorni* and *stiliza-tsia* KUDs of urban folk performing dances they might otherwise never have performed. The fifth, of course, represents state sponsorship of culture. The latter three situations demonstrate, as noted by ethnochoreol-ogist Andriy Nahachewsky, the divorce of professional ensembles from experiential knowledge of traditional folk dance performance. To paraphrase the title of the influential handbook on recontextualizing traditional folk dances to the stage by Croatian choreographer Ivan Ivan-can, the connection between *folklor* (traditional participation) and *scena* (stage performance) has been severed.18 In light of my thesis here, there is an important difference between categories one and two and categories three and four. Categories one and two represent an actual memory of dance as a part of everyday life. The third and fourth categories represent the shaping of the experience of urban folk, giving them a cultural memory of a time and a place (premodern rural life) they may not have personally experienced.

Pleasant memories of the enjoyment of performance inspired a number of members of one Sarajevo KUD from this early era to reconstitute themselves in the 1980s as the Veterani section of U/AKUD Slobodan Princip-Seljo. This was the first such instance that I have found in Bosnia of a 1940–50s "A" section recreating itself decades later. Rather than performing the dances of their own ethno-national group or ancestral/ traditional village repertoire, they rehearsed and subsequently performed the dances of the all-Yugoslav repertoire that they had first encountered decades earlier as members of an urban KUD. In this sense, this older generation literally embodied in performance the successful creation of a Yugoslav national identity.

An example of how personal experience and memory shape meaning in dance relates to performances of the *Partizan kolos* (partisan round dances) in various regional and national festival situations. During the Second World War, according to the 1942 Statute of the Proletarian Liberation Brigades, every partisan unit was required to have a culture team.19 The culture team's mission had a folk dance section, often accompanied by agitprop (agitation-propaganda) theater and the like. The later reenactment of the *Partizan kolos* evoked the brotherhood and unity of the anti-Fascist struggle, and although partisan dances had already been included as a component in other festivals, according to a Saraje-van informant, specific festivals of partisan dances appeared first in Bosnia only in 1984–85.20 In their original context, partisan dances were often simply traditional round or line dances renamed and thus made ethno-nationally neutral. These ethnically neutral, war-contextualized dances served two functions.

On the one hand, they existed in the memory of the postwar audiences as something they may have performed around campfires and under the direction of partisan culture teams as Yugoslavs, not as Serbs, Croats, Slovenes, and so on. Seeing these dances performed, albeit on stage and by dancers too young to have fought together and then to have danced around military campfires, validated this generation's experiences of comradeship and sacrifice. At the same time, partisan *kolos* served to create a memory in audiences too young to have experienced firsthand the unity of the Second World War. Thus, choreographed and recontextualized folk dances contributed to the creation myth of the new Yugoslavia. Croatian musicologist Naila Ceribasic notes that one folk dance in particular, *Kozaracko Kolo,* was simple enough to be easily recontextualized as the main partisan dance, and this simplicity allowed performers and audiences to make an affective connection. In a way, this process is analogous to the many Second World War movies produced by postwar Yugoslav studios, which simplified the war narrative for a postwar audience of the victors, and which emphasized the comradeship and sacrifice of the participants to create a common social memory for the generation that experienced it.

A Yugoslav Eutopia

If the utopian period considered above is examined as a period during which the new state used existing folklore to create a fresh image, then the eutopian period, painted here with a broad brush as existing from the early 1960s until the outbreak of civil war in 1992, was one in which that image was consolidated both at home and abroad. Tensions, however, existed. In the early 1960s, the attempt to create a unified national Yugoslav culture was abandoned. The Constitution of 1963 replaced "the brotherhood and unity [*bratsvo i jedinstvo*] of the peoples of Yugoslavia" with a pluralist, multinational self-image. It was felt that Titoism and the Yugoslav version of socialism would be enough to hold the state together. Self-management was extended to the role of culture. But who would be the managers in self-managed culture?

In folklore, this eutopian period is best characterized by two themes, commodification and consolidation, and is exemplified by a period known as the

KUD *Kriza* (the KUD Crisis). Lasting until the early 1970s, the KUD *Kriza* began in the mid-1950s when socialist realism was abandoned and culture became less "mass" and more concentrated in the hands of culture workers. In the consolidation phase of amateur folklore, tensions arose between being what was described in ethnographic interviews as "a really good, professional-like KUD," where only the best performers were on display, and the ideological need to be open and democratic and so inclusive of all standards. Because of these conflicts, a number of KUDs ceased to function during this era, including some quite distinguished ones, such as KUD Veselin Maslesa of Banja Luka.

Folklore performances also became transformed into more than the *symbolic* commodities of the immediate postwar period. As well as being replaceable units of ideological production and consumption, staged choreographies based on folk themes became *actual* commodities, as performing groups came under pressure to address economic imperatives. KUDs, in order to meet their financial needs, began performing at other venues, taking contracts with tourist hotels, for example. Thus, KUDs also became packaged as part of the value-added segment of a tourist economy, enhancing foreign visitors' memories of their holidays in a romanticized Yugoslavia. In a certain sense, choreographed folk dances may be thought of as particularly "robust" forms of cultural commodities. So long as audiences appreciate them, they can be repeated ad infinitum locally and even be exported internationally, both to make money and to represent the state. Indeed, some suites of dances became iconic representations and would frequently appear in ensembles' repertoires: a Sumadija suite represented Serbia, a Posavina suite represented Croatia, a "silent *kolo*" stood for Bosnia, the *Lindjo* (a couple dance) stood for the coastal region of Dalmatia, and so on.

In comparing utopia (1945 to the early 1960s) and eutopia (the early 1960s to 1992), it is helpful to think of the earlier period as one in which Yugoslav socialism was being built. Dance and music performance was one of its aspects, along with ideologically driven national projects such as railway roadbed projects constructed by idealistic socialist youth. The eutopian period, on the other hand, was one of the consolidation of socialism. A generation had grown up with stage-oriented folklore performance as a normal part of, primarily, urban and modern life. The KUD Crisis represents this process of consolidation of performance under actually existing Yugoslav socialism.

Urban youth were the target of the KUD's primary ideological mission, particularly in Bosnia. Midhat Ridjanovic, a distinguished Bosnian linguist and veteran of Sarajevo's U/AKUD Slobodan Princip-Seljo, used the descriptive phrase *peljovan od* (inoculated against) to indicate the role that amateur folklore groups were assumed to play in creating counterweights to ethno-nationalism. But the youths' principal interest was less in national ideology performance than it was in the opportunity to travel, especially abroad. Bosnian ensembles that had performed at the Eisteddfod (an international festival of traditional folklore, held in Wales) thought it especially ironic, given that festival's particular emphasis on authenticity, that none of them were rural people performing their own traditional material; they were city people from Sarajevo (notably from the RKUD Proleter) from different ethnic backgrounds.

The social memories created for them were much more personal: it was their experience of stage performance as part of a KUD, not as part of a traditional dance context that had meaning for them. When Muslim, Serb, and Croatian Bosnian *Ve t e r ani* would gather for a *teferic* (picnic) in the 1980s and 1990s, their memories as a group were of their experience as stage performers. In one sense, the state's attempt to build a nation through performance had some effect. People valued their performance experience, but no "Yugoslav" dance emerged, no dance became "the" dance that represented a unified Yugoslav ideal. Dances of the individual Yugoslav republics, presented as part of the all-Yugoslav program, were always potentially available for nationalist re-appropriation. Attempts were made to continue the supranational dance tradition of *Par-tisansko Kolo* and *Titovo Kolo* (as some of these recontextualized dances were called) at specific festivals.

One such festival I attended in the late 1980s was held in honor of Tito's birthday, with all the KUDs of Sarajevo participating. After the performances of various standard suites, the grand finale took the form of a mass performance of a specially choreographed dance with the dancers remaining in the costumes they had worn during the performances of the various suites that they had performed previously in the program. It should be remembered that the KUDs of Sarajevo were, almost by definition, multi-ethnic. Thus the grand finale mixed both apparent (as indicated by costuming) and actual Serbian, Croatian, and Muslim youth, epitomizing the unity amid diversity that Bosnia, and Yugoslavia, should ideally have represented. This was an interesting parallel to the performance by Sarajevo KUDs at the opening of the Olympic Games in Sarajevo in 1984. Attired in snowsuits, each group in one of the five Olympic colors, they performed a mass, choreographed folk dance representing the submersion, but not the eradication, of national identity in the utopianism of the Olympic movement.

In broader terms, it might be argued that the potential of a socialist utopia had yielded to the actuality of a socialist eutopia. *Utopia,* mostly used to suggest a fantasyland of perfection, in effect, means "no place": the unachievable political and social dream beyond human grasp. *Euto-pia,* on the other hand, translates from the Greek as "good place" and arguably, at least, could be perceived as a desirable goal. If not a perfect place, or even a good place, perhaps a good enough place would still be something to be desired in the Yugoslav context. The projected past of a socialist utopia, the projected future of a united but culturally diverse country, was highly visible at staged folk performances. After 1980 and Tito's death, folklore performances became privileged venues for extravagant displays of loyalty to Tito's memory; the slogan "Tito, This We Swear to You, From Your Path We'll Never Deviate" always appeared somewhere near the stage at each performance. The two ideas were thus connected: Tito's vision of a united Yugoslav state and multinational folklore performance. Another popular slogan also appeared, "After Tito—Tito!" presaged not hope but desperation. Again, a social memory of the utopian socialism of the Tito era was evoked, as the country slid far from the goal of eutopian socialism.

By the late 1980s, living standards had declined as a result of hyperinflation and the mistakes of workers self-managing their own failing industries. As some of the constituent peoples of Yugoslavia began to say: it might be better being out than being in. What Marvin Harris has aptly deemed "ethnomania," an especially aggressive and virulent form of ethnocentrism, began to consume the Serbian imagination, and the country started to collapse in the wars of Yugoslav succession/secession. Yugoslav eutopia for many, especially in Bosnia, soon became quite the reverse: a true distopian nightmare, as Yugoslavia seemed poised to join the ranks of post–Cold War failed states.

(Former) Yugoslavia in E.U.-topia

In the post–Bosnian War era, relationships between folklore performances and political aspiration have continued. Some, indeed most, of the choreographic material from the former periods of utopia and eutopia has been used to represent the contemporary political situation and the projected future of the emergent states from the former Yugoslavia. Not every performer in the various folklore ensembles, however, found a common meaning in the relationship between repertoire and symbolic representation during this postwar period. As I discovered from field-work in Bosnia, especially in multi-ethnic, urban KUDs, for many performers their common memory of performance was an important part of their shared memory as Yugoslavs; their interests as folklore performers did not automatically relate to their present and future status as members of the new states or indeed as members of specific ethnic communities. Former war correspondent Steven Erlanger notes the emergence of the phenomenon of "Yugo-nostalgia," of older people remembering when Yugoslavia was supported by the West as an independent Communist state. This Yugo-nostalgia represents a connection to the utopian future past, a "future history" (a familiar trope in science fiction literature) that was not.

Less nostalgic meanings, however, could be determined in the folklore performances, and these related to the new future signaled by plans for Bosnia-Herzegovina eventually to become a member of the European Union. Since the conclusion of the Yugoslav war with the signing in 1995 of the Dayton Peace Accords, the advantages of economic inclusion and political affiliation with the European Union had became apparent for Bosnia-Herzegovina. Membership in the E.U. requires adherence to criteria for democracy, equality, and respect for minority and human rights. In Bosnia in the early twenty-first century, folk dance is used to illustrate such ideals of fair and tolerant social and cultural inclusion.

During the early part of the war against Bosnia, for obvious reasons, KUDs had eliminated almost all local Serbian (and later many Croatian) dances from their repertoires, at least in Sarajevo. They did, nonetheless, continue creating memory through dance. People attended KUD rehearsals and scheduled performances, even during the darkest hours of the Serbian siege of Sarajevo. It was understandable that performers might not want to celebrate the culture of the former Serbian neighbors who were sniping at them on their way to rehearsal, or when Serbian or Croatian ethnic militias were driving their rural relatives from their homes. I remember yet another example of the emotional resonance of dance during times of war, once again captured and broadcast by CNN. As United Nations troops entered a small town east of Sarajevo, the camera focused on a group of women who began dancing a traditional Bosnian dance in celebration.

After the signing of the Dayton Peace Accords, which ended the active military stage of the dismemberment of Bosnia, ensembles began to reintegrate Serbian material into their performances, particularly those performances that might be viewed by foreign dignitaries. In the modern E.U.-topian period, the first step was to perform those national dances that had become iconic standards from before the recent war, dances that many KUD members had performed growing up. Classic choreographies of pre-1992 material filled this need. The next step was to perform integrated dances, that is, those in which the performers were in the costumes of the three main prewar ethnic groups but performed the same dance medley.

A medley of dances called *Sarajevo Zavrazlama* was revived and neatly fitted this bill. The final step in the use of folk dances in E.U.-topian Bosnia was to perform a stand-alone suite of Bosnian Serb dances. I witnessed this in 1999, though the organizers were careful to dust off a pre–Bosnian War suite of Serbian dances, *Okolina Sarajeva* (Around Sarajevo) with which audiences were already familiar, as was I. A reference to viewing a performance that included *Okolina Sarajeva* first appears in my field notes in 1985.

Sarajevo, Bosnia's capital, also now plays an active role on the international folk festival circuit. Like its long-established Croatian counterpart, the main festival in July is composed of lectures, costume exhibitions, parades, and performances. I remember one outdoor performance during the festival, in what is certainly a concession to the role of religion in contemporary Bosnia. As a KUD finished one dance in its suite of dances, they stopped, and a pause ensued for several minutes while the dancers and musicians stood idly by on the stage as the muezzin of the nearby mosque began the electronically amplified call to prayer from the minaret.

A BRIDGE NOT TOO FAR: THE ETHNOGRAPHIC CHRYSALIS UNFOLDS

Viewed through the heuristic devices of utopia, eutopia, and E.U.-topia, this consideration of folklore ensembles and their repertoires demonstrates the shifting and situational meanings of dance in relation to political economies. Furthermore, it highlights a key issue in the production of ethnographies and histories of performance.

Anthropologists, undoubtedly influenced by Clifford Geertz's elegant and accessible writing style, and certainly stimulated by the appearance of George Marcus and Michael Fischer's *Anthropology as Cultural Critique* in 1986, as well as Derek Freeman's powerful and persuasive critique three years earlier of Margaret Mead's research in Samoa, came face to face with what has come to be a central question of a postmodern ethnology.

That is, when we write ethnography, are we writing facts as they appear on the ground, or are we writing fictions, essentially pleasant and entertaining memoirs from our time in the field? Are we recording an ethnographic reality, or is the field a palimpsest upon which we place our own constructions? The answer, of course, is that we are doing something of both. We see the cultures under study through the lens of our experience, our memory, and our theoretical orientations. Emic and etic (insider's view and outsider's view), both past and present, exist in constant inter-penetration. In my research work on the folklore performances in various parts of former Yugoslavia, what I am writing about is, in some ways, the conflation and creation of both social and personal memories of the performers and of their audiences.

For the performers, there are the formal, culturally created memories of an imagined idyllic past, created on stage for a receptive audience, aided by the individual memories of performers who literally made the performance and who remember, not an idealized rural past nor the creation of a socialist Yugoslav utopia, but rather their own experience of performing the dances and music of the many peoples of former Yugoslavia. For the audience, these dancers and the dances that they perform carry a number of complex and mutable meanings about ethnic and national identity in embodied movement, in bodily habitus. Returning to my original metaphorical moment, during which a curious ethnographer watches CNN, three young women dancing in the dark in Belgrade come to symbolize the complex relationship bridging memory, history, and ethnography.

5

Qualities of Memory

Investigating the role of embodiment in practices of knowledge and memory, this chapter considers in particular the felt, somatic aspects of movement knowledge. I argue that thinking itself, including the way we access, organize, retrieve, and present information, is as much a matter of somatic understandings as of semiotic ones. Whereas identity has been considered in terms of ethnicity, race, gender, and class, here I suggest that the way kinetic energy is organized to carry meaning constitutes a "difference" that has yet to be investigated. Drawing on field research with dancers in the annual fiesta of Our Lady of Guadalupe in Tortugas, New Mexico, I review findings resulting from a somatic approach.

CONCERNING THEORY AND METHOD

In the 1970s, Richard Bandler and John Grinder, students of anthropologist Gregory Bateson and originators of the popular therapy Neurolinguistic Programming, showed that different people access memory via different sensory modalities. Further, the sensory mode by which an individual *accesses* a memory is often different from the one in which he or she *represents* the memory. All thinking occurs in one or another sensory modality, but the ratios are different for different individuals, and perhaps for the same individual in different circumstances. At about the same time Bandler and Grinder were analyzing sensory access to memory, Clifford Geertz, leading the "interpretive turn" in North American cultural anthropology, wrote that works of art, including dances, are meaningful because they "connect to a sensibility they joined in creating." Since then, scholars working at the juncture of sensory anthropology, performance studies, and dance ethnography have queried the relationship between the sensual and the ideological in the organization of cultural knowledge and memory. For many, the goal has been to return sensory modes of knowledge, and bodily consciousness in particular, to a central place in the study of cultural performance. How do we, in Geertz's terms, "sense with understanding"?

In 1988, James Clifford issued an invitation to assess critically how participant-observation "obliges its practitioners to experience, at a bodily as well as an intellectual level, the vicissitudes of translation," in effect opening the door for a "sensory anthropology." Following Marshall McLuhan, who wrote that "[a]ny culture is an order of sensory preferences," David Howes and Constance Classen suggest, for example, attending to differences in "sensory profiles," the relative emphasis placed on different sensory modalities in different cultural communities.

"What if," Howes writes, "there exist different forms of reasoning, memory, and attention for each of the modalities of consciousness (seeing, smelling, speaking, hearing, etc.) instead of reasoning, memory, and attention being general mental powers?" This is promising, its premise borne out by the work of Bandler and Grinder cited above. Howes and Classen, however, omit kinesthesia, the proprioceptive sense of movement within our own bodies. While kinesthesia might be subsumed under touch, as the changing contours of touch within our own bodies, omitting it from the sensorium leaves us with no sensory reference point for addressing movement as a way of knowing. Is kinesthesia, then, excluded from the sensorium because it refers to no external object and can only be apprehended proprioceptively, that is, within one's own body?

Philosopher Edward Casey distinguishes "body memory" from "memory of the body," the first working primarily through feelings in the body, the second through representations of the body as an object of awareness. For Casey, the first would be properly called *remembering*, the second *recollecting*. He suggests that whereas remembering manifests in terms of "its own depth," recollection is "projected" at a "quasi-pictorial distance from myself as a voyeur of the remembered." In recollection (as well as in verbal reminiscing), Henri Bergson wrote, we "peer" back toward a past that seems to have independent being distant from the present; in body memory, the past is enacted in the present, as a kind of *immanence*. Casey's distinction is useful for thinking about dance history and memory. One might say that dance can work as either recollection or remembering, or both. Recollection, "seeing" a dance in the mind's eye, is the traditional mode of studying dance history. But, remembering, or "feeling" movement memory as immanent kinesthetic sensation, is essential to dancing itself and to its continuation and transmission over time. It is critical to communication via dance and to the cultural knowledge and values negotiated through dance. We cannot exclude it from attention.

Kinesthetic sensations, much less their meaning, are rarely the focus of everyday awareness. As Marcel Mauss and, after him, Pierre Bour-dieu have pointed out, the bodily patterns we master are then enacted outside of conscious awareness. We remember how to drive a car without focusing on the motor skills needed to turn the key in the ignition, depress the clutch, shift into gear, and rev the accelerator. Dancers step up to the barre and begin a daily routine that includes so many brushes, so many pliés, so many relevés, without needing to relearn each day how to do each move. Bourdieu recognized that the very roteness of the "habitus" disguises cultural and historical predispositions, social schemes of perception and thought passed from one generation to the next in patterns of movement. The unconscious braiding of movement practices and ideologies constrains people to perpetuate social structures at the level of the body. For Bourdieu, people are not in possession of the habitus; rather, they are possessed by it.

But the hold of the habitus is not absolute, and we do sometimes transcend its automatic and efficient grip. Performing a plié in the studio, perhaps a dancer has lucid moments of seeing herself, as if from a distance, lined up among the others, holding onto a wooden pole in order to drop and rise "gracefully" over and over again, understanding, in that moment, her complicity with a socioaesthetic system that values "ballet." Her lucid moments may occur in the opposite direction, consciousness diving inward and immersing in the minute sensations of spine extending, wrists softening, breath suspending. In the first kind of lucidity, one calls on visual imagination to project across distances to "see" the larger system; in the second, one calls on proprioception, turning awareness inward to "feel" one's body as a continuum of kinetic sensations. In either case, the hold of the habitus is broken, inviting opening beyond routine.

These two imagined possibilities of transcendence are encapsulated in the polarity of "sensibility and intelligibility," loosely representing, on the one hand, somatic organizations of knowledge and, on the other, the socially sedimented meanings and values embodied in movement systems, especially in their political dimensions. The most succinct elaboration of their complementarity is given by psychological anthropologist Thomas Csordas, who weaves together Maurice Merleau-Ponty's phenomenological analysis of perceptual processes and Pierre Bourdieu's sociopolitical analysis of collective practice. Csordas recognizes that the phenomenologist's "lived experience" is never merely individual and subjective but develops as relational and cultural constructions in social space. He understands that the sociologist's "practice" is not only a collective sedimentation passed on through generations but an opportunity for individuality, agency, and somatic awareness.

Distinguishing between "the body," as biological and material, and "embodiment," as an "indeterminate methodological field defined by perceptual experience and the mode of presence and engagement in the world," Csordas addresses embodiment as "the starting point for analyzing human participation in a cultural world." He coins the term "somatic modes of attention" to refer to "culturally elaborated ways of attending to and with one's body in surroundings that include the embodied presence of others."

Following Merleau-Ponty, Csordas suggests that before we come to perceive ourselves as objects, we are first subjects to ourselves in a "pre-objective" world that experiences embodiment but not "the body." Child psychologist Daniel Stern provides clarification of the problematic term *pre-objective* and supports Merleau-Ponty's ontological order. Stern shows that before we are able to differentiate objects, including ourselves as objects, we perceive and organize sensory experience. Stern, like Csordas, considers the processes by which we become objects to ourselves, or, in his terms, how infants begin to have an emergent sense of self. Experiments show that in an infant younger than two months old, a sense of self first develops in relation to its body, "its coherence, its actions, its inner feeling states, and the memory of all these," through the process of organizing sensory experience. This is the framework for his discussion of pre-objective organizations of sensory experience.

Specifically, in the pre-objective phase of development, Stern writes, the senses work in tandem. We are born with the innate capacity to "transfer perceptual experience from one sensory modality to another," translating, for example, between what an object feels like and what it looks like. The same cross-referencing occurs in translating sound intensities (loudness) to visual intensities (brightness) and with recognizing temporal patterns (beat, rhythm, duration) between visual and auditory modes. Before infants recognize that an impression "belongs" to a particular sense or a quality to a particular object, they make global abstractions of shape, temporal pattern, and intensity across the senses. When Csordas says that we are first subjects to ourselves in a "pre-objective" world where we experience embodiment but not "the body," I understand him to be referring to this phase and process.

Philosopher Mark Johnson offers an elegant model for thinking about the pre-objective processes Stern describes. Johnson challenges objectivism, the notion that meaning occurs as objective structures transcendent of human embodiment and independent of human engagement, recognizing meaning to be an *event* of human understanding. For Johnson, both logical and metaphoric thinking are meaning-making processes that depend on imagination, which is, in effect, the capacity to structure experience by organizing perceptions into patterns. Like Stern, he focuses on the prelinguistic and pre-objective phase of ordering bodily experience across sensory modalities. The resulting extrapolations, which he calls "image schemata" or "embodied schemata," are neither perceptions nor reflections, but cross-modal recognitions of pattern, whether of form or of quality, that emerge from and structure perceptions. For example, the spatial embodied schema of "up and down" or the dynamic embodied schema of "rushing" are built cross-modally from movement sensations, seeing, and hearing.

The combination of Stern's concept of amodal perception and Johnson's concept of embodied schema offers a framework for understanding how innate capacities for combining perception and conception are differentially developed in different cultural communities. Although, as anthropologist Brenda Farnell notes, phenomenology carries the danger of positing a "universal bodily experience" that separates "the body from language and culture," here are grounds for a phenomenological approach to knowledge that addresses embodiment as culturally informed right from the start. Specifically, while the capacity to abstract patterns from sensory experience, via amodal perception, is innate, the metaphoric process of schema-building is indeterminate, open-ended, creative, and continuously active.

In other words, schema-building is inherently open to cultural, as well as individual, variation. Sensations in the womb, even though they are not organized objectively, in terms of "my" sensations in "your" womb, are influenced by a social milieu—the mother's movement patterns, her breathing rhythms, intrusions from the environment. In Csordas's words, our bodies, from the beginning, are "in the world," part of "an intersubjec-tive milieu" that includes others' bodies; thus, it is not subjectivity but intersubjectivity "that gives rise to sensation." Pre-objective and pre-linguistic do not imply pre-cultural. From the womb onward, in different sociocultural and historical circumstances, we learn to emphasize and value different sensory details of form and quality, different perceptual and expressive media, and different ways of processing somatosen-sory information.

Concerning the argument for qualitative factors in cultural constructions of meaning and memory, Stern reports that just as infants extrapolate between quantifiable elements like shape and temporal pattern, they also cross-modally "yoke together" qualities of feeling. Stern is emphatic that these feelings are not "categorical affects" like happiness, anger, surprise, and so on. Rather, they are "vitality affects," the complex qualities of kinetic energy inherent in all bodily activity. An infant can recognize, for example, the similarly lightly caressing quality of vitality in the way her mother might brush her hair, sing a lullaby, and smile at her, before she can distinguish her mother or herself as objects, and before she can recognize singing, hair brushing, or smiling as discrete actions.

Unlike the terminology of emotion, Stern writes, vitality affects are "better captured by dynamic, *kinetic* terms, such as 'surging,' 'fading away,' 'fleeting,' 'explosive,' or 'crescendo,' 'decre-scendo,' 'bursting,' 'drawn out,' and so on." Vitality affects are most revealed, Stern writes, in events like music and dance that have no "content." Indeed, he acknowledges, they are equivalent to what Suzanne Langer calls the "forms of feeling" embodied in dance. Likewise, if the phenomenologist's "lived experience" is understood to be the ongoing dynamic changes in vitality affects over time, what Stern calls the "activation contours of experience," then lived experience is not, as anthropologist Drid Williams protests, "some mystical bodily event of shared experience," but the cross-modal apprehension of kinetic dynamics as they are differentially developed in different cultural communities.

Until we attend to kinetic dynamics, the way vitality affects are organized in specific movement systems and actions, we lack a crucial dimension in understanding the meaningfulness of movement performance in and as social memory. As Howes calls for "sensory profiles," I am calling for "vitality profiles." The dynamic factors of rhythm, speed, and duration; force; degree of muscular tension or relaxation; and degree of giving in to or resisting gravity (weightiness and lightness) encode cultural dispositions as much as the shapes and spatial patterns of movement do. Labananalysis, as Rudolf von Laban's schema of qualitative factors is now called, offers a systematic way of observing such dynamics.

The system focuses on eight core qualities: light or strong use of weight, quick or sustained time, direct or indirect use of space, and bound or free movement flow. As dance critic Marcia Sie-gel notes, the system has flaws. It is prejudiced toward the extremes, omitting neutral territories that are, for example, neither quick nor sustained. Siegel also recognizes that the Choreometrics system based on Laban's categories is biased toward the Western emphasis on shape and spatial design, with little attention given to rhythm, interaction, continuity, and change. I would add, first, that the eight core qualities do not cover all possible kinds of vitality. Most important, neither Laban-analysis nor Choreometrics addresses social interaction or cultural constructions of meaning at all. Although the Laban system is in need of cross-cultural modification and development, it is, for the moment, all we have for guiding observation beyond the shapes and spatial patterns of action toward qualitative factors. If Laban's categories are taken to be aids to observation rather than a catalogue of all possible qualitative factors, they can be useful.

Dance anthropologist Cynthia Cohen Bull's comparison of ballet, contact improvisation, and Ghanaian dance offers a sampling of the possibilities. Working with qualitative factors, she finds that whereas "[b]allet practice and performance hone visual sensibility, giving the dancer an acute awareness of the body's precise placement and shaping in space," contact improvisation, as an oppositional practice to ballet, "seeks to create a sensitivity to touch and to inner sensation." Ghanaian dance emphasizes neither shape and line nor weight and touch, but "the rhythmic dialogue among participants." An early, more detailed comparative study of gesture, conducted in 1941 by anthropologist David Efron, a student of Franz Boas, went further.

Undertaken to refute Nazi notions about the correlation of race and gesture, Efron studied and compared the conversational gestures of two relatively homogenous and stable European communities whose members had migrated to New York. These were Jewish immigrants from the ghettos of Lithuania and Poland, and Neapolitan and Sicilian peasant immigrants.

Although he found marked differences between the groups in the immigrant generation, in the following generation, depending on the degree of assimilation, the original gestural patterns had disappeared. Both groups' gestures in the younger generation more closely resembled those of other New Yorkers than those of their immigrant parents. That significant differences in gestural patterns are determined, not by inherent physiological, psychological, or mental differences, but by the interaction between learned traditions and social conditions was predictable even in 1941.

In the course of his study, however, Efron found something less predictable; that differences in gestural systems embody differences in the aesthetic structuring of thought. In short, the Sicilian immigrants employed gestures that depicted the *content* of their thought, like a sign language. Their gestures were largely presentational and connotational, as if they carried "a bundle of pictures" in their hands. They either pointed to objects or referred to the forms of objects, to spatial relationships, or to bodily actions. Gesturing among the Jewish immigrants was neither pictorial nor connotational and referred to the *process* rather than the objects of their thought. The Jewish immigrants used gestures to "link one proposition to another, trace the itinerary of a logical journey, or to beat the tempo of mental locomotion." Their embroideries and zigzags resembled "gestural charts of the 'heights' and 'lows,' 'detours' and 'crossroads' of the ideational route." Where the Sicilians' gesturing emphasized the "what" of thinking, the Jewish Lithuanians' emphasized the "how." Challenging the popular misconception that gestures are a kind of semiotic hieroglyphics that occurs "naturally," Efron concluded that pictorial gesturing occurs among only some cultural groups and that nonpictorial, ideational kinds of gesturing are of equal significance. "We conceive of gestural behavior as an intrinsic part of the thinking process," he writes.

The comment is significant, suggesting that "mind" is as much a matter of kinesthetic as of verbal or visual organization. This organization occurs, Efron's data show, as the aesthetics of thinking, in terms of sensory profiles and formal kinetic elements. For example, a sensory profile of the Italian immigrants' gestural thinking would emphasize the visual shapes of thought content, whereas for the Jewish immigrants, the auditory rhythms of thought process were emphasized. In Labananalysis terms, the Italian immigrants' thinking emphasized continuous flow and direct pathways, whereas the Jewish immigrants' thinking favored interrupted flow and indirect pathways.

Efron set out to observe only the spatio-temporal and referential aspects of gesturing; had he been skilled in observing qualities of vitality, we might also have learned about the force of the two kinds of gestural thinking, their changing intensities, and their use of weightiness and lightness. These aesthetic patterns point, in Johnson's terms, toward different embodied schemata of "thinking." What if, then, we conceptualize "thinking" in different cultural communities as different genres of aesthetic, even kinetic, improvisation whose structural rules organize sensory modalities, formal elements, and vitality affects? Thus conceived, we would have a model for thinking about thinking as a matter not only of symbolic representations but also of kin-aesthetic orderings.

If, as Howes has shown, sensory ratios are different for different cultural communities, and, as Efron has shown, different among community members at different historical moments, then the way memory and history are embodied is also different in different cultural communities at different times—not only the content of memory but the aesthetic processes and structures involved in knowing and remembering.

CASE STUDY: THE TORTUGAS DANCES

Inevitably, dance and movement researchers, too, have habits of preference among sensory modalities, favoring one or another dynamic and structuring perceptions and conceptualizations according to different embodied schemata of "thinking." Maybe we "see" spatial patterns but are numb to the proprioceptive subtleties of force. Maybe we think in rhythmic processes but are blind to nuances of shape or line, or care nothing about the structures of thought and only about which foot a dancer begins on. We may be trained in either quantitative or qualitative analysis and loyal to our training. Indeed, sometimes I wonder if academic disagreements about methodologies are more a matter of competing pleasures than of conflicts of intellectual conviction. Our sociocultural and personal preferences manifest in choices made about subject matter, theoretical models, and methodological approaches.

Movement, for me, has always been a matter of the pleasures of kinesthetic sensation. Although I was schooled early in modern dance, my studies and performance career were in theater, especially Etienne Decroux's corporeal mime and New York's ensemble movement theater of the 1960s and 1970s, in the mode of Jerzy Grotowski's "poor" or "spiritual" theater and the Open Theatre's improvisational ensemble work. I also grew up folk dancing in a utopian socialist community. Perhaps not coincidentally, when I switched from theater to academic work in dance ethnology and performance studies, I chose to do field research on a communal religious ritual performance, the annual fiesta of Our Lady of Guadalupe in Tortugas, in the southwestern U.S. state of New Mexico.

It was the affects and effects of the fiesta I wanted to understand, what it was to "feel the Virgin's presence," as the people said, and what that presence meant in the fiesta. I hypothesized that religion in Tortu-gas was as much a matter of somatic as of textual, or liturgical, meanings and that qualitative movement analysis could lead me to appreciation of the fiesta's spiritual work. I did not aim for a structural study of the fiesta's movement events but for a study of the way the meanings of movement comprised a web of sensibility and intelligibility. As I wrote in my ethnographic monograph, *Dancing with the Virgin:*

"Sensibility" and "intelligibility" imply mutually permeable cultural processes. Sensory perceptions are molded by cultural epistemologies; abstract conceptualizations refer to culturally specific sensory orderings. All our actions in the world are at the same time interpretations of the world. Movement in other words combines felt bodily experience and the culturally based organization of that experience into cognitive patterns. Ways of moving are ways of thinking.

Relying on participant-observation, tacking between movement analysis and extensive verbal exchange, as well as on reviewing the relevant literature, I sought instruction about the weaving of somatic and verbal detail. I brought both my knowledge (academic skills, theater skills, and the multiple accumulations of biography) and my ignorance (about the community, the fiesta, and local processes of making meaning) to learn how to learn. My framework was epistemological, linking bodily sensation with the other senses and with verbalization, and all of these with the processes of coming to know. What follows is the story of my discoveries about the fiesta's two dances. Letting the dances, and people's words about them, lead me, I discovered that they demanded different approaches and pointed to different but complementary aspects of identity. They also demonstrated different ways history and memory can be embodied in the same community.

Unlike the Protestants who killed or "removed" the indigenous people they encountered in New England, the Spanish Catholics required native labor and coveted, in the name of God, indigenous souls. Along the Rio Grande in what is now New Mexico in the southwestern United States, they coerced or convinced many Pueblo people toward religious conversion, while imposing a policy of forced servitude *(encomienda)*. They also banned dancing. Thus, unlike the Jewish and Italian immigrants in Efron's study, for the Puebloans conquered by the Spanish, assimilation was enforced rather than sought. In 1680, the Pueblos revolted and drove the Spanish south, from the Rio Grande Pueblos in northern New Mexico to the Spanish stronghold at El Paso del Norte. Now divided into the U.S. city of El Paso, Texas, and the Mexican city of Juárez, this "pass of the north" was originally settled as a rest stop at the spot where the Camino Real, or "royal road," from Mexico City crossed the Rio Grande on the way to the Pueblos in the north.

In 1692, twelve years after their retreat, the Spanish regrouped and returned north to conquer the Rio Grande Pueblos. The conquered Puebloans chose to continue dancing "underground," in a sense ghetto-izing their own corporeal practices to protect them from Spanish, and later American, censorship.

When the Spanish first retreated south after the 1680 Pueblo Revolt, some Puebloans, either by choice or by force, joined the retreat. In El Paso del Norte, they lived in mission communities among the larger Spanish and *mestizo*, or mixed Spanish and indigenous Mexican, population. They embraced Catholicism while sustaining many Puebloan ritual practices, including dance. They also adopted *mestizo* clothing, language, and social practices, somewhat like the "hybrid acculturation" Efron found among some of the second-generation Jewish Lithuanian-Americans. In the mid-

1800s, about 150 years after the mission communities were established, a band of El Paso del Norte *indios,* as they called themselves and are still called, again migrated. Responding to internecine Mexican wars, land scams, and Anglo-Texan invasion, they moved about forty miles northward up the Rio Grande to the area that is now Las Cruces in southern New Mexico.

This area was almost immediately ceded to the United States in the 1848 Treaty of Guadalupe Hidalgo, and the immigrants became American citizens. Helping the group to acquire land for a church and ceremonial buildings that would ensure the survival of their religious traditions, an Anglo stagecoach driver who had married "a princess of the tribe" helped the *indios* to incorporate as an American-style benevolent association. Since then, the annual celebration for the Virgin has evolved in the village of Tor-tugas in Las Cruces, but it is still sponsored by the *Corporación de Nuestra Señora de Guadalupe.*

During the years I participated, between 1984 and 1998, the annual fiesta followed a consistent scenario. On the first night, 10 December, an all-night *velorio,* or wake, honored the Virgin with prayers alternating with rounds of a *matachine* dance that is locally termed *la danza.* Weaving together elements brought to America by the Spaniards with indigenous features, *matachine* dances from Mexico City to the Rio Grande address, in movement elements and meaning, the Hispano-Indian encounter. On the 11th, as many as 250 visitors spent the day in pilgrimage to the top of Tortugas Mountain. On the 12th, a High Mass in the morning preceded a day of dancing in the church plaza.

Here the participants of *la danza,* known as *los danzantes,* were joined by other members of the community in the *indio* or "Pueblo dance," similar to the corn or tablita dances performed at all New Mexico's Rio Grande Pueb-los. It was also referred to as the "Tigua dance," Tigua being a Spanish spelling of Tiwa, the Rio Grande Pueblo linguistic group from whom many of the El Paso del Norte *indios* claimed ancestry. At midday on the 12th, the *Corporación* offered a feast for several hundred people at the community dining hall, and at dusk, in a climactic procession, the Virgin's image was passed into the care of the next year's *mayordomos,* stewards responsible for the smooth running of the whole event. The fiesta ended with a reception and informal dance when anyone could join in the *danza* or *indio* dance.

When I first looked at the *indio* dance, its general similarity to the Rio Grande Pueblo dances was immediately apparent: a group of approximately ten male singers, one of whom carries the drum; two lines of dancers moving in synchronized unity;

the cumulative rather than climactic dance structure; the dance outfits (*mantas*, which are the traditional one-shouldered black dance sheaths worn by Pueblo women; moccasins, shawls, men's decorated dance shirts, downy feathers). As in northern New Mexico, the dancing began with slow songs accompanying a processional choreography. The men in Tortugas used the same basic knee-lifting jogging step and the women the more subdued and flat-footed inching walk as in the north. As in the north, the dance changed to a faster section of choreographic figures. These variations in the north might include turns in place, exchanges of place between the two lines, or circling in small groups. In Tortugas, there was only one pattern of advance and retreat. During the fast section, both Tortugas and northern dancers performed a duple-beat or accented step; between each footfall they gave a small foot tap forward, or downward against the ground, or against the standing leg, before the foot descended.

People in Tortugas did not discuss either the meaning of the dance or their dancing experience; rather, they talked about the technicalities of performance, debating the fine points of step and music. For the men's basic step, though everyone agreed on the injunction to "lift your knees," there was intense debate about whether the hunting bows they carried in the left hand should be held above or below the gourd rattle, carried in the right. They considered whether the men's body position for shaking the rattles in the fast song's transitional section should be a squat or a lunge, and, most controversial, whether, at the pause when the man has lifted his knee in the duple-beat step, there should or should not be a quick and tiny punctuating forward kick. Qualitative analysis revealed the Tortugas style to be lighter and more direct than the northern styles, the endpoints of step and gesture more punctuated, giving the dance a sharp and angular quality. "Too sloppy," a Tortugas companion commented as we watched the more lyrical dancing style at Ysleta del Sur in El Paso, Texas. Of the dancing of the northern Pueblos, one woman remarked, "That may be the way they do it up north, but it's not the way we do it here." This kind of scrutiny and commentary suggested to me intentional movement choices that made fine degrees of kinesthetic distinction between an "us" and a "not us."

The distinction referred in part to religion. While many northern Puebloans are Catholic, Pueblo religion and cosmology continue to be their predominant reference system for the dances. Though few Pueb-loans now farm and hunt for subsistence, the dances occur in an annual cycle corresponding with the growing and hunting seasons, and multiple symbolic elements help dancers harmonize body, thought, and prayer with these cycles. Except for one family, these references were absent in Tortugas. No one spoke any of the Puebloan or other Native American languages, and no one could translate the song texts, except one sung in Spanish honoring the Virgin. At one dance practice, an elder next to me explained that the ubiquitous Pueblo vocables "heya, heya" really mean "for her, for her," the Virgin of Guadalupe.

Movement choices reiterated this orientation. For example, the choreography in the first slow, processional section consisted of following a circular path while changing direction every few steps via a zigzag from side to side. This pattern enabled the dancers to face the four directions in the course of circling, an orientation prevalent throughout the Pueblos. An additional injunction, however, has entered the Tor-tugas choreography: "Never turn your back on the Virgin." A portrait of Our Lady of Guadalupe hung before the dancers during every rehearsal and performance. The injunction to never turn your back on the Virgin translated choreographically, so that when the dancers neared the portrait, rather than zigzagging to face the four directions, they maintained a single focus forward. The shift was both choreographic and symbolic. The dance had changed from the four-directional spatial and cosmological system of the Pueblos to the one-directional orientation of church architecture and cosmology.

The dance worked as a mnemonic, a way to remember, in the sense of re-embody, a time "before the missionaries came and Christianized us," as one elder put it. In Tortugas, the missionizing process was, for the most part, viewed not as a loss, but as goodness, a gift. The reference to a pre-Christian past was not religious nostalgia but an assertion of ancestry and autobiography. The combination of observation and conversation directed my attention to the problem of biography. The dance, I learned, commemorated a historical link to the northern Pueblos while asserting a differentiation from those same Pueblos. That problem was embodied in the dancing in various ways: in outfits and paraphernalia, in spatial choreography and body shape, and in the qualitative dynamics of movement style.

Where the *indio* dance drew from the north, the *danza* drew from the south, from Mexico. Similar to *matachines* performed throughout northern Mexico and the southwestern United States, its origins lay in Mexico City when the first Spanish missionaries grafted Christian concepts and European dance elements onto Aztec dances to teach the new religion. The dance spread with missionaries and settlers, shaping to local customs and meanings.

In Tortugas in the 1980s and 1990s, it was danced by eighteen men, in two parallel lines, accompanied by a violin. Led by a *monarca,* the dance leader, an *abuelo,* his assistant, and a *malinche,* a pre-pubescent girl, in each of ten *sones,* or songs, the dancers unfolded a different *figura,* a choreographic design in space. Except for two of the *sones,* the dancers used a basic repeating step, alternating initiation between left and right feet: three steps in place punctuated by a stamp and a forward kick. Like the *indio* dance, the *danza* was dedicated to the Virgin. Here, however, talk about dancing did not focus on the correct execution of steps. The *monarca* dismissed my questions about the steps, simply saying they were mostly the same for all the dances. Rather, he drew attention to what the dancers "do" in the changing patterns of the dance, its symbolic action.

While most *matachine* dances refer to the story of the Aztec monarch, Montezuma, and his conversion to Catholicism, the Tortugas version made reference only to Our Lady of Guadalupe. In talking about the *danza,* the men emphasized their devotion to and sacrifice for the Virgin and the personal, transformational effect of the dancing. Both the *indio* dance and the *danza* addressed religion, but where the *indio* dance provided opportunities for negotiations about ancestry, the *danza* provided opportunities for the experience of religious meditation on the Virgin. This was not apparent from a structural analysis of the *figuras* or the step. However, qualitative analysis revealed contradictory movement qualities. The men performed the basic three-steps-in-place, stamp, and kick pattern low to the ground, with a forward-driving momentum: the triplet, a light and tight bounce, followed by the slow, heavy stamp, catching the momentum off the rebound to propel the kick forward, quickly recovering to begin again. Performed in unison, the repetitive stamping and propulsion forward gave the impression of insistent and driving force. In spite of this, however, there was an elusive quality of softness, even vulnerability, in the men's dancing whose source I could not locate in the movement itself.

When I watched the men at rehearsals, dancing without their face-covering *cupiles,* or headpieces, I was struck by their eye focus. Although they occasionally looked around to see where *monarca, malinche,* and *abuelo* were in the choreography, the men's focus was not primarily material. Rather, the gaze was inward directed. The dance leader confirmed this: "When I'm dancing as the *monarca,* I don't see nothing of the people that are standing around. All I see is the dances and the vision to the holy Mary. That's all I see. I don't even know who is around me, if anybody's around me. That's the way I feel. . . . And I never lift my head up. I shouldn't lift my head up. I'm there for one purpose." It was as if the men were already under the *cupiles* that during the fiesta would separate them from their material surroundings.

At rehearsals, the dancers faced a portrait of the Virgin. During the all-night *velorio,* her altar was before them. The *monarca* was adamant that her portrait had to be in front of the men before they would dance. The image the men faced was the image they carried within. The *monarca* clarified further: "When you're dancing it's the same as dancing with the Virgin. It's something like if I were talking to her, expressing our gratitude for what she had done. . . . Every time we're dancing there, it's like we were saying thank you and just talking to her, giving her our thanks."58 I understood at this point that the elusive quality of softness that contradicted the driving power of the men's dancing was not a structural element of the dancing, but a manifestation of the men's meditation on the Virgin. The *danza* worked somatically, as a meditative space in which conversion could be repeatedly experienced.

Both the *danza* and the *indio* dance were brought from El Paso del Norte, and both commemorated the Virgin and the community's past as a kind of "home." But that home continued to be a home-at-a-crossroads. Where the *indio* dance asserted identity in terms of historical ancestry, the *danza* did so in terms of ongoing religious conversion. Both embodied memory, but the bodily experience of remembering was different for each. The dances offered different profiles of the process of remembering. *Indio* dancers emphasized the look of the dancing, its details of shape and dynamic. The *danzantes* emphasized focus of attention, both somatic and symbolic. Indeed, when I asked one man what made a good dancer, he said, "One that isn't just there for the dance, one that's really there for the sacrifice to dance for the *virgen,* not just to dance because it looks good." Others also specifically directed my attention away from the dance's visual effect.

We cannot ignore the experiential somatic aspects of dancing in favor of the formal, especially if the dancers lead us toward it. Following the *danzantes*' lead, I sought to understand the *danza,* and the fiesta as a whole, in terms of how it enabled the experience of "feeling the Virgin's presence." I found that there was no other way to it than through my own body, sampling, for example, the qualities of time, intensity, and focus of attention I observed. This work demanded a rigorous attention to detail as well as repeatedly checking my understanding with informants, in words. After I left the community I ran headlong into the problem of recuperating the combination of somatic and verbal memories that had been woven in the emergent process of performance. I have written elsewhere about the path of remembering and evoking I followed; here, I will only report that I came to the theory summarized in this chapter by necessity, as it seemed crucial to find models and language with which to talk in ethnographic terms about the somatic dimensions of embodied cultural knowledge and memory.

In the search for theoretical models, I have been led beyond the toolkit of dance, through sensory anthropology, to child psychology and philosophy and back to dance ethnology. The journey of participant-observation, memory recuperation, and analysis has taken me from the visible forms of movement into the phenomenological, cultural particulars of sensory schema and somatic awareness. This is not only a Geertzian quest for social breadth, but a descent into sociosomatic depth. Now, in response to Merleau-Ponty, Csordas, and Stern, I find myself asking, not how we become objects to ourselves, but how we might cease being objects to ourselves. Can we *attend* our bodies, rather than only attending to or with them? Is objectification inevitably simultaneous with sensation, or is this a particular cultural construction? In other words, might we attend, not even "the body" or "the person," but simply sensation, as Buddhist Vipassana meditation instructs? And might such attending open new possibilities for appreciating cultural constructions of embodiment? From the perspective (or the sitting place) of Vipassana, I cannot help but remember that "person" and "self," "body" and "thought," are verbal symbols (embodied schemata) that we come to believe define reality whereas, in effect, they create the territories to which they point. Entering this territory with a "new mind," I offer these thoughts, not as answers, but as openings toward further questions.

6

Dancing Through History and Ethnography

A bharata natyam dancer, clad in a tailored silk sari and bedecked in jewelry, sinks gracefully onto one leg. She smiles as her arm arcs gently and her articulate fingers lead her hand from a high diagonal in toward her torso. Her legs fold out into a rotated, bent-knee position, and her feet beat out a sharp rhythm. With her torso floating gracefully above her dynamic feet, she traces intricate hand shapes that ornament the angular positions of her limbs. She dances in a courtyard, before a temple, a setting that suggests that her solid, graceful movements are as enduring as the pillars and carvings of the temple compound. She is the very emblem of classicism, traditionalism, and the endurance of ancient values in present-day India.

BHARATA NATYAM AND THE PRODUCTION OF THE PAST

Bharata natyam relies upon the choreographic practices of the past. The dancer's movement vocabulary, for instance, derives from *sadir,* the dance practice of *devadasis,* courtesans, and ritual officiants who were associated with the temples and courts of South India until the early twentieth century. The *mudras,* or hand gestures, parallel, in both shape and meaning, those described in the *Natyasastra,* a canonical dramaturgical text written in the ancient, elite lingua franca of Sanskrit. A standardization of concert practice by the nineteenth-century Thanjavur Quartet, a renowned group of musicians, produced the *margam,* or concert order.

Despite these commonalities between bharata natyam and past practice, many elements of present-day performance are new. Dancers transformed the style of rendition of the movements over the twentieth century (in some interpretations more than others), extending lines out into space and augmenting the angularity of positions. Some performers have also broadened the floor patterns of the choreography, covering more ground than *sadir* dancers did, in order to suit the larger, proscenium theaters of the contemporary performance context. Similarly, dancers have amplified and "theatricalized" the facial expressions of the *abhinaya,* or dramatic elements of choreography, again with the aim of rendering the expressions legible to a less proximate audience.

Repertoire also changed during the twentieth century. Even the most "traditional" choreography is not completely fixed. A dance piece consists of a compilation of phrases, set to a piece of music that belongs to a dance style's customary repertoire. A dancer or, most commonly, a dance teacher arranges phrases, learned from her own mentor, but assembled according to her decisions. The amount of decision making increases as a practitioner takes on more responsibility for teaching. Repertoire, therefore, changes in the process of its transmission. Present-day practitioners also commission music and devise new items of repertoire. Likewise, they choreograph pieces outside conventional genres, create works of ensemble choreography, and compose evening-length pieces based on the bharata natyam movement vocabulary.

In addition, many elements that frame the performance are new. The name "bharata natyam," for example, is a twentieth-century appellation. The "traditional" bharata natyam costume developed out of changes to concert attire in the 1930s. Even the temple performance context, despite its suggestion of antiquity, is itself a product of the changes that the dance form underwent in the nineteenth and twentieth centuries. In 1892, activists mobilized against the performance of dance in Hindu temples and succeeded in banning such events in 1947. Only in the 1980s did dancers return to temple performance, bringing with them the movement vocabulary and repertoire of the concert stage. Present-day temple dance events have therefore developed out of a fractured tradition.

A possible conclusion to draw from this scenario is that the dance form derives solely from an intentional, self-conscious engagement with the past and not from an unbroken oral tradition. One could, in looking at such a situation, call bharata natyam an "invented tradition." An alternative conclusion might be that there is a single authoritative history, which aligns with one set of choreographic choices, while the other versions of history are inaccurate.

I want to suggest, however, that the actual situation is more complex than such assertions would indicate. Bharata natyam is neither entirely "ancient" nor is it solely a product of the twentieth century. Furthermore, none of the histories that practitioners put forth is spurious: dancers describe different versions of the past through the selection of competing sources, each of which constitutes a potentially valid historical "truth." Twentieth-century dancers, through their choices in repertoire, choreographic themes, and movement vocabulary, connected their performance work to practices of the past. This explicit and intentional use of historical sources separates their practice from that of nineteenth- and early-twentieth-century dancers. They have selected a wider range of influential materials, using them in divergent ways and making their engagement with the past more apparent in choreography and pedagogy than it had been previously.

Most dancers who define their work as classical bharata natyam agree that a sense of continuity should undergird choreographic endeavors. Nonetheless, individual dancers disagree as to what the most important aspect of the dance form's history is, what elements should be maintained or revivified, and how best to express allegiance to that history. Concepts of authenticity, tradition, classicism, and history do not necessarily invoke agreement; rather, they form the bases of diverse points of view. Such a situation raises several questions. Why are notions of tradition and classicism, rooted as they are in ideas of consensus, points of departure for different interpretations?10 Why does this dance form appear to need history at the same time that its practitioners vary in their approach to that history?

ETHNOGRAPHY, PERFORMANCE PRAXIS, AND ANTHROPOLOGICAL CONCERNS

These questions developed out of my personal experience, as a performer and scholar, with bharata natyam. At present, I write primarily as a dancer and cultural historian who has investigated choreographic and political strategies of the past as they inform current practice. My study of bharata natyam since 1988 has, however, used methodologies from anthropology and history as well as from choreographic analysis, critical theory, and cultural studies. A dual attention to social significance and change over time has enabled me to investigate transformations in bharata natyam's form and content over the twentieth century. Each approach, however, especially coupled with my own performance practice of bharata natyam, has complicated and challenged the other methodologies.

Despite these changes in interpretative strategies, I have returned, on several occasions, to ethnographic field methods. For my initial study, I undertook ethnographic fieldwork in 1989. During subsequent trips to India in 1995–96 and 1999 (at the same time as researching diasporic practice in Toronto in 1998 and 1999), I conducted formal and informal interviews, viewed performances, and researched written accounts. I have moved into and out of ethnography, valuing immediate experience but questioning some of the anthropological assumptions that undergird ethnographic practice and drawing upon historical methods.

My inquiry into bharata natyam's twentieth-century history has negotiated the concerns of performance, historiography, critical theory, dance analysis, and ethnography. Because I have drawn on a blend of methodologies, I cannot identify myself as solely a performer, historian, ethnographer, or dance analyst. This shifting methodology reflects not only my changing interests but also, and more importantly, the complexity of the field of study itself. Therefore, the pages that follow trace the phases of my study of bharata natyam as they deploy ethnographic, historical, and analytical methods. I do this to comment on these methodologies as they engage with the study of dance, generally, but also to illuminate why bharata natyam has required such theoretical maneuvers. In doing so, I hope to indicate how ethnography and history have served this study and how, in themselves, they remained incomplete.

I entered this field in 1988 as an undergraduate student in dance and anthropology at Wesleyan University in Connecticut. I began training

T. Balasaraswati at Veterans Auditorium, San Francisco, 1972.

in the Thanjavur Court style of bharata natyam, from the South Indian state of Tamil Nadu, a style associated with the legendary *devadasi* practitioner T. Balasaraswati. My initial study (1989–90) followed an ethnographic pattern of immersion in a situation—the study of bharata natyam—and the generation of interpretations from that experience. The dance study itself and my interactions with other dancers yielded insights about how a bharata natyam performer develops a characteristic way of moving and how she learns to think about her body. This period of research hinged on questions about choreographic priorities, repertoire, format of performances, training methods, criteria for the evaluation of student and professional dancers, and the "worldview" of the dance field.

This inquiry relied upon on my experience with anthropological thought and raised questions about the cultural relativism of dance aesthetics, dance technique, and therefore the dancing body itself. Using an anthropological model proposed by Adrienne Kaeppler and further developed by Cynthia Novack, I argued for a complex and multifaceted relationship between dance and other social practices.

I relied upon anthropologists Marcel Mauss and Pierre Bourdieu in order to suggest that corporeal techniques created the dancing body as much as they relied upon it. Initially, I was more interested in the anthropological construction of a bodily subject than in the production of historical narratives in dance practice. The study, therefore, attended to technical requirements, especially as put forth in dance pedagogy. My research focused on the specific muscular strengths and postural stances developed through dance training; on culturally specific notions of what is beautiful, virtuoso, feminine or masculine, and age appropriate; and on the selection or nonselection of different body types.

Yet, from the beginning, some aspects of bharata natyam urged my study out into other methodological fields. Bharata natyam already had a long history of representation and, thus, unlike a traditional field-worker, I could supplement my interpretations with the writings of others, including Indian musicologists, dancers, dance critics, and literary and religious studies scholars.

My teacher Nandini Ramani's father, the distinguished Sanskritist and musicologist V. Raghavan, had written extensively on bharata natyam. An archive of his work was made available to me during my stay in India. The Music Academy, Madras's renowned dance and music venue, has its own library. The city also houses dance and music archives such as Sampradaya and features publications, like *Sruti* and *Kalakshetra Quarterly,* dedicated to classical dance and music.

The use of such materials began to align my project with historiography. As the study progressed, the theorizing behind it also intersected with questions of history. The social construction of the body, I argued, occurred through a worldview that surrounded the dance, as well as through studio practices. This argument led into historical concerns as the study contended with bharata natyam's recontextualization. Originally, courtesans and ritual practitioners had performed *sadir.* Dance reformers recrafted the form in the 1930s and renamed it "bharata natyam." On the one hand, the present-day social significance of bharata natyam hinged on the religious and courtly function of its predecessor.

On the other hand, present-day dancers diverge in their approaches to the dance form's complex history.

My interest in the form itself, rather than with dance practice as a marker of broader social values, also shifted my interest away from anthropological concerns and toward historical ones. My project was ethnographic and informed by anthropological thought and not a work of dance anthropology *per se.* In Adrienne Kaeppler's terms, because of the emphasis on dance works and a concern with geographic-political alignment, gender identity, and class status, my study might be classified as more "ethnological" than "anthropological." As the form became more familiar to me, I also noted its multiple interpretations. This inquiry, then, moved from generality to increasing specificity, focusing on individual strategies rather than providing an authoritative account of what bharata natyam is or was. The more I wanted to address these competing versions of the dance practice's identity, history, and social meanings, the less useful I found the traditional anthropological concept of culture. My inquiry shifted away from traditional anthropology when I realized that the cultural meanings of the form had changed dramatically over the twentieth century.

As I became more closely involved with bharata natyam, I became increasingly uncomfortable with some of the underpinnings of conventional anthropology. Traditional anthropology relies upon cultural difference as its basic premise. The global circulation of bharata natyam, including my own practice of it, complicates the notion of cultures as discrete, bounded entities. Moreover, I am not the first foreigner to cross into the realm of bharata natyam performance. The bharata natyam revival hinged upon the inclusion of those hitherto outside the form, including South Indian brahmans, non-Tamils, non-Hindus, and dancers from countries other than India. The extension of bharata natyam into a global performance milieu through an internationalization of pedagogy draws dancers from North and South America,

Europe, Africa, and other parts of Asia to the form. Bharata natyam's twentieth-century history has, therefore, shifted the constitution of belonging within the form.

My participation in dance study and performance may have worn away boundaries of inside and outside more quickly than other ethnographic situations. The people who would, in a traditional ethnographic model, be "other" to me are my colleagues and mentors; I interact with them as part of my quotidian, nonfieldwork experience. Bharata natyam thus became less a foreign form to be understood and more an integral part of my life. This transition challenged assumptions about the distinction between scholar and "informants."

I am likewise not the first to straddle performance and scholarship. Numerous bharata natyam dancers have pursued their study of the form through both performance and scholarly avenues. Kapila Vatsya-yan, whose groundbreaking studies initiated the critical history of Indian dance, pursued extensive training in Indian classical dance forms.16 Dance theorist Avanthi Meduri began her career as a bharata natyam and *kuchipudi* performer and subsequently turned to scholarship and theater direction. Dutch scholar Saskia Kersenboom-Story and Canadian sociologist Anne-Marie Gaston have integrated their study of bharata natyam into their research. Choreographer Padma Subrahman-yam trained in dance before turning to scholarship in order to further her inquiry into the form. She has brought her intellectual investigations back into performance by proposing a new dance form, *bharata nritya,* based on the reconstruction of material from Sanskrit texts. For many of these dancers, scholarship underwrites a particular interpretation of bharata natyam.

Here, too, traditional anthropology provided an uneasy fit with this subject matter. Traditional anthropology assumes an imbalance between an articulate scholar and a largely inchoate "other," as Lila Abu-Lughod has argued from within the discipline. Joann Kealiino-homoku's influential essay of 1970 on the cultural investments of ballet represents a significant exception to the then existing trend of anthropologists studying others abroad and the disempowered at home. The imperative to represent an other group was challenged in the 1980s by disciplinary critiques like native anthropology and minority discourse. A field like bharata natyam, populated by articulate artist-scholars, each with her or his own version of history, provides a further challenge to an attempt to represent the field as a whole.

My own studies of anthropology (1986–90) had occurred at a time when the inclusion of history in anthropological studies was not typical. One way of addressing my concerns about the traditional culture concept could have involved a deeper inquiry into postmodern and experimental anthropology, by following the subdisciplinary critiques of native anthropology, dialogic anthropology, feminist anthropology, and transnational anthropology. I elected instead to employ historical approaches because I found useful the attention that the discipline of history conventionally gives to individual action. In addition, historical perspectives informed my inquiry because dancers articulate their competing understandings of bharata natyam through reference to the past. Historical narratives legitimize particular choices, and, therefore, comprehending such decisions required knowledge of history.

Furthermore, many practitioners, even those with divergent choreographic projects, agree on the importance of the bharata natyam revival from 1923 to 1950. Therefore, I found it necessary to gain an understanding of these events, which I developed through historical inquiry, stimulated by my interest in the work of individual artists. This latter concern shares an emphasis with the focus of traditional aesthetics but, as I detail below, also diverges from it in the attention I give to social context.

CRITICAL HISTORIOGRAPHY AND CONSTRUCTS OF TRADITION

If my first study borrowed from ethnography, then the second relied on critical historiography. This investigation began with a simple but productive theory: if several practitioners claim that their approaches are classical, traditional, and "authentic," and yet these approaches vary, the practitioners must define classicism and tradition in different ways. In revisiting the material I gathered in India, I realized that most performers and viewers agreed on the importance of tradition. They offered contrasting opinions as to what constituted tradition and what lay outside the boundaries of a classical performance.

The source of this discrepancy lay in bharata natyam's recontextualization, during the period from 1923 to 1950. The debate about what constituted tradition emerged out of questions raised during that time regarding the dance form's "disreputable past" and how to contend with it. Drawing on political studies, especially those of Benedict Anderson and Partha Chatterjee, I argued that the "revived" version of bharata natyam, represented most clearly by choreographer and dance reformer Rukmini Devi, addressed the concerns of the emergent nation-state. It, like the nation, contended with a paradox in which indigenous identity articulated itself in negotiation with Western-defined systems and structures. So, for example, Devi referenced Western theatrical protocol and ballet technique as a model for the recrafting of bharata natyam. In addition, Devi mobilized the orientalist nationalism of the Theosophical Society that supported her efforts by looking to the distant past and

6.2. Rukmini Devi ca. 1940s. Photo courtesy of Jerome Robbins Dance Division, The New York Public Library for the Performing Arts, Astor, Lennox and Tilden Foundations. Used with permission.

to Sanskrit theoretical texts as an indicator of bharata natyam's true identity. *Devadasi* practitioner Balasaraswati, by contrast, responded to this nationalist reconstruction by emphasizing regional, Tamil origins for the form, highlighted the recent historical past, and privileged praxis over aesthetic theory. As such, she provided a counter-discourse to the shifts bharata natyam underwent in the 1930s and 1940s.

This project focused on two influential figures from the past, Ruk-mini Devi and Balasaraswati. The study framed areas of debate key to early- and mid-twentieth-century bharata natyam, focusing on the dominant history and one major counter-discourse. I returned to material, mostly published, that I had gathered in India and supplemented it with further research into textual sources, focusing on the plethora of writing that surrounded both Devi and Balasaraswati. Each produced her own body of literature, through lectures, essays, and debates, that commented on her choreographic practice. I augmented this material with the accounts of those in the present who were closely linked to these dancers, such as Kalakshetra exponents V. N. and Shanta Dhananjayan and Balasaraswati's disciples Nandini Ramani and Kay Poursine.

My interest lay largely in understanding how each dancer defined bharata natyam and in highlighting that each identified the form in strikingly different ways. Both used historical narratives to authorize her version of bharata natyam. Each dancer also expressed a different politics of representation through her understanding of the form, offering competing opinions on regionalism, nationalism, caste, class, and gender identity. How Devi and Balasaraswati portrayed their choices discursively held as much significance to this inquiry as the choreographic decisions themselves. As such, their public representation of such points factored into the investigation more than how they thought about them privately or how they had approached them in a class context.

Devi maintained that bharata natyam descended from a pan-Indian high culture rooted in the classical language Sanskrit. She privileged ancient Sanskrit aesthetic theory texts and Sanskrit drama as the origins of bharata natyam and claimed to access their spirit, if not precisely their form. She maintained that dance and theater were once, and should rightfully be again, the domain of "women of good families." She therefore drew on the tactics of anti-colonial nationalism by "rewriting the script" for bharata natyam and finding in it the glories of a shared tradition that could unite a diverse subcontinent.

For Balasaraswati, by contrast, bharata natyam derived from the literary, religious, and musical heritage of the courts of the South Indian state of Tamil Nadu. She located the sources for bharata natyam in ancient Tamil poetry, local temple rituals, and the cultural traditions of the Thanjavur Court. Nonetheless, she acknowledged parallels with pan-Indian Sanskrit sources such as the Vedas, the Upanishads, and the Puranas and upper-caste practices like yoga. She rejected attempts to "improve" bharata natyam by aligning it with the tenets of Sanskrit aesthetic theory texts. The dance form, she maintained, found its proponents in the hereditary community of *devadasis.* She traced an unbroken chain from the artistic practices of the eighteenth- and nineteenth-century Tamil courts to twentieth-century bharata natyam. For Balasaraswati, attempts in the present to improve, purify, or modernize bharata natyam threatened to sever this connection. A profound sense of loss accompanied her version of history.

Devi thus eschewed the very past that Balasaraswati celebrated. Devi located bharata natyam's authenticating history not in the nineteenth-century *devadasi* temple and court traditions of South India but in ancient Sanskrit drama, the values of which could be reconstructed in the present. For Devi, the *devadasi* were subject to a system that restricted and degraded them. She thus maintained that the twentieth century was a time of rejuvenation, not of a threatened destruction.

6.3. Rukmini Devi ca. 1940s. She is wearing the modified dance costume introduced during the revival. Photo courtesy of Jerome Robbins Dance Division, The New York Public Library for the Performing Arts, Astor, Lennox and Tilden Foundations. Used with permission.

6.4. T. Balasaraswati performing abhinaya *(dramatic dance) at Mills College, Oakland, California, 1984.*

Their two perspectives lined up into sets of binary oppositions. Devi privileged a Sanskrit tradition, Balasaraswati a Tamil one. Thus, Devi identified bharata natyam as a national form; for Balasaraswati, its roots were regional. Devi celebrated the new generation of brahman (upper-caste) practitioners, while Balasaraswati maintained that the form rightfully belonged with the relatively lower-caste *devadasi* practitioners who had nurtured it for centuries. Devi saw herself as purifying and revitalizing a form in decline, whereas Balasaraswati saw herself as upholding a threatened tradition.

This historical and discursive paradigm yielded important insights, as, through it, I was able to analyze a dominant narrative of bharata natyam's "revivification" and to begin to theorize resistance to this narrative. This model indicated how choreographic projects yielded particular sociopolitical strategies. The distinction between these two practitioners indicated a split at the roots of present-day bharata natyam. This approach, therefore, opened up a means of investigating discrepancy as well as consensus within Indian classical dance.

At the same time, this study encountered limitations, some of which point out the boundaries of a historical discourse analysis. For example, the history that this inquiry built did not address choreographic practice directly. Traditional historical methods offered a means of understanding only those choreographic decisions that had already been documented, leaving, in this case, more of an emphasis on how dancers represented their decisions than on how these two versions of history articulated themselves in theatrical form.

In addition, my study of bharata natyam began with, and continues to hinge upon, the practices of the present. Classical historiography became less useful as I returned to present-day choreography from the reconstruction of the past. The aim of this study was also to understand and to highlight the nondominant narratives about the form. Despite significant challenges issued from the subdisciplines of social history and cultural history, traditional history privileges the actions of a few, luminary individuals over those pushed to the margins.

Because of such limitations of conventional historical approaches, my resulting argument rested on a binary model that featured one hegemonic and one resistant narrative, providing for two positions:

brahman-nationalist-Sanskritic or *devadasi*-regionalist-Tamil.

Because Balasaraswati was always cast in the responsive role in this binary, it was difficult to theorize her position. My continued investment in Balasaras-wati's historical narrative was even more difficult to contend with. In this regard, my role as dancer carried over into my entry into historiography. I was less able to theorize Balasaraswati's history simply because, in part, I still thought of it as "true." It took a return to immediate experience and, thus, to an ethnographically based inquiry to challenge these assumptions further.

ETHNOGRAPHY AND THE POLITICS OF CULTURE: HISTORY AS STRATEGY

I returned to India in 1995 for nine months' intensive technique and repertoire training, having applied for admission to the Ph.D. program in Dance History and Theory at the University of California, Riverside. My aim in going to India was twofold: to immerse myself in performance practice, while supplementing this with preliminary "fieldwork" that would prepare me for further academic study. I arrived in India retaining my Devi-Balasaraswati focus and, largely unwittingly, my investment in the Balasaraswati version of the past. Contemporaneous choreographic practice and verbal accounts pushed me to contend with the present and to problematize Balasaraswati's version of the past.

In early 1996, I met artists and scholars who identified themselves as activists and who aligned their positions with the early Dravidianist movements, combining a class critique with an embrace of Tamil identity. They questioned what they called the "brahman" version of bharata natyam's history, critiquing the Madras arts milieu from a socioeconomic position as well as from a large-scale political one. These colleagues encouraged me to extend my critique by pointing out that most *devadasis* had been more marginalized than Balasaraswati and that my research should address the position of those outside the elite, urban sphere.

My response to such a challenge was to embark on a project that bridged oral history and ethnographic methods. I traveled from Madras to towns and villages of Tamil Nadu and met artists from these communities, seeking out *devadasis* and men of their community—now collectively known as the *icai vellala* caste—who participated in the dance field as dancers, musicians, and teachers.

This project drew on the methods of oral history in its emphasis on change over time. I spoke with people who had a direct connection to pre-revival dance and who could address it through their own memory and through what they recalled of their older relatives' experiences. My aim was to reconstruct *devadasi* practice of the past as it contrasted with the stage performance of the present.

One of my main concerns in these discussions pertained to the use of aesthetic theory texts as the source of and basis for dance practice. My inquiry into Devi's project suggested that the revival initiated an integration of theoretical study into dance training.

I wanted to find out if *icai vellala* practitioners shared Balasaraswati's suspicion toward reconstruction. Rather than simply corroborating the Balasaraswati version of history, these conversations provided a third version of history, one that drew on the same sources as Balasaraswati but interpreted them differently.

Like Balasaraswati, these practitioners maintained that the arts of Tamil Nadu had always been the domain of the *devadasis* and their male counterparts, the *nattuvanars*. (A *nattuvanar* conducts the musical orchestra that accompanies a dance performance and is traditionally also the dancer's mentor.) Indeed, the *icai vellala* practitioners suggested that their communities were the true authors of Tamil tradition. Several of these practitioners rejected the Sanskrit language and texts in a way that Balasaraswati did not.

These artists, however, did not accordingly distance themselves from theory; instead they gave aesthetic theory a South Indian past. Some practitioners like violinist T. S. Ulaganathan spoke in overtly politicized terms when he maintained that "this is a Tamil tradition. They [brahmans] destroyed it in Tamil and re-created it in their own language [Sanskrit]." By contrast, T. R. Navaneetam, a musician, replied to a question about the current interest in Sanskrit texts, as follows: "[T]here was more of that then than there is now. Like if present now, today's dancers were to dance in front of them [*devadasi* dancers], they could quote the text and say where these people are going wrong. They didn't have books as they have now, but still they knew." She then went on, however, to say that "they learned most of these things through Telegu [the language of the state of Andhra Pradesh and a major literary and musical language of Tamil Nadu]."

Comments like this revealed several insights. At first, the political implications of dance had seemed to me to hinge upon nationalist politics.

The perspective of those marginal to the Madras milieu, combined with the politicization of linguistic and caste identity in the daily life in Tamil Nadu, indicated how regional and linguistic affiliation, alongside caste and class issues, intersected with and, in some cases, interrupted projects of nation making.

At the same time, such overtly political interpretations of history indicated that the nonhegemonic history was just as constructed and just as ideologically based as that of middle-class dancers like Devi and her students. Such encounters indicated that bharata natyam provided for the crafting of multiple affiliations and multiple histories. They also suggested that identity, whether established through caste, class, or training lineage, did not yield predictable responses to questions about past and present practice.

Multiple, competing versions of the past replaced a dialogue between one dominant and one resistant history. It now seemed impossible to locate—and write—a singular, "accurate" history. I therefore became concerned less with uncovering the authoritative history and more with the divergence within these inquiries into the past. My inquiry developed into a history of the competing histories created from different perspectives within the bharata natyam field.

I decided then to approach bharata natyam not through metaphors that emphasize wholeness and social cohesion but through those that foreground individual action. On my return to academic study in September 1996, I sought out methods for understanding how individuals politicized aesthetic practice through history.

6.5. The Banyan Tree. Lakshmi Viswanathan in attire re-created after the costume of Rukmini Devi.

Another encounter, earlier in 1996, fostered my shift toward competing versions of history: witnessing a performance of Lakshmi Viswa-nathan's *Vata Vriksha,* or *The Banyan Tree,* on 1 January 1996.34 The piece has a Sanskrit title, and its choreographer is a middle-class brahman woman who followed in the footsteps of Devi, receiving her training as a result of the events of the revival. Viswanathan has not followed the still-conventional pattern of training in dance with one teacher. She began studying as a child but learned with several different teachers as "at that time, no one wanted a career as a dancer, it was part of [her] education." It was only following her university study that she trained under Ellappa Pillai, a mentor of the Thanjavur style of bharata natyam. In addition to this dance education, Viswanathan has conducted ethnographic fieldwork and textual research on bharata natyam's history, which she has then channeled into both written and choreographed works.

6.6. The Banyan Tree. Rukmini Devi's encounter with Pavlova as The Dying Swan. Photo courtesy of V K Rajamani.

Vata Vriksha opens with the choreographer's onstage introduction of "the story of the dance of my people." It soon becomes apparent, through depictions of the folk dances of the Kaveri River delta, possession rituals, and the accomplishments of the temples and courts, that the people to whom she refers are not Indians generally but Tamils.

Like Balasaraswati, Viswanathan celebrates the early *devadasi* legacy, draws from Tamil poetry, and foregrounds the accomplishments of the Than-javur courts. Yet, like

Devi, she treats the nineteenth century as a period of decline and distances her vision of bharata natyam from remaining twentieth-century *devadasi* practice. The piece concludes with a celebration of the efforts of Devi and of the revival.

This piece provided a history that, to me, was unexpected. Viswanathan draws upon similar sources as Balasaraswati when she invokes the Tamil literary canon. Like Devi, she references the *Natyasastra* as "the basis of all Indian performing arts." She also, however, highlights the importance of praxis over aesthetic theory, stating, "I don't think dance grows out of text. It grows out of the life of the people." She foregrounds the temple and court dance traditions but, like Devi, celebrates a distant past, albeit a Tamil, not pan-Indian, one. As did Devi, she represents the mid-twentieth century as a time of restoration, not of threatened disintegration. Although Viswanathan acknowledges the significant difference between her view of history and Devi's, she nonetheless credits the revival-period choreographer for her efforts to "make [dance] credible." Unlike either of the early-twentieth-century practitioners, Viswanathan also explicitly acknowledges the globality of the revival when she refers to Devi's "inspiration during colonial times from seeing [Anna] Pavlova."

Vata Vriksha developed out of an extended period of research in which Viswanathan investigated local and regional origins for bharata natyam, producing written works that emphasize bharata natyam's origins in Tamil Nadu. She embarked on this research in order to uncover "the multiple influences over centuries" on dance in South India. Like Balasaraswati, she highlights the importance of the mentor-disciple tradition and the contributions of the Thanjavur Quartet musicians to the present-day repertoire. In her monograph *Bharatanatyam: The Tamil Heritage,* Viswanathan also acknowledges the influence of Sanskrit sources on the dance, when she maintains that "[i]nfluences, both Vedic and Aryan, bringing with them the richness of Sanskrit scholarship were absorbed, adapted, and modified by an already fully developed Tamil Culture." She uses the *Natyasastra,* however, as a source not that prescribes the form that bharata natyam should take now, but that describes the nature of an early South Indian dance form.

Her history draws together the divergent sources that Balasaraswati and Devi used to different ends. Upon encountering this, and other equally complex narratives, I could no longer fix bharata natyam even as a site of contestation. The writing that followed this research emphasized individual decisions and specific strategies. Pieces like *Vata Vriksha* also encouraged me to locate these projects not only in a dancer's discursive representations but also in choreography. I thus deployed the idea that choreography operates as a strategy for negotiating a multifaceted field of social and political concerns. I defined choreography as the planned and intentional selection of movement that includes the arrangement of conventional items of repertoire, material generated through improvisation, and the composition of entirely new work.

All of these forums offered dancers opportunities to express their perspectives on history, politics, and the social meanings of bharata natyam. The concept of choreography-as-strategy suggests that through their choices individuals negotiate a field of discourse not of their own making. The metaphor of strategy rather than, for instance, that of "creation" acknowledges that although broader concerns—social, political, cultural, and economic— inform a dance practice, they do not determine it. As such, the concept of choreography acknowledges the interplay of social, political, and historical concerns, while foregrounding a circumscribed agency.

Although anthropology and sociology have, in recent years, attended to individual agency, critical, especially poststructuralist, history has contested the idea of individual action. The anti-humanist critique pushed scholars to look at social context as determinative of individual actions; anthropologists, by contrast, have already traditionally privileged context over individual decisions.46 Thus, while poststructuralist historians have treated the notion of agency with skepticism, contemporary social scientists now include individual decision making in their inquiries. For those concerned with non-Western forms the situation is made still more complex by the endurance of an orientalist framework that identifies practitioners of such forms as constrained by "tradition." With their practices rendered fixed, such artists have been denied agency in traditional scholarship. In such a situation, a wholehearted anti-humanism can replicate the orientalist assumption of a static, unselfconscious culture that simply reiterates itself through its practitioners. My discussion of choreography represents an attempt to negotiate between these two disciplinary perspectives by suggesting that practitioners select from a set of possible options and, in doing so, creatively respond to larger social and political discourses.

This interest in individual interpretations also urged a return to ethnographic methods. While historiography emphasizes individual action, ethnography can provide a means of uncovering and understanding such strategies. Upon returning to India in 1999, I conducted formal interviews with dancers, dance teachers, and promoters, ranging across generations and levels in their careers. This involved raising questions about individual perspectives and particular experiences rather than general insights. I wanted to understand how dancers articulated their point of view within a professional sphere and, thus, how they spoke about their work in a relatively formal setting. I also selected formal interviews because I preferred interviewees to know when they were speaking on and off the record. Likewise, I intended for this choice to respect the difference between public and private selves. The dancers interviewed spoke about their procedures for performance, choreography, and research as well as about their understanding of history, their perspective on the revival, and their sense of the current dance milieu, including its economic conditions.

CONCLUSION: ETHNOGRAPHY, METHODS, AND PRACTICE

In my study of bharata natyam since 1988, I have drawn on ethnography, history, performance practice, and choreographic analysis. These methods have come into play less as a means of ascertaining the "truth" about this dance form and its past, and more as a way of tracing different choreographic strategies and their politics of representation. Through these inquiries I have realized that twentieth-century bharata natyam challenges boundaries between the disciplines of history, ethnography, and cultural studies.

When dancers participate in projects of intentional cultural production, they present "culture" as a site not of implicit consensus but of divergence. This suggests that culture as articulated in bharata natyam choreography is not seamless, organic, or implicit. Culture is not a single identity that dance reflects or contributes to. Rather, culture is a set of politicized "belongings" that shift in relationship to concerns that are local and contemporaneous. This phenomenon challenges older anthropological notions of generality. While traditional forms of anthropology continue to seek out commonalities among members of a community, ethnography can be used for other ends. The ethnographic method of participant-observation, through its emphasis on immediate experience, generates a personal involvement that can challenge dichotomies and problematize assumptions of unity within a form. It also produces a familiarity with a practice that can highlight difference in practice and interpretation. Interviewing, too, although perhaps originally used to glean insights about a shared culture, provides a vehicle for soliciting individual perspectives and understanding how the approaches of individuals differ from those of their peers, as well as how they are in accord.

Choreographic practice within bharata natyam likewise complicates an academic inquiry into history as practitioners deploy historical sources to divergent political and aesthetic ends. Practitioners produce social and political affiliations through historical narratives. This challenges a search for historical "truth." At the same time, however, because bharata natyam choreography produces social meanings through historical narratives, such strategies can only be understood through attention to the practices of the past.

This proliferation of social meanings and historical narratives, with their accompanying multiple truths, can be freeing for dancers, choreographers, historians, and for those who bridge these categories. Since the early twentieth century, this dance genre has looked back into the past in order to find its rightful place. Inquiries into the past have legitimized different interpretations of form and history. These divergent notions of past-ness have, in turn, fostered the emergence of different choreographic visions. The very presence of these multiple historical narratives, then, provides bharata natyam practitioners with a means of looking forward.

This study has also offered me an opportunity to look forward. I began this study as a dancer who wanted to unravel the complex narratives that I encountered through my participation in the Thanjavur Court style of bharata natyam. Through this inquiry, I have ended up, literally, dancing through and between ethnography and history. The process of writing these multiple histories has illuminated both the validity and the constructed nature of all of them. As such, it has shaken— and ultimately challenged—the faith I had invested in one particular version of history. Although productive, this left me temporarily without a place for my dancing in this field. As I wrote this chapter, however, I returned to performing bharata natyam after a three-year hiatus. The traditional repertoire of the Thanjavur Court style will, I trust, continue to undergird my danced inquiries of the future, but perhaps I will not be constrained by a particular version of history and aesthetic quality. I hope that through performing in and writing about such projects, I, too, can consider bharata natyam's future as well as its past.

7

Interpreting the Historical Record

When I began field research on Korean dance, I made a conscious decision to focus on the analysis of contemporary performances of older dances. As a dance ethnologist, I planned to use my specialized movement analysis skills as an entrée, and then branch out and deepen my understandings by digging into history and by learning about such other cultural manifestations and belief systems as religion, music, and philosophy. My research in Korea began in 1979 and since then has involved four extended periods of residence and numerous short visits. While learning to perform a number of dances, transcribing the dances into Labanotation, and trying to understand better the nature of the movements and choreography, I began to see how intricately interwoven were the ethnography of the present and the historical records of the past. Documenting the dances of the present was important, but a real understanding of the present could not ignore the impact of the past and a careful examination of its records.

As I sought to understand contemporary performances, Korean colleagues and consultants continually referred me to the past. They identified events they believed contributed to the present, pointed me to historical documents, and justified current practices on the basis of records of the past. When I began to study some of the historical records that were repeatedly referenced, however, I often became puzzled. I could not always see in them the validation of the present that my Korean associates espoused.

My purpose here is to examine selected iconographic representations of Korean dance, one particular type of historical record, to show the interface between history and ethnography in researching the dances of this country. Along the way I comment on my discoveries and dilemmas, as well as on the responses of Korean colleagues and consultants to things that struck me as of particular significance. In doing so, I call into question the assumption that Korea's iconographic representations of dance, even when commissioned by the royal court for the explicit purpose of documenting events, represent actual dance moments.

This resonates with contemporary thinking on historical dance research. For example, Susan Manning tells us: "An event bound in space and time, a performance can be read only through its traces— on the page, in memory, on film, in the archive. Each of these traces marks, indeed, distorts, the event of performance, and so the scholar pursues what remains elusive as if moving through an endless series of distorting reflections. But this pursuit leaves its own sort of illumination, and that illumination is what the scholar records, in effect penning a journal of the process of inquiry."

Georgiana Gore states the belief that the "discovery of historical knowledge or disclosure of historical truth are no longer tenable research objectives," but what is possible is "the mapping of a multiplicity of authorial voices through the deployment of interpretive strategies which acknowledge that all writing is situated." And Joan Erdman advocates contextualizing historical events, examining them in relation to contemporaneous occurrences, in order to obtain the clearest understanding of them. The emphasis of these authors on the situatedness of writing, the use of interpretive strategies, and the value of establishing multiple "truths" applies equally to iconographic records and points to the importance of examining historical records, regardless of their format, from many points of view. I offer selected examples from my studies of Korean dance that reinforce the necessity of fully embracing multiple perspectives in order to comprehend historical documents and the relationship between history and ethnography.

Ch'qyongmu: Realistic Depiction of Performance Moments?

The primary focus of my early research was *Ch'qyongmu*. The dance is performed today by five masked dancers, usually men, each wearing a different colored tunic. Written historical documents tell us the dance began in ritual contexts, and contemporary Korean dancers and scholars acknowledge this origin. The dance is now generally described by Koreans as a court dance, since that is the primary context in which it was performed for countless centuries prior to the demise of the court in the early 1900s. As I began to explore the history of *Ch'qyongmu* in order to understand the nature of today's version of the dance, colleagues referred me to paintings and woodblock prints of the dance in addition to textual manuscripts. Fully cognizant of the many challenges involved in using iconographic representations of dance in historical research, I became particularly interested in the paintings and prints for two reasons. First, I thought their visual nature might yield more information than such instructions as "do the poking the sky gesture," one example of the kind of description contained in manuscripts. Second, because many of these images were commissioned by, and done under the supervision of, the royal court to record, for posterity, important events, I assumed considerable attention would be paid to accuracy of detail.

I encountered a number of fascinating images of *Ch'qyongmu.* They portrayed various settings in which the dance was previously done and costumes and suggestions of choreographic moments that appear in today's dance. The latter often took the form of circular or diamond formations through which the dancers pass, and displayed a sense of liveliness, which characterizes certain portions of the dance. I found one painting especially intriguing because of its direct relationship to a sequence in today's dance. Figure 7.1 documents the entertainment at a banquet honoring elderly gentlemen.

When I juxtaposed this image against the contemporary choreography of *Ch'qyongmu,* I realized that while the artist appeared to have captured a moment in the dance, this moment was both similar to and different from one in today's performances. At one point in contemporary presentations the dancers place themselves in a diamond formation, as shown here, with one dancer in the center. The central dancer then faces and performs with each of the other dancers in a canon (a movement sequence in which the remaining dancers each join in succession). The moment suggested here could easily be a canon, with the dancer at the bottom awaiting his turn to join the others, but the order in which the dancers appear to join the canon is different from the order followed in today's performances. The original image from which this detail is extracted is in vibrant color, and the order in which the dancers join the canon, based on the tunic color of the figure who appears to be waiting for his turn, suggests a difference from current performance practice.

Another difference between this painting and contemporary performances is the way the dancers' movements relate to each other. Today, once the dancers have joined the canon, they all perform exactly the same movement. While the central dancer and the one to our right are shown doing identical movements here, the dancers at the top and to our left, although animated and apparently dancing, are doing something different: they do not have one leg lifted so high nor one arm thrust upward.

7.1. Detail of King Sukjong's Private Party for Elder Ministers, from **Kisa kyechbp** *(Album of Gathering for Officials Over the Age of 70), 1719-20. Color on silk, original 44.0 x 67.7 cm. Photo by Kim Chin-yo et al., Ho-Am Art Museum.*

JUDY VAN ZILE

In this image the formation shown and the suggestion of a movement canon parallel things seen in contemporary performances. Details of the canon portrayed here, however, are different. This raises at least two important questions. First, did the artist intend to record a realistic moment, or take artistic license in using the techniques allowed by his medium to capture only the flavor of a particular moment and the fact that the dance was performed? This latter possibility is suggested by Korean art historian Pak Chong-hye when she says that painters "could not easily represent all details ... on a picture plane. Sometimes a painter's discretion or ability yielded changes in the paintings."

Because today's version of the dance has been reconstructed on several occasions (see discussion below), the second question is posed by turning the first question around: is the painting an accurate representation of what transpired, while reconstructors of today's version of the dance took liberties in modifying movements and choreographic sequences as they brought the dance to life again?

Ch'oyongmu: Who Is the Choreographer?

As I continued to seek out images of *Ch'oyongmu* I encountered a number that puzzled me in a different way. Figure 7.2 is representative of these kinds of images. Here we see five masked dancers as well as four additional unmasked dancers. (In this case, based on the costumes worn, the additional dancers are likely to be men. In some similar images, again based on costumes, the unmasked dancers are likely to be women.) Performances of *Ch'oyongmu* today rarely include more than the five masked dancers, and my Korean colleagues never referred to additional dancers. As I showed some of these images to them and asked about the additional performers, they seemed surprised. If they had seen the images before, they never bothered either to look closely at them or to question the presence of additional performers. Some simply stated they did not know why the additional performers were included; some speculated they were ceremonial attendants, who were often present during court dances. I turned to textual manuscripts for possible clues to the extra performers.

7.2. Ch'oyongmu illustration from Sunjo muja chinjak idgwe (1828). Courtesy of Kyujanggak, Seoul National University.

The *Akhak kwebbm* (Guide to the Study of Music), an important fifteenth-century court manual, contains verbal descriptions of two versions of *Ch'oyongmu,* one performed as part of New Year rituals to expel evil spirits and that is described as elegant *(Chbndo Ch'oyongmu),* and one that was done for entertainment and that is described as lively *(Hudo Ch'oyongmu).* The dance done for entertainment was part of a suite *(Hak ybnhwadae Ch'oyongmu hapsol)* consisting of three dances—the Crane Dance *(Hangmu),* the Lotus Pavilion Dance *(Ybnwadaemu),* and *Ch'oyongmu.* Because of a number of textual references that translate as "spirit," as well as text included directly on some of the pictorial images that contain the additional figures, it is possible the extra dancers were used when the dance was part of New Year rituals. Does this mean all images that include more than five dancers record ritualistic performances?

Or did some artists include the additional dancers because of the elaboration, or ornamentation, they contributed to the painted image? Once again the issue of realistic depiction as opposed to artistic license emerges. And again, the question can be turned around: did such images contribute to today's performances?

Ch'qyongmu is first described in a late-thirteenth-century document *(Samguk yusa—*Memorabilia of the Three Kingdoms) and subsequently in numerous records up through the twentieth century. Despite this long history, there have been at least two breaks in the tradition of performing *Ch'qyongmu,* both caused by the country's engagement in political battles. Each time, however, the dance was reconstructed, either from the memories of living dancers or on the basis of extant documents such as those described here.

The dance performed most often today is said to replicate a version reconstructed in 1923. Following a hiatus in court performances during the early days of the Japanese occupation (1910-45), *Ch'qyongmu* was reconstructed by members of the court music academy (Yiwangjik Aakpu). Because of a belief that the nature of the movements made *Ch'qyongmu* more suitable for men than women, and because there were no men alive who had previously performed the dance, young boy musicians were given several months of dance lessons so that they could perform. At that time, only *Ch'qyongmu* was restaged, not the set of three dances constituting the suite described above. Thus, claims of "authenticity" regarding the dance performed today are based on the belief that it is essentially a continuation of the dance reconstructed in 1923, which, in turn, is considered "authentic" and "accurate" because it was based on information in historical documents.14 In subsequent years, other extant documents were consulted to refine performance details as well as to reconstruct the other two dances of the suite, but with only two exceptions, no effort was made to perform the dances as a suite.

A major departure from the independent performance of *Ch'qyongmu* with five masked dancers was staged in 1983. At that time *Ch'qyongmu* authority Kim Ch'on-hung decided to reconstruct the entire suite.15 Although several textual records attempted movement descriptions of each of the three dances, none described how they were linked to create the suite. Based, in part, on some of the same pictorial representations described here, Kim Ch'on-hung staged the full suite of dances. Following the three dances in the suite, all performers joined together in a kind of grand finale. During this culminating section, women performers joined the men *Ch'oyongmu* performers to dance, at one point, in between each of the masked dancers and, at another point, in a circle surrounding the masked dancers. In mixing the masked male and unmasked female dancers, Kim replicated the configuration shown in a number of iconographic representations of *Ch'oyongmu.* Interspersing unmasked female dancers with the five masked dancers in this 1983 performance was consciously based, at least in part, on iconographic representations in historical documents, documents assumed to represent a historical reality. In addition, since no masks from former times could be located for the 1923 reconstruction, an illustration in the *Akhak kwe-bom* was used to create new ones, an image that continues to serve as the model for today's masks.16

The mixing of masked and unmasked dancers in a series of configurations similar to those in the 1983 reconstruction was used in 2001 when staff of the National Center for Korean Traditional Performing Arts (Kungnip Kugagwon) presented a reconstruction of an abbreviated version of a 1795 banquet at which documents indicate the full suite was performed.

Since we know that there have been several breaks in the continuity of *Ch'oyongmu* performances and that the dance has been reconstructed several times specifically based on various historical documents, do we know who choreographed today's *Ch'oyongmu?* Although many of these documents were commissioned by the court to record actual events and are assumed to be accurate in detail, we also know that movement is extremely difficult to represent in a two-dimensional medium, either textual or pictorial. Once again, it is possible that while documenters, particularly those creating pictorial records, sought to represent the actuality of individual events, they also took artistic license. Although based on reality, they in fact may have created a kind of mythical performance moment. When people tried to reconstruct *Ch'oyongmu* after periods of inactivity and turned to pictorial documentation for inspiration, they developed a performance based on artistic license taken by the documents' creators—ultimately establishing a new reality based on a mythical reality. When contemporary dancers and scholars use such documents as the basis for reconstructing dances as they believe them to have been performed in the past, artists may, unwittingly, become contributors to the choreography.

Chinju kommu: Court Dance or Folk Dance?

A second dance that has been the focal point of some of my research is *Chinju kommu,* a knife dance from the city of Chinju that is performed by women. My interest in this dance grew from curiosity relating to several distinctive movement patterns, patterns not typically found in other "traditional" dances performed today, and which are the antithesis of stereotypically appropriate Korean female deportment. Among these movements are a displaying of the palms and a sequence in which the dancers tilt their torsos slightly backward and open their arms sideward, "presenting" the front surface of the torso in an explicitly open fashion. While virtually all sources, both written and living, trace the origin of the dance to a likely legendary story of a young boy dancer, significant debate revolves around whether today's dance is a folk dance or a court dance: whether it originated in entertainment for royalty and their guests in the central court, or among women entertainers in outlying districts. In fact, there are now three quite different categories of knife

7.3. The torso-display movement of Chinju kommu, in a performance by dancers from the National Center for Korean Traditional Performing Arts. Courtesy of Kungnip Kugagwon.

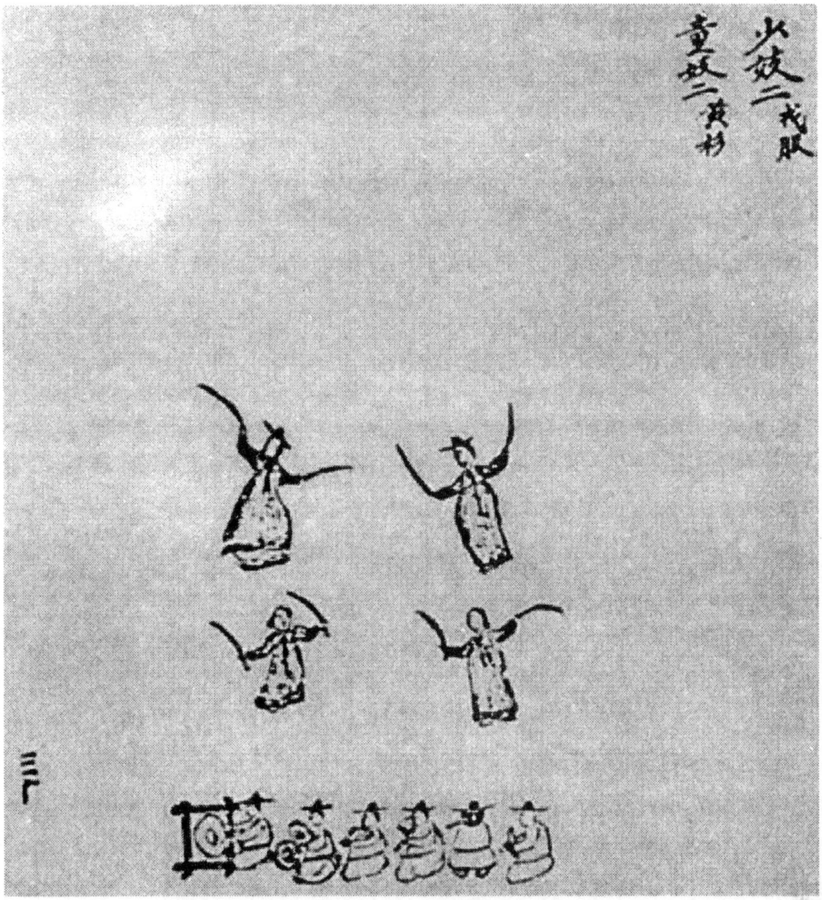

7.4. Kommu (Sword Dance) illustration from Kyobang Kayo (Text Collection of Court Entertainers' Training Institute), 1872. Courtesy of National Library of Korea.

dances: one that retains many of the movement features of other court dances and that is classified as a "court dance" *(kungjung muyong)*; several that are quite lively, acknowledged as having been created toward the middle of the twentieth century and which are categorized as "folk dance" *(minsok muyong)* or "new dance" *(shin muyong)*; and several regional variations, including *Chinju k¢ommu.* In discussing these diverse versions with colleagues, various historical documents were again cited, but this time no one ever referred to countless woodblock prints and court paintings I was discovering of knife dances.

As I tried to sort out the court/folk origin of *Chinju kommu* I found myself increasingly returning to these iconographic images. With such distinctive movements in *Chinju kommu* and the absence of even hints of these movements in the images, why had my Korean colleagues not used these records to point out the distinct differences between the court version of the dance and *Chinju kommu?* Other images, such as those discussed here of *Ch'qyongmu,* captured predominant features of individual dances even though not precisely aligning with today's performance realities. Could the iconographic images of court versions of knife dances be used to support the argument that the origin of *Chinju kommu* might lie elsewhere? Why were existing sources not being mined to the fullest extent to approach answers to acknowledged questions?

Were Many Dances Really So Similar?

As my interest in iconographic images grew I began to look increasingly at different representations of the same dance from different time periods.22 What struck me was the similarity of many of the group formations in these images as well as the similarity in positions of many dancers. Why had so many artists chosen to record the same moment in the dance? And why were the positions of individual dancers identical— sometimes within the same image and sometimes in images from different time periods?

Most of these images, such as those in Figure 7.2, are woodblock prints, in some instances with color added during the initial rendering, a format used for many other contexts besides dance. Korean art historian Yi Song-mi has carefully scrutinized images that record formal processional activities, such as that in the detail of Figure 7.5.23 She believes that many of the figures were produced by multiple stampings from a single woodblock, and that after the woodblock was stamped the image was sometimes modified by hand to create *seemingly* new figures, as in Figure 7.5; discretely backgrounded beneath the layer of paint that forms the skirt of each of the women in the upper portion of this image is a pair of legs with knee breeches identical to those of the men just beneath her.

This exemplifies Yi's conviction that the creator used a single block to produce all of these images and, when appropriate, transformed individual figures by hand-painting details. The similarity between individuals in a single representation of a dance suggests the possibility of a parallel technique.

Another explanation for similarities in images from different time periods lies in the training of painters. It was common practice to copy earlier images when learning requisite skills. Thus, whether intentional or not, details of images created by predecessors may have found their way into the works of later artists.

7.5. Detail from the 1696 Record of the Superintendency of Royal Weddings' Painting of the Wedding of Crown Prince Kyongjong (Wangsaejo Kybngjong karyae togam idgwe panch'ado). Photo by Yi Song-mi. Courtesy of Han'guk Chongshin Munhwa Yon'guwon (The Academy of Korean Studies).

I propose that in some instances the dance images were stamped out by an artist using a woodblock created by an earlier artist, and then occasionally modified by hand, and in other instances training practices contributed to the inadvertent replication of images created at another time. The implication, then, is that these images simply serve as a printed program that makes the statement "This dance was done," rather than representing an actual moment from the performance of the dance on a specific occasion. This then means that assuming such images are a kind of realistic photograph of a historical moment and relying on them for accuracy in reconstructing past choreographic details are questionable practices.

Simultaneous Performance of Different Dances?

Many court paintings, such as those in Figure 7.6, raise an issue relating to time. In these images several dances are depicted in a single "frame." If read literally, the images suggest the dances were all performed simultaneously. Is it likely this would have been the case? Would there have been a sufficiently large number of dancers available to engage so many performers at one time? Would accompanying music have been the same for all the dances shown? Would there have been a grand finale in which portions of several dances were, indeed, performed simultaneously, as in the suite reconstructed by Kim Ch'on-hung? Or do these images show us the creations of painters who took artistic liberty with the element of time? Did they simply combine, in one frame, all or many of the dances done over a period of time at a particular event?

Did painters try to suggest the elaborateness and full content of the event in a single image rather than create separate illustrations for each dance? Does the painting, once again, serve as a kind of printed program that tells us which dances were done rather than suggest an actual moment from the event? That such images were composite renderings rather than temporally realistic moments is suggested by Song Hye-jin in her analysis of a nine-panel folding screen when she states that one panel of the screen includes dances performed in 1902 at a morning banquet as well as those danced at an evening banquet. In her analysis of a number of images in relation to textual descriptions of the events they record, Kim Eun-hee suggests that vertical alignment in a single frame represents the order in which dances were presented.

CONCLUSION

Korea's history of iconographic representations of dance extends back at least as far as the sixth or seventh century A.D. to the now-famous paintings on the walls of the Dance Tomb *(Muyong ch'ong)*. Because of this long history, because in many instances court painters were officially commissioned either to document events after they transpired or to create manuals that could be used as scripts to plan and stage events, and because both dance and iconographic images are visual media, I was tempted to rely on such images as accurate depictions of a past reality.

7.6. Detail of hand scroll, Inaugural Celebrations Welcoming the New Governor of P'yongyang, attributed to Kim Hong-do, late-eighteenth/early-nineteenth century. Courtesy of National Museum of Korea.

This temptation was, I believe, the same as that to which many of my Korean colleagues had succumbed. Their reliance on the veracity of the content of historical documents, however, is also attributable to a long-standing Confucian tradition of the unquestionable authority of history and the historical record. Despite my colleagues' references to these documents, close examination of them to determine what they did or did not reveal was not a research concern for them. This acceptance of historical records was exemplified when, in the late 1990s, I gave a public presentation in Korea on several of the aspects of iconographic representations of *Ch'oyongmu* discussed here. Instead of reiterating the validity of the historical records that I was calling into question, a validity they took for granted, several individuals expressed surprise and disappointment that I had not magically discovered some new historical documents.

Korean historian Choe Yong-ho stresses the Confucian use of historical records, by their creators, to teach moral lessons. He points out that contemporary scholars believe this intent may have contributed to the distortion of reality in order to justify a particular point. I do not suggest here that the creators of iconographic representations of dance sought intentionally to distort a truth. Rather, I consider that the nature of dance and the iconographic medium may have contributed to a fictionalized reality and that, until recently, adequate attention has not been paid to interpreting the documentary veracity of these records and their possible contributions to the present.

The unquestioning acceptance, or unscrutinizing examination, of iconographic records of dance is changing. Several examples of recent research point to the kinds of analysis and interpretation that have now begun, such as that mentioned above by Song Hye-jin. Because of her background as a musicologist and specific interests, she pays particular attention to representations of music, but she also offers occasional comments on dance.

In 1990 she shared with me a database she had developed that catalogued court paintings and the individual dances depicted in each of them. The database is an extremely valuable approach to ascertaining when different dances were performed. It includes records of more than a dozen events and information on the location of each event, gender of the audience and performers, person in whose honor the event was presented, and names of dances performed. In 1997 art historian Pak Chong-hye published an article in which she briefly discussed the sociocultural context in which many court paintings of the Choson era (1392-1910) that included dance were created, as well as details relating to some of the events they recorded.

This was followed in 2000 by her book, based on her doctoral dissertation, which elaborated on the topic in significant detail. In 1999 Song Ki-suk, a dance researcher and writer, authored a chapter in which she examined one important image from the Dance Tomb.

Besides the fact that it was written by an individual trained in dance, this chapter is noteworthy because its analysis of the relationships between figures in the image is based on information contained in archaeological reports about the site as well as on Song's own reasoned interpretation. In 2002 graduate student Kim Eun-hee compared movements represented in sixteen images of *Ch'byongmu* to movements in the dance performed today. Her work is important because it is the first by a Korean researcher that is rooted in movement analysis, and it points out the anatomical impossibility of positions shown in some images.

Growing concern with understanding more fully how to interpret historical iconographic records in the context of Korean dance, as well as an interest in the views of someone not native to the culture, is reflected in attention to some of my own work. This has taken the form of an invitation to contribute an article on the topic to a Korean dance journal, and to contribute an essay on related ideas to a book, published by the National Center for Korean Traditional Performing Arts (Kungnip Ku-gagwon), of court paintings of music and dance. In both instances the material is published in Korean as well as English, and the content focuses on broad issues relating to the interpretation of images specifically in the context of Korean dance; analysis of individual images serves to exemplify points raised rather than to treat any individual one in depth.

Although some issues described here are unique to Korean dance and artists who represent it, they are of broader concern. Thomas Heck tells us that "art usually imitates *art* more than it imitates life" (emphasis in original), and cites an example from theater that points to paintings as commodities: replication resulting from the selling of wares rather than the recording of actual events. And French painter Edgar Degas expresses his belief in the importance of artistic license: "A painting is above all a product of the artist's imagination, it must never be a copy. . . . the air one sees in the paintings of the masters is not the air one breathes." In another statement he remarks, "a painting requires a little mystery, some vagueness . . . the fantastic; when the i's are always dotted and the t's crossed, it gets boring in the end."

It could be argued that these points are irrelevant to Korean court painting, in which artists were specifically tasked with accuracy. Indeed one Korean writer describes court images as "photo-journalistic," commenting on the dispatch of court painters to areas struck by natural disasters so that their paintings could assist officials in assessing damages, and to the imposition, in 1431, of punishment on painters "who failed to draw an exact representation of a dragon for the box of a diplomatic letter which was to be sent to China." But because dance exists in time as well as in three dimensions of space and is not a physical object, representations of it have unique problems of interpretation, and they must be evaluated especially carefully.

At the beginning of the twenty-first century, issues such as those raised here, as well as others, were being addressed from multiple geographic perspectives by members of the substudy group on dance iconography of the Ethnochoreology Study

Group of the International Council for Traditional Music. At meetings in 2002, 2003, and 2004, participants focused on issues relating to dances in Poland, Greece, Italy, Hungary, Tonga, and Malaysia.

That events of the past contribute to the present is widely acknowledged. That historical documents represent *the* truth is increasingly being questioned. And that iconographic representations of dance in Korea, or elsewhere, can be assumed to be any more valid than verbal documents is now an issue. It is important that the extraordinary quantity of iconographic representations of dance in Korea be critically analyzed for how they relate to other forms of documentation, realistic feasibility of human movement, and relationships to contemporary practices. In Korea the tension between history and ethnography plays itself out not only in coming to grips with trying to understand events of the past, but with interpreting the historical records of that past, regardless of their format, and ultimately in understanding how the past and its records contribute to the present.

8

Romani Dance Event in Skopje, Macedonia

The longitudinal study described in this chapter presents an ideal opportunity to examine ethnographic and historical dimensions in relation to a specific dance event, and also to reflect upon the context of the pioneering academic development of dance ethnology at the University of California, Los Angeles (UCLA) in which the research was pursued. Several histories intersect in this personalized narrative: influences upon research, such as the changing means of documentation available to the dance ethnographer, the emergence of a sociopolitical Romani cultural identity during the years in which the study was conducted, and generational interpretations of a continuing annual dance event.

My initial purpose was to document dance events in their social contexts among the Roms living in Skopje, Macedonia, in 1967. This became a foundation for a methodology with multilevel contacts in multiple time frames. Tangible visual data provided a comparative view in continuities and changes of a dance event within the continuities and changes of the social, cultural, and political fabric of an otherwise marginally recognized population. The study became a historical record, but given the involvement of dancing bodies in particular spaces, it also provided a basis for uncovering layers of social history that had been implicit through the dancing occasions.

DANCE ETHNOLOGY AS A UNIVERSITY DISCIPLINE

"Dance ethnology," "ethnochoreology," or "dance anthropology" had not yet appeared as a university academic subject within a dance curriculum when I was a graduate student in the early 1960s. The founding of the Department of Dance at UCLA in 1962 under the umbrella of a College of Fine Arts with three other departments—music, theater, and art—was in itself an innovative curricular development. The college within the university environment provided a major step toward recognizing dance as an arts discipline, with its own body of knowledge. Prior to 1962, various dancing classes (folk dance, social and square dance, modern dance, tap dance) were offered as "body activity" classes within the Department of Physical Education, which trained students as teachers for sports programs. Within the newly established Department of Dance under the leadership of Dr. Alma Hawkins, a visionary in dance education, an undergraduate or graduate student could focus on dance and dancing (albeit creative dancing) and earn a Bachelor of Arts and then a Master of Arts in dance.

The emphasis in the curriculum was to produce a broadly educated dancer/ performer/choreographer/ teacher who could pursue a profession in dance or in advanced dance education. One of the required courses of all dance students was the history of dance, but the emphasis here was on a survey of "art" dance seeped in Western cultures of Ancient Greece, medieval, Renaissance, and Baroque dance styles leading to dance as a performance art in contemporary times. Also in the earliest years of the 1960s only a beginning and advanced "folk dance" class offered a preliminary experience of "social" dances from an international array of countries, but mainly examples from northwestern Europe.

I entered this new Department of Dance as an older graduate student with a set of experiences differing from that of most American-born dance students: first as a child in Los Angeles growing up in South Slavic "ethnic" communities (Croatian, Serbian, and Slovenian) that offered dancing and music at most every community- or family-sponsored social event (almost a weekly occurrence), and then as a young adult performing in Skopje, Macedonia (then part of Yugoslavia), with the professional Tanec Folk Dance and Music Ensemble.

After a period of looking after my two young children, I returned to academia into the newly formed graduate dance program of UCLA, to expand my knowledge about dance and to prepare myself for teaching dance in higher education. I realized with Allegra Fuller Snyder, a colleague who had also just returned to academia, that there was a major lack in the literature about dance beyond ballet, modern dance, and Western history of dance. We were seeking a broader knowledge about dance in other parts of the world and to learn about the social and ritual contexts of dancing.

Among readings, the most satisfying was in a newly published and seminal article by Gertrude Prokosch Kurath. I was inspired, for Kurath had recognized the Yugoslav-based Janković sisters and their contributions to the description of dances, their creation of a dance notation system, and their attempts at structural analysis. Kurath's article expanded my thinking toward possible studies among populations located in Slavic areas of southeastern Europe, where I had already had personal experiences. I began to consider the possibility of recording and describing dancing events rather than recording only the dances as found in many field collections and publications of dance, such as those collated for use by teachers of "folk dance" classes in physical education curricula.

Philosophically within the Department of Dance, all dancing was considered an art form. I began to be strongly aware of a difference in that "art" dance was "formally organized" and intended to be performed for an audience, whereas the social forms that I encountered as a child within the South Slavic community events were unrehearsed and spontaneous in participation. Were these dances art? The kind of dancing that I performed with the professional dance ensemble in Macedonia was "art," but the dances were derived from spontaneous social forms. The extent of their adaptation for the staged performance was dependent upon the "choreographer," who was not of the community from where the dances were taken. The dances were out of their social context and became crafted as "art."

Seminal writings for studying or understanding dance learned through field participation and observation had not yet appeared. Thinking about dance in social contexts came later. My models in the 1960s came empirically by way of UCLA graduate courses in folklore and ethnomusicology and readings in anthropology. "Going into the field" was a method of study in all three disciplines. Anthropological ethnography recognized dancing within a culture, but there was no mention of dancing characteristics, structural form, the body movement, numbers of dancers, and so on. "People danced." Furthermore, the anthropological fieldwork tended to be within Native American, African, or Asian groups of peoples who were unfamiliar to my own living experiences and to the search for understandings of my own experiences.

Folklorists, such as the head of the Program of Folklore at UCLA, Wayland Hand, conducted fieldwork in Western-based cultures, but these folklorists were principally interested in the "oral traditions" and made extensive comparative studies of oral texts independent of their social contexts. The texts as products were analyzed and compared with each other. Ethnomusicology at UCLA (a fledgling field of study under the leadership of Mantle Hood) was the closest model to my dance interests: the music was recorded within a cultural context, as far away as Indonesia, but also closer to Los Angeles, in northern Mexico and southwestern United States. The dancing that was accompanied by the music, however, was usually not considered by the young graduate ethnomusicologists. They too were not prepared to understand the body movement or interrelationship of the music to the dancing. With dance at UCLA as a newly recognized field of study, there was clearly a need to conduct our own fieldwork with a focus on dance within its social and cultural contexts.

Who are the people who do the dancing? When? Where? How? Why? At the time of my graduate studies at UCLA, ethnographic descriptions answering these questions for peoples from southeastern Europe were rare. Joel Halpern, a young anthropologist who was at UCLA before me and who had done fieldwork in Yugoslavia for a doctoral dissertation, published *A Serbian Village* but like most other anthropologists, he did not include dancing in any of his analysis of lifestyle.6 As a result of my childhood experiences in Los Angeles and those as an adult performing in Macedonia, I knew that dancing was a vital expressive activity in the geographical area of his studies. There was, however, another unexpected and important outcome of Halpern's time in Yugoslavia in the 1950s. The chancellor of UCLA had assigned Halpern to acquire publications for the university during his fieldwork in Yugoslavia. Hal-pern with his anthropological background collected all forms of publications, old and new, and created the largest and fullest collection of publications in humanities, history, and folklore from that part of Europe. I had at my disposal an unequalled fund of written materials from pre-Yugoslavia and the then current Yugoslavia, a collection not available anywhere else outside Yugoslavia. At the time of my graduate studies, I was not aware of this wealth but learned of its significance in following years.

Also owing to the new program in dance at the university, there was a policy of enriching the collection of dance literature for the UCLA Research Library. Available at the time were early-twentieth-century published collections of "folk dances" particularly from northwestern and western Europe; the 1950s international handbook series of folk dances from many countries in Europe; the International Folk Dance and Song Society yearbooks that happened to include Felix Hoer-burger's folk dance survey and his suggestion of first and second existence of "folk dance." His survey reinforced existing emphasis on the dance product, rather than the ethnographic information about the dancing contexts. The models for "folk dance" study were limited to the "product" and not the context of the dancing. In the geographical area of the South Slavs, eight volumes of "folk dances" *(narodne igre)* were published by sisters Ljubica and Danica Janković between 1934 and 1962, a full set not available anywhere else in the United States at that time (thanks to Halpern's collection).

Their and other descriptions of dances from all parts of Yugoslavia through the 1950s produced an extensive resource, but I was interested in understanding the social context of the dancing of these dances and not just the described dance product. Another area of unique expansion in the library supplemented the course on the folklore of the Gypsies taught by Visiting Professor Walter Starkie. The UCLA Research Library added readings and studies on the Romani peoples, also not equaled at any other university. In an assignment for his class, I used this collection in a bibliographic search on dancing of the Roms, and I saw that almost nothing was written about their dancing or their dancing contexts, even though the "Gypsies" were reputed to be a dancing culture.

New recording technology had become available at this time, which facilitated understanding of how dancing forms continue or change over time. Portable reel-to-reel audio tape recorders and hand-held 16-millimeter film cameras with portable battery packs revolutionized the ability to make tangible the study of a whole dancing context, rather than needing to extract and describe the dances (the product) independently of the context. Even a single person could record spontaneous dancing during social events. No longer was a multiperson crew necessary to invade the context for recording purposes. Furthermore, there was less dependence upon the vagrancies of memory and less drilling native dancers to perform their dances repeatedly (and out of context) with the objective of notating the dance.

With the personal experience of growing up dancing in "ethnic" events in the United States, I was particularly sensitized to immigrant groups and their descendants. My questions became polarized toward a comparative view of emigrant and immigrant dancing customs. Both the South Slavic and Gypsy communities in Los Angeles sparked my inquiries into comparative continuities and changes in dances and their dancing. Serbian Gypsy families happened to live nearby the part of the city where my family lived, so that I had an awareness of their mixed Serbian-Romani language and familiar customs. Then while a university student, I had the opportunity to attend their family events, which included open-circle chain *kolo* dancing and solo dancing. Eventually, funded by the United States Department of Health, Welfare and Education, in 1967 I traveled to southeastern Europe for several months, supplied with a 16-millimeter film camera, rolls of film, a reel-to-reel tape recorder, and a still camera with an attachable telephoto lens. Little did I realize that this first professional dance ethnology project would become a basis for a longitudinal study.

The tantalizing excitement of my first experience at a massive social event with dancing and music motivated me to "revisit" the community and its multiday celebration of St. George's Day (Gjurgjevden in Macedonian), also known as Coming of Summer (Erdelezi in Turkish), in Skopje, Macedonia. This annual festivity (hereafter referred to as St. George's Day) was celebrated exclusively by the Roms in Skopje and offered an ongoing base from which to note selected markers of continuities and changes. I conducted an audiovisual documentation of the multiday event (5–9 May) six times over a thirty-year period: ten-year intervals in 1967, 1977, 1987, 1997, with two interim years, 1995 and 1996. The hundreds of still photographs along with movement documentation on film and videotape of this single event over a span of years provides a tangible means to study this event against a background of sociocultural and sociopolitical changes.

DOCUMENTING ROMANI EVENTS IN 1967

Because of my memories of many Gypsies in Skopje during the time I spent with the Tanec professional dance and music ensemble, I had decided to begin my documentation of dancing within social events in Skopje. I knew that I could "find" Gypsies in that area even though I did not know very much about this particular community. Although I had planned to arrive in time for a national holiday (1–2 May), with the expectation that there might be dance and music, followed by the celebration of Macedonian Orthodox Easter (discouraged during the Communist regime, nevertheless observed on a limited basis), I was not aware of the overlapping of the St. George holiday dates that these Gypsies celebrate. After watching dancing at the crossroads in a Gypsy neighborhood and making visits to several other neighborhoods in the city during early May, I was told that I should go especially to the hill adjacent to the old Gypsy quarter, Topaana, on Tuesday afternoon, 9 May. I did and was awed by what I witnessed.

Imagine a mass of about 10,000 Gypsies on a green and wooded hillside, dressed in their finest—the women in pantaloons made of twelve meters of colorful lightweight fabric with matching billowing sleeves and delicately decorated headscarves—and at least twelve bands of musicians scattered throughout the hillside, each accompanying from twenty to seventy dancers. The sounds of *zurla* (double-reed wind instruments) and *tapan* (large but portable double-headed drums struck on one side by a stick and on the other with a type of twig), saxophones, tambourines, violins, accordions, and bagpipes all intermingled into a din of rhythmic sounds. This was an extraordinary participatory social dance event. Families feasted on foods brought from home, while sitting on brightly woven rugs spread out along the hillside, and with hundreds of musicians and dancers, negotiating their space between these family groupings. Furthermore, based on the manner of dress and body behaviors, I noted that there were almost no "outsiders" (non-Gypsies) at the event. By sunset, the hillside was empty; the families had returned to their homes to continue socializing among themselves. Unknown to me at the time, I had observed the most significant annual event of the Gypsies in Skopje.

Over the next months, I filmed and recorded dancing at several social events, mainly family celebrations of weddings, circumcisions, and naming of babies. There were basically three types of dancing—two in public, that is, outside of the home, in the streets, or in another public setting, and one that was restricted to private contexts. One public type of dancing was performed by people, linked by a handhold either at shoulder height or down at the sides, moving in open circles that progressed in a counterclockwise direction. The other public type was performed in linked handholds as the dancers paraded frontally, using a repetitive step, through the streets in forward-moving lines. Such public open-circle dancing might have included anywhere from three or four to thirty or forty dancers performing a repetitive step pattern.

The music accompaniment consisted of *tapan* and *zurla* or a small band in some combination of clarinet, accordion, *darabuka* (clay-based hourglass-shaped hand drum), trumpet, or saxophone (electrified instruments had not yet been introduced). The rhythmic meter was usually an uneven pattern, identifiable by a combination of slow and quick beats: slow, quick, quick ($-^{7}_{8}$), or quick, quick, quick, slow ($^{9}-_{8}$). Dancing to one melody could last several minutes, and a medley of tunes might last up to a half hour or more. The tempo of the music was usually moderate, but quickened when the musicians warned the dancers that the piece would soon end. At the right end of the chain, the leader could be female or male.

The other type of dancing took place at gender-exclusive parties in private settings where dancers took turns performing the solo form known as *cocek*. The solo was danced only during private segregated occasions, such as part of the five-day wedding cycle, or a three-day cycle for the circumcision of a son, or at the naming of a newborn child. During the event, every female at the party was expected to rise up from her floor-seated position to dance a type of "belly-dance" producing a vertical up-and-down movement of the abdomen (in Labanota-tion terms this is a somersaulting movement of the pelvis); the arms are moved in an improvised range at about shoulder level, with snapping fingers, while the feet are stepped in place to the rhythm of the music— usually in a $^9{-}_8$ meter. The music accompaniment was by a hired Ro-mani woman, who sang and held a tambourine in an upright position with her left hand, while tapping the skin with her right hand; more affluent families used a phonograph player for 45-rpm records of Turkish melodies in $^9{-}_8$ meter. This type of solo dancing tended to occur at all-night parties, involving light drinking (sweet liquor and beer) and feasting. Men and women partied in separate rooms, and each with their own musicians or phonograph players. Young children, who would also be encouraged to dance the *cocek,* joined the female members of the family.

Because of the large numbers of Gypsy families in Skopje, there were multiple events most every week. Since the dancing during these events tended to be "public" (that is, in the streets), there was ample opportunity to watch along with local Gypsy spectators and, when I had been given permission, to record with still photographs or film footage. In addition, whenever I was invited to join the dancing line, I took advantage of dancing next to other females and tried to emulate their style. I did not feel that it would be appropriate to dance next to a male or to lead a chain of dancers. Although nonfamily members could participate in the public dancing, it was, of course, noticed when this "Amerikanka" participated. Although I loved dancing with them, I only participated when invited. While attending the private events with *cocek* dancing, however, I was expected—and even urged—to dance, because every female at the event danced. No excuse was valid. If one did not feel well enough to dance, then one did not go to the party.

Wherever I learned of an event in Skopje and later elsewhere in the Balkans, I brought my cameras and tape recorder. Since I had use of a car, it was possible to be mobile. As a result, I experienced and recorded an overview of Gypsy dancing in southeastern Europe preceding the arrival of "Rom" advocates (particularly from England) to Gypsy suburbs and communities. This was still a time when Gypsies had not yet been sensitized to a "Rom" identity in place of the degrading identity of "Cigan." In most countries, sizeable Gypsy populations were not even included in official census statistics; this was the case in Yugoslavia until 1971. The Gypsies had no political representation, no literature, and very few studies had been done about them. The events that I attended and the contacts that I made were all achieved through personal references.

Although this was a very fulfilling learning experience, with exposure to various styles of dancing among the Gypsy populations in much of southeastern Europe, I was not able to proceed with my underlying interest of comparative continuity and change of immigrant and emigrant contexts owing to my lack of proficiency in the various dialects of Romani. My focus then shifted to Croatian communities with whose language and traditions I was more familiar. It was this latter study that brought me back to southeastern Europe for an extended time of research during a university sabbatical leave in 1976–77. Remembering my 1967 experience of the extraordinary St. George's Day in Skopje, however, I planned to revisit Skopje in May (but now with portable video equipment) to observe and record this event again. So it was not until ten years later that I realized it would be possible to take an event such as St. George's Day and compare it with itself. Although I continued with the Croatian research, the St. George's Day event turned out to be a long-term field study.

ROMANI HISTORY AND IDENTITY IN SKOPJE

Although the population of the Skopje-based Roms is one of the largest in Europe, there is scant written information about their history in Skopje or in Macedonia. The chronicling of Roms into Europe begins in Constantinople (Istanbul) in the tenth century. The earliest record of "Egipchani" (Egyptians) in former Yugoslav lands is in Dubrovnik (Ra-gusa) in 1362. By the middle of the sixteenth century there are more numerous records, including a count of Cigan (Gypsy) households in Skopje. During the Ottoman Turkish advances into Europe, there are notings of Gypsies who provided blacksmith and music services for the Turkish army garrisons in Skopje, Beograd (Belgrade), and other centers.16 In Skopje, the Romani presence began at least by the fourteenth century. The Roms in Skopje are not nomads, but "settled" peoples with traditional occupations. Itinerant Roms *(cergari)* do come and go through Yugoslavia, but in the twentieth century at least, they did not integrate or intermarry with the sedentary Skopje Romani population.

Two sets of census records, almost a hundred years apart, are significant markers of the count of Roms in Skopje. Statistics gathered in 1891 list 1,920 Cigani (240 houses) in Skopje, making the Roms the third largest population in Skopje at the end of the nineteenth century. A hundred years later, the official 1994 census shows that the Roms continued to be the third largest population in Skopje, with 20,070 (4.5 percent of Skopje population), while in 1997 they were the fourth largest population in the Republic of Macedonia, following the Macedonian, Albanian, and Turkish language groups. Although there have been shifts in the size of other nationalities, the Roms have maintained their proportionate numbers since the late nineteenth century.

When I went to Skopje in 1967 to document dances of the Gypsies during their social events, the old Gypsy quarter, known generally as Topaana, was in a state of flux. Due to the disastrous earthquake four years earlier, when many families had suffered damage to their homes, they were placed in temporary housing on the safer outskirts of the city. Within four years a new suburb, Suto Orizari, was under construction north of the city, and families were given plots of land and financial credit toward building new homes. Hundreds of Romani families began to resettle in this suburb, and although the St. George's event began to be observed in both Romani settlements of Topaana and Suto Orizari, the height of the event on 9 May, with its music and dancing, continued to take place on the hillside near the older community in Topaana.

During the early 1970s advocates of human rights for Roms initiated changes in self-identity. The First Romany Congress held in London in 1971, and the Second Romany Congress in Geneva in 1978, firmly established the shift in self-identity terms from "Cigan," "Gypsy," and "Gitano," considered to be degrading terms, to Rom or Roma, a word taken from their Romani language; a tri-colored (red, blue, and green) flag with a centered wagon wheel was designed to represent the Rom; and a popular song "Gjelem Gjelem" was selected as an anthem. The 1971 census added "Roma" (instead of "cigani") as one of the multinational categories in Yugoslavia. The growth of Skopje's industries after the earthquake provided opportunities for employment, resulting in scheduled work hours and scheduled public transportation, which in turn influenced the timing in the celebration of family events that included music and dancing. Greater educational opportunities were provided, leading to developing professionals and political leaders, who became influential in later decades.

Beginning in the 1980s the community in Suto Orizari became more involved politically, both internationally and locally. Romani leadership and performing artists from Skopje were invited to participate in the next World Congress (held in Sweden), and a Romani festival and scholarly meeting was held in Chandigar, India, where Prime Minister Indira Gandhi embraced the Roms as peoples from India. In the late 1970s and 1980s, the newly composed Romani music in Skopje included Indian music themes (taken from Indian-produced films shown in Skopje).

Macedonia became independent from the "former" Yugoslavia in 1991, but the political and economic situation was tense owing to border closings caused by Greece in the south and Serbia in the north, followed by tensions with Kosovo Albanians. The seeds of education that had been sown in the 1970s, however, provided a growth of leadership from within the Romani community. For the first time there was Romani representation in the democratic state of the Republic of Macedonia, with political parties and political self-determination in the government. Romani television and radio stations were established by and directed by Roms, with dissemination of

Romani news in Romany language causing language standardization and programming that provided affirmation of Romani identity.

The entire Romani population, however, continued to be involved with the St. George's Day celebration. There were changes in the melodies (more Indian themes), the addition of electrified instrumentation, and less use of the "traditional" dress in public. Dancing and music continued all five days. As music bands became more and more dependent upon electricity, only *tapan* and *zurla* instruments continued to accompany dancing during the St. George's Day event in the next two decades. Dancing and costuming (festive dress of the past) have become identity markers of their community. The pantaloons and colorful headscarves that were once worn daily, only to be embellished with "new" outfits for St. George's Day celebration, weddings, and other family events, now are reserved for wear during a part of the wedding or for special occasions that display a "Romani" identity to non-Roms, such as political rallies and stage performances. *Cocek* solo dancing has become a staged identity for Roms.

In 1967 the *cocek* was a "behind closed doors" dance, which by 1997 had become a public performance dance as an identity marker with amateur organized dance ensembles. Young people see their "costumes" as making a statement or symbolic show of the past, but their dancing continues to be a reality of the present. The "public" open circle chain dancing is still a community-wide social form, and everyone still knows how to participate in the dancing. The solo *cocek* dancing has become more specialized. It is acceptable for this dancing to be done in public, and it is this dance that is the Romani identity marker for music and dance ensembles who give professional staged performances—now an "art" dance rather than a spontaneous social form.

Against the background of these major sociopolitical changes among the Skopje Roms since my recording of their events in 1967, the five-day holiday continued to be celebrated as the most important event in a year's cycle of social activities. "We must celebrate St. George's Day . . . if we have the means—but for St. George's Day, if we cannot or can, we must. Spring comes only once a year."

TIME, TECHNOLOGY, AND DOCUMENTATION

Reflecting upon the continuities and changes within this community has led me to consider how technology may provide a means of revealing and reflecting upon the past. Regardless of the advances in recording live dance events and my care to take advantage of the very latest equipment available, it was an already established technological means for documentation—the still photograph—that unexpectedly provided insight into the past. What had been the capturing of an ethnographic moment in 1967 became, in the late 1990s, itself a historical source that enabled older members of the community to communicate a hidden knowledge to myself and to younger generations of their own people.

Unknown to me as a researcher at the time, I had happened to document my first St. George's Day in one of the early years of transition after the catastrophic earthquake of 1963, which had its epicenter in Skopje. Dancing in Topaana in 1967 occurred on each of the three days, 6–8 May, at the crossroads *kod cesma* ("by the water fountain"), while on 9 May, the height of the event, most of the Romani population gathered on a hillside adjacent to Topaana. My documentation of ten, twenty, and thirty years later showed that the dancing no longer took place at the crossroads, nor anywhere else in Topaana, for the St. George's Days, although 9 May, the last day of the holiday, continued to be held on the spacious hillside adjacent to Topaana.

I was curious why the dancing on 6–8 May 1967 took place in the narrow streets near the crossroads, with cars, trucks, or buses frequently honking their way through the thick lines of dancers, when there were other more spacious areas nearby with no passing vehicles. My understanding of the dancing on the street at this particular intersection developed indirectly, thirty years later, after tracing genealogies of musician families, and through discussion with the participants I had recorded in 1967.

In 1996, I took an album of photographs from 1967 to elicit comments from those participants. The 3x5-inch photographs seemed easily viewable to me, but an unexpected problem surfaced. The people in the photos were, in 1996, aged in their late forties, fifties, or sixties and had poor eyesight, with no access to eyeglasses. In 1997 I returned to the same families with the same photos, which had been scanned to large-size paper and placed into a binder. Also I supplied a magnifying glass to help those with very poor eyesight, and I paid particular attention to visiting them during good daylight hours. Conversations about the dancers represented in the photographs and about the *tapan* and *zurla* musicians revealed information about the neighborhoods prior to 1963. These discussions brought to light a Romani self-identity that was based on a territorial distribution of the Roms in Skopje, which hitherto had not been mapped or studied.

When I came to Skopje in 1967, the rebuilding of the city following the earthquake and the partial removal of the *ciganska maala* (the old Gypsy quarter), a part of Topaana, were in their early stages. Many Ro-mani families had suffered damage to their homes and had been placed in temporary housing on the safer outskirts of the city. By 1967, a new suburb, Suto Orizari, was under construction north of the city, where hundreds of Romani families had begun to resettle. In 1967 the St. George's event was split in its celebration between the old Romani district of Topaana and the new suburb of Suto Orizari.

There was a notable distinction in the musical accompaniment provided for the celebrations in each of these districts. Music for the celebrations on the hillside was and has continued to be provided by sets of musicians playing *tapan* and *zurla*. The *tapan* and *zurla* musicians did not play for the dancing at the crossroads. The traditional *tapan* and *zurla* were played only within musician families who passed on the skill of constructing and playing their instruments. These musicians supplied the accompaniment for family events (such as weddings) only in their own neighborhoods. The event that took them to the Topaana hillside was 9 May, where ali neighborhoods converged for feasting and dancing. But even on the hillside, the musicians tended to play for those families who knew them in their own neighborhoods. Music for the dancing at the crossroads in 1967, on the other hand, was provided by "modern instruments" such as clarinet, trumpet, hand drum, and accordion, played by musicians who did not come from a long family tradition.

Not until I began to trace genealogies of musicians did I uncover that there were distinct neighborhoods prior to the 1963 earthquake. The *tapan* and *zurla* musician families came from two of the oldest parts of the *ciganska maala* that had been erased as a result of the earthquake and subsequent urban renewal. These changes had also brought about intermarriage between the families of these two old neighborhoods. The adjacent neighborhoods were considered to be of "newcomers." The presence of these different families and their residence patterns were the result of new Rom migration into the area following the withdrawal of the Ottoman Turkish Empire from its northern territory during the nineteenth and early twentieth centuries. Those Roms who were not Christian found haven in the Skopje "Turkish" Romani quarter, and each major migration seems to have settled on the fringes of the older neighborhoods.

Before the earthquake, marriages were controlled by the families and did not integrate the groups of Roms from different migrations. In 1967, although I noted that many marriages had been brokered between families, a large proportion of the marriages appeared to be "love" marriages—that is, the young people knew each other before the marriage (which, I was told, in the days of their grandparents and great-grandparents was not the case). Most of my informants in 1967, in fact, had been married after the earthquake and lived in either Topaana or Suto Orizari, where their own neighbors were of "mixed" marriages— that is, between families from different (although contiguous) neighborhoods. My photographic record on 7 and 8 May happened to document two late afternoons when there was dancing at the crossroads, and which did not happen in later years, because most of the homes in Topaana had been demolished for apartment buildings, and families had moved into the new Suto Orizari suburb, where the prior distinctions of migrations had become erased physically and eliminated in the dancing events.

Those who were dancing at the crossroads in my 1967 documentation thus represented a mixture of neighborhood populations. The year was part of a transition when there was a physical breakdown of the neighborhoods, and families from these neighborhoods were becoming integrated by marriage. The St. George's Day in 1967 was the only event in the year when dancing was the key means for once separate groups to have social mixing, and this was at the margin of the old and new neighborhoods. The crossroads marked the nonverbalized, unmarked neutral space dividing the older and newer migrations into Skopje, representing the territorial division between the Romani neighborhoods and distinct identities.

As a result of combining my own past documentation with present interpretations from the local people depicted in the photographs, a shift in residence and marital patterns was thus revealed to me, an aspect that was manifested in the manner in which St. George's Day had been celebrated over the thirty-year period and before. This historical perspective was revealed only through my previous documentation of the event.

Such collaboration with local people, using technology as a research tool beyond its immediate function of documentation, has similarly led to fresh insights into the continuity of the celebration. Advances in technological capabilities over the years have facilitated my understanding of local implicit interpretations. For the dance researcher, developments in the long-play capability in both audio and visual recordings to allow for "real time" and whole dance sequences rather than "selected" moments have been of undoubted benefit for analysis.

Also, it is now easier to be unobtrusive in the field, both because the equipment is smaller and capable of operating in low light levels and because the equipment itself is no longer particularly novel and hence distracting. Indeed, it has now been possible to hire local videographers to document those moments that are not possible for a dance ethnologist to access as a result of being an outsider to the community. It is never possible, of course, to make a "complete record," but supplementary tangible visual data is helpful to the understanding and interpreting of the context.

By the 1990s, videographers other than me were common at Romani events. Professionals with their own video cameras were hired by families to record whole events just as still-camera photographers were once engaged to take photographs. These video images are used in a manner similar to that of home movies or as photo albums for the event.

With the advent of Romani-produced television programs, freelance or station videographers were also employed to cover events in the community for broadcast purposes. In 1997 I hired local videographers who had experience in recording events for local Romani television stations. I explained that I wanted their perspective of the St. George's Day event. In looking at their first tapes, I realized that they were accustomed to taping short takes, and I could not understand a sequence without their verbal input. They were so familiar with the context that a short take was all that was necessary. But as an outsider, I needed more explanatory footage.

I then directed them to do nonstop video "scenes." They went on to document aspects of the holiday that I, as an outsider, could not or would not. Especially useful was their videotaping of private family aspects of the holiday, such as the bathing of the children (placing herbs and gold jewelry in the bath water) and dressing the children in new clothing, preparation of special foods for the holiday, neighborhood and family visitations, at-home spontaneous dancing to audiocassette music, multiple recordings of lamb sacrifices over a two-day period in neighborhoods of varying economic strata.

Although they had freedom to record events, we discussed ahead of time their suggestions and ideas for recording. My interests in the ethnographic purpose behind video-recording do not, however, seem to have left any long-term influence upon them. There was no sense that the videographers were recording for posterity; rather, they were simply recording as paid professionals.

Given this change in the nature and profile of technological documentation, to what extent has this influenced kinetic transmission of the dances? The dances occur mainly during wedding and circumcision events at which musicians (now with electronic music) are hired, and space is consciously provided for participatory dancing.

As large family events, these parties are partially "public" so that children and youngsters are frequently exposed to the dancing in their homes and in their neighborhood streets. In the Romani community there are no teachers or demonstrators. Dancing in close proximity, with a handhold contact with dancers on either side of oneself, one may easily blend into the group body action with the repetitive dance steps. Technology does not play a direct role in the transmission of these dances. Since the early 1990s, however, dancing has been regularly viewed on the Romani-produced television programs and videocassettes produced by Romani music groups, both of which regularly show the *cocek* dancing in costume.

Although the rapid advances in technology for consumer use are incredibly useful for the documentation, preservation, and analysis of dance movement, the dancing within the Skopje Romani community has, nonetheless, continued to be transmitted through imitation learning or teaching (I prefer the term "body movement transmission" rather than "oral tradition").

In the thirty-plus years of my tracing of their lifestyle and dance events in Skopje, the dancing repertoire and style of dancing during group dancing in open chains has not, however, been influenced directly by television and video intervention into their lives. So long as the dancing has continued to fulfill social needs within the communities and there are musicians (such as *tapan* and *zurla*) who still accompany the outdoor dancing, specific technology has not changed the manner of transmitting the dances. The dance repertoire of the "public" dancing during weddings and circumcision celebrations has continued. There are changes in the music accompaniment, clothing, and frequency of dancing, but the basic dance repertoire, the manner of dancing, and the acquisition of knowledge of dancing have remained. The repertoire that was danced in 1967 accompanied by such "outdoor" music instruments as the *zurla* and *tapan* was danced in 1997 accompanied by a younger generation of *zurla* and *tapan* musicians.

CONCLUSION

The Romani population in Skopje has come a long way since 1967 in terms of educational levels, political self-determination, media communication, introduction of social services, and living conditions, and has set a model for Romani communities elsewhere in Europe. Family support for education has produced professionals within the community and for the Macedonian state at large, such as community leaders, journalists, attorneys, medical personnel, educators, theater directors, internationally esteemed professional entertainers, and more. The five-day St. George event with its dancing continues to be a major annual celebration, and dancing remains a vital ingredient within life-cycle events. No one, however, in the community or in the country of Macedonia has ventured into an ethnographic documentation of these festivities. Consequently, my own thirty-year study of a contemporary dancing event has now become their historical record.

Initiated prior to the development of a dance ethnology curriculum in the United States, this study, using the latest technology as a means of documentation, became the first dance ethnology project at UCLA to emphasize the importance of experiencing, observing, and recording dance in its context over a long-term period. It demonstrates that a dance ethnology study is not based upon one-time contact but upon multilevel contacts in multiple time frames providing a continuity of data making for a historical record. This longitudinal ethnographic investigation developed into a model for future research projects that commence with contemporary forms of dancing, with understandings of continuities and changes not otherwise possible, except through tangible images and through direct observation, participation, and interviews with the living. Such ethnographic strategies, as evidenced above, may offer unexpected opportunities to uncover hidden historical dimensions and to celebrate the rich rewards that may be gained through moving across past and present.

9

Being Traditional

Neat divisions into traditional and revival practices of dance frequently obscure often complex relationships to the past and present. A particular case is English morris dancing, a dance type that boasts six hundred years of recorded history, although in some quarters it is believed to date from prehistoric times. In serious decline by the end of the nineteenth century, morris dancing underwent documentation and revivification in the early 1900s, within the framework of the national English Folk Revival. This movement included song, music, drama, and other dance forms that were designated by the collectors as authentic folk practices worthy of being recorded for revival. A handful of the older teams of morris dancers that had not disbanded by the early 1900s performed throughout the twentieth century, continuing to the present day.

Such long-established morris teams, together with those that had died out, and other pre-twentieth-century folk performance arts, became collectively categorized as the Tradition. In order for a dance to be judged traditional, a key criterion was an origin that predated the folk revival movement of the early twentieth century. The oppositional category of the Revival was used to designate those folk activities, including teams of morris dancers, that largely owed their inception and existence to the program of national recovery.

These constructs of the Tradition and the Revival were thus created by the collectors of folk material and employed by those who took up performance of the nationally delineated folk repertoire to distinguish between the existing practitioners and contexts of performance and those inspired by a national, self-conscious movement of revivalism.

The concepts of the Tradition and the Revival exist through mutual and exclusive definition, signaling dichotomies of old versus new, authentic versus invented, and genuine versus spurious.3 They also signal different aspects of the past. The Tradition is usually accorded a mythic past, as the origins of most customary practices are deemed to lie beyond living memory and written and iconographic records. The Revival, on the other hand, demonstrates a documented past, since the origins of revival practices, deriving their inspiration from the folk collections of the early twentieth century, are demonstrably retrievable through the typical written and oral memory-type source material of history.

The late twentieth century witnessed some revisionism of this once accepted distinction, however. Scholarly investigation of nineteenth-century records and, where available, earlier source material sometimes revealed a starting point for some customs much later than popularly held. Since the 1980s, the disclosure that a so-called traditional practice is actually a comparatively modern phenomenon has been the fate of a number of British annual customs.4 Similarly, in the critical discourse on dance that examines the uses of tradition in legitimizing performance, it has usually been the researcher's role to interrogate these tensions between the mythic past and the documented past, exposing dances with assumed credentials of extreme longevity to be more recent creations than hitherto believed.5 Revelations about the presumed antiquity of certain morris dances do not, however, provide the principal focus for the historical and ethnographic exploration in this chapter; for other pasts are at stake in this discourse, not least of which is the past of myself as researcher. I wish, instead, to challenge the neat division into mythic and documented histories through the complicating factor of a personal history created through memory and reflection upon my own documentation of morris dancing. In this respect, aspects of this chapter fall between the categories of ethnographic writing characterized by sociologist Amanda Coffey as "tales of the self " and as "partial/autobiographical."

John Lofland and Lyn Lofland, in their guide to qualitative observation and analysis in ethnography, observe that "the norms of scholarship dc not require that researchers bare their souls, only their pro-cedures." Revelation and re-evaluation of my past procedures as a researcher, quite obviously, make public the pitfalls of my former training in older models of ethnographic and historical inquiry.8 The return to my past as researcher and to the intertwined pasts of those I researched has, more awkwardly for me, also highlighted my frequently unconscious construction of discrete selves and others as essential to pursuing the investigation. In carrying out the research, I had unwittingly drawn upon different versions of my own self, versions that drew upon personal experiences and senses of identity that I failed to realize profoundly influenced how I conceived of and treated the people who helped me in my study.

Throughout the conduct of my research, however, I had believed that only one self was legitimately in operation in relation to my material, that of the scholarly self. Revisiting my ethnographic notes, correspondence, and, latterly, the field has demonstrated my comparative ignorance. Finding bias in the work of others, in the sense of past writings of scholars, is a critical directive in academia; finding it in the work of one's own is a less comfortable experience. In discussing such self-revelatory discourse, anthropologist Drid Williams points out that reflexivity serves no purpose for the reader and academic community unless made to inform beyond the personal and sub-jective.9 Taking heed of this, my aims in this chapter are not to rehearse transformational experiences in my life as a dance researcher, purely for their own sake, nor merely to repeat criticism of the folk paradigm in which the concept of tradition has long been enshrined.

Both approaches in relation to the subject of this chapter would only posit a simplistic dichotomy between my present self and my past self. Instead, I wish to explore the mutually constitutive nature of the researcher and the researched, through my past and present attitudes toward the ethnographic communities, historical sources, and dancing.

DIFFERENT HISTORIES: STUDYING MORRIS DANCING IN NORTHWEST ENGLAND

In the nineteenth century, the period for which most primary sources exist, morris dancers would appear at regionally specific holidays. As performed throughout England today, however, the form is usually the preserve of adult amateur enthusiasts. From the early twentieth century, when the custom underwent the large-scale revival, morris dancing transformed from a local cultural activity to that of a nationally distributed recreation, performed mostly at weekends throughout the summer months.

Morris dancing increasingly since the 1920s came to be perceived in England as a somewhat anachronistic affair, revived by aficionados who came from a more privileged social and economic background than that of its former practitioners, who were principally drawn from the laboring classes. Such a contrast was encapsulated by the early-twentieth-century distinction made between the Tradition and the Revival. The former designated the genuine folk, the supposedly uneducated, preferably rural, working classes. The Revival, on the other hand, was dominated by the educated, socially and geographically mobile members of society, whose reason for performing the folk repertoire often stemmed from a false nostalgia for a vanishing cultural past.

In the mid-twentieth century, the folk performing arts underwent a second national regeneration, in effect spawning a further morris revival in the late 1960s and 1970s.11 These later-twentieth-century revivals attracted a more socially diverse following, a phenomenon that remains to be fully investigated. One result was a higher public profile for morris dancing with, in some quarters, a strong emphasis on adhering to the practices of the Tradition. These neo-traditionalists, here also referred to as purists, in part sought to re-create the past through the re-appropriation and reconstruction of regional variants. Unlike the earlier national Folk Revival that had tended to focus upon one geographically distinct form of morris dancing, the 1960s and 1970s movement sought to revive regional variants.

These different types of morris dancing are distinguished by the number of dancers, the type of implements that the dancers carry in their hands, costume, choreography, and musical accompaniment. The northwest variety of morris dancing, which formed the subject of my research, is typically performed by eight or more dancers who carry decorated short sticks, semi-flexible rolled-up handkerchiefs, or garlands. They wear brightly colored clothes and wooden-soled shoes known as clogs. The music is often a brisk, almost military-style rendering of popular eighteenth- and nineteenth-century popular tunes, played by a mixture of brass instruments, concertinas, melodeons, and drums, to accompany a processional street dance.

In the second half of the twentieth century, two broad approaches had come to typify the Folk Revival: the longer-established approach of revivalists who performed material regardless of its regional provenance, and the new approach of neo-traditionalists who sought to create regional identities in contradistinction to the older national Folk Revival. This latter aim was mainly pursued through close attention to the former contexts and practices of the Tradition. It was in this framework that I began my doctoral research on northwest morris in 1976.12 Prior to this, I had never been engaged with the Folk Revival, nor indeed consciously exposed to dance practices categorized as the Tradition. Instead, I began my investigation with a background in ballet and modern dance and an undergraduate degree that included folk life studies.

Academic training continued to insist upon a critically neutral stance toward any subject intended for scholarly investigation—a normal practice for most researchers, and especially so in folk life studies, in the days when a positivist stance was the aim, well before reflexive ethnography had gained widespread acceptance. Given the low academic status of dance and the absence of scholarly research into folk dance in England at that time, my choice of topic was quite radical in the context of an English university. Most of the limited publications available on English "folk culture" had been written within a nineteenth-century evolutionist framework that had long been discredited in the social sciences.

Accepting without question the interpretations of the English folk dance collector Cecil Sharp (1859–1924) and his followers, most writers regurgitated the belief that morris dances were an ancient tradition handed down from prehistory and thus beyond documented history. Like many of my academic contemporaries in the study of folk performance, I believed that the phenomenon of morris dancing could be understood through access to a demonstrably lived past, identifiable through rigorous scholarship and the evidence of tangible records. It could also be explored as a lived present through ethnographic investigation of contemporary practice. I worked across the frameworks of European folk life studies, the British new social history, and North American folkloristics.

My interests lay in the analysis of multiple and variant forms of this dancing, in providing sociohistorical contexts for its performances, and in humanizing the activity in terms of individual agency within social groups and institutions. Responding to the frequent integration of historical and contemporary concerns of the intellectual disciplines across which my research was principally located, I sought to understand the phenomenon of morris dancing through both synchronic and diachronic perspectives.

The timing of my research, unexpectedly for me, coincided with the flowering of interest in the revival of northwest English morris dances in the 1970s and 1980s. Revivalist performers were also searching through local history libraries and traveling around to film and interview old morris dancers. My purpose, unlike theirs, was not principally to collect notations of dance and music for reconstruction, and I was sometimes irritated by their unsystematic, highly selective inquiries that occasionally resulted in publicity pamphlets and short populist articles with no academic referencing.

After over a year's research, it was clear that I could not investigate every instance of morris dancing in the region, whether designated revival or traditional, within the time frame of a doctorate. Decisions on how to limit the scope of my research were influenced by the attitude of some revivalist dancers who jealously guarded historical sources for their own revival of northwest morris dances, refusing to make them public. My period of research (1976–84) had also coincided with the contested emergence of women's morris teams within the national Folk Revival, a factor that similarly placed bars on my access to material.

Being female meant that, in some cases, male revival teams, fearful that I would steal their dances, treated my inquiries with suspicion, despite my protestations of being a scholarly "honorary male" with no desire to perform or pass on morris dances. Even some female teams resisted my research, convinced that I would learn their dances in order to start up my own team.

Rejecting most of the politically fraught contemporary scene, I eventually settled upon the period 1780 to 1914—the classic long nineteenth century—as one trajectory for my study. The other trajectory facilitated both historical and ethnographic dimensions. I would concentrate upon one unusual team in the region—the Britannia CocoNut Dancers—who demonstrated a comparatively continuous record of performance from the mid-nineteenth century to the present. Both the historical records of pre-1914 morris dancing and the Britannia Coco-Nut Dancers were unquestionably recognized as belonging to the Tradition. In the process of data collection and analysis, I hoped to shed further light on what constituted traditional practice.

By turns frustrating and fascinating, the revival morris teams thus became marginalized in my inquiry; though not before I had collected, in the manner of "ethnographic reconnaissance," some field notes, records of telephone calls, letters, and films of revival performances.[15] Through later family connections with northwest morris dancing and a growing involvement with the Folk Revival, I maintained an interest in the debates and performances, which continued into the 1990s.

In 2001–2, I revisited some of the revival teams to find out what had happened to that passion for revivification of a distinctive northwest style of morris dancing in the 1970s and 1980s. In reflecting on my methodological procedures over this time span, it appears to me that several histories are at play, manifested through written and visual material, memory, and bodily reenactment.

These constitute the history of northwest morris dancing in the long nineteenth century; the history of my own ethnographic and historical research during the late 1970s and early 1980s; the history of the revival of northwest morris dancing; the history of my return to the field in 2001–2; and the longer, less tidily defined history of my involvement with the Folk Revival from the late 1970s to the present day.

FROM THE NATIONAL TO THE LOCAL: ASPIRING TO BE TRADITIONAL

The concept of tradition was a rallying call among several morris team leaders in the 1970s and 1980s, indicating their preference for a neo-traditionalism in revivalist practice that made their performances and policy distinctive within the larger national frame of the Folk Revival. Often rejecting the recent past of the early-twentieth-century first revival—as represented by the institutions of the English Folk Dance and Song Society (EFDSS), founded in 1911 as the English Folk Dance Society, and the Morris Ring, founded 1934—the neo-traditionalists often sought to return to an earlier lost but retrievable past, reinterpreting and discovering source material for nineteenth-century examples of morris dancing.

It was thus believed that the notion of tradition might be given new life through the reexamination of the field manuscripts of Cecil Sharp and other early-twentieth-century collectors, or by finding new source material in newspapers, in photographs, or, indeed, from surviving morris dancers of the period and their relatives. The other major source of inspiration constituted performances and practices of the so-called living tradition: that is, continuing teams that had been originally encountered by Sharp and his colleagues, or else teams that had apparently experienced little previous contact with the Folk Revival, such as the Britannia Coco-Nut Dancers.

In northwest England, one impact of the first major revival of the early 1900s had been to introduce the regional variant known as Cots-wold morris to the area. Cotswold morris is the name given to the style of morris dancing found mainly further south in the counties of Oxfordshire, Gloucestershire, and Warwickshire, which formed the basis of the national morris revival. Even in the twenty-first century, the style dominates, and most of its practitioners are to be found in the south and midlands of England, as indeed are most morris teams, regardless of what style is performed. Cotswold morris is typically performed by six men in two files of three who, waving handkerchiefs and clashing sticks, perform in a light aerial style. This style of morris dancing constituted the original repertoire of the Manchester Morris Men, the revival team based in one of the largest cities in northwest England. Largely made up of university academics, this team was established sometime prior to 1936.

During the 1950s, interest in retrieving local variants of morris dancing, through a mixture of oral history and reexamination of manuscripts of dances collected before the Second World War, resulted in the Manchester team adding northwest dances to its repertoire. In 1960, two team members published a survey of northwest morris dances in the *Journal of the English Folk Dance and Song Society*. They listed their sources, plotted the dances' geographical distribution, considered the sociohistorical context of historical performance, and speculated on reasons for distinctive choreographic variants within the region. The collecting, publication, and teaching activities of the Manchester Morris Men were hugely influential. In 1960, only two adult male teams in the region performed local dances; by 1996, the figure had grown to thirty-four. This growth occurred in the context of a growth in revivalist morris dancers across the country, some of whom espoused the neo-traditionalist cause.

There are two striking features in the citation of tradition in the northwest morris revival: the first relates to gender, the second to place. Searches in archives and for old morris dancers in northwest England had revealed a regional peculiarity. There had been female morris dancers in the past, a discovery that contradicted the nationally accepted view that morris dancing was an exclusively male activity. This revelation was at first considered problematic by the EFDSS and was clear anathema to the fiercely male bastion of the Morris Ring, most of whose teams performed Cotswold morris. History and the notion of tradition were cited to justify the exclusion of women from performing Cotswold morris, but as new research was disseminated through workshops and specialist folk revival magazines, it came to be more accepted that the northwest repertoire might legitimately be performed by women. All-female morris teams performing northwest dances expanded in number, the most well known and influential being the Poyn-ton Jemmers of Cheshire, founded in 1975.

Interpretations of morris dancing and its relationship to place embraced another shift in thinking during this period of contestation. In the early 1900s revival, the concept of folk signified the older cultural practices of rural communities. Cotswold morris had mainly been performed in the nineteenth century by agricultural laborers; thus, in this rather circular argument, its enactment by such personnel contributed to its authentication as a genuine folk activity. In contrast, the occupations of morris dancers in northwest England had frequently been those of coal mining, quarry working, hat making, or, more especially, cotton spinning. The region, particularly in the city and hinterland of Manchester, is, in fact, considered to be the oldest in the world to undergo extensive industrialization and urbanization.

This might be considered an illegitimate site for recovery of authentically traditional dances. A landscape of industrial towns and villages certainly contributed to the neglect of this part of England by Sharp and his colleagues as a potentially fruitful collecting ground for folk culture. According to the constructs of traditional and modern, the former term was properly applied to practices in rural contexts, whereas the industrial was recent and an aspect of modernity. By the middle of the twentieth century, however, as a partial consequence of the decline of the British Empire, the urban and industrial glory days of the nineteenth century were no longer perceived as standing in opposition to tradition but had emerged instead as a newly authentic industrial cultural heritage. The industrial "workshop of the world" was now silent and the nineteenth century suitably distanced in time.

The criterion of "place" was to exercise yet greater force in the northwest morris revival. Place in the sense of the past origin of morris dances was an essential criterion for authenticity, but soon questions of place in relation to present performance were being raised. Cotswold morris dances had already been disseminated across the nation in the first revival, the dances taken away from their regional roots in a transmission that was regarded by purists as having weakened any attempt to honor genuine traditional practice. Was the same fate now to befall northwest morris?

TIME, PLACE, AND PEOPLE: A VIEW OF AND FROM THE NORTH

By the mid-1970s, following the Manchester Morris Men's example, most newly revived morris teams in northwest England performed a general repertoire drawn from specific communities across the region. The nineteenth-century practice of a specific choreography being performed exclusively by one team in one local community was no longer tenable to sustain twentieth-century audience and team member interest. Morris teams now needed several dances to entertain, and finding sufficient dances of local provenance proved a problem. The race to recover, and indeed to create, was on.

Another race had emerged that further troubled morris teams in the northwest. Across the country, a number of the revival teams were donning clogs and performing northwest morris dances. This situation caused an outcry from purists. New teams, formed in the locality of the dance's original provenance, sometimes sought to reclaim dances that were now in the national public domain. The rhetoric propagated by such neo-traditionalists placed a high premium on ownership of the dances through the criteria of locality and birthright. They thus positioned themselves as other to a national folk revival that they viewed as essentially southern. As noted above, the majority of morris teams, whatever repertoire they were performing, were located in the midlands and south of England. The strong sense of "northernness" was not peculiar to neo-traditionalist morris dancers in the region during this period.

On the contrary, it drew from and continued a long-held and deep feeling about northern England, often perceived by its residents in the twentieth century as marginalized and under siege from the more affluent south. The decline of heavy industry and widespread closure of factories in what had been the engine room of the British Empire left a sense of economic and political neglect, made worse by the redundancies in the area during the years of Margaret Thatcher's premiership (1979–90). Such themes are evident in the correspondence in national folk periodicals complaining of the perceived appropriation of northwest English culture by southerners. For such neo-traditionalists, revival by northerners betokened authentic longevity, whereas southerners were merely swayed by passing fashion:

A lot of us in the North West feel that after many years of being a social and educational backwater which no one South of Birmingham wanted to know about, it is now the "in thing" to dress in clogs and shawl and speak "Lanky" [i.e., Lancashire dialect].

Sometimes we think of it as the London attitude: squeeze the provinces dry so that we can have a good time.

These territorial claims to cultural heritage were undoubtedly indicative of resistance to sociocultural and political changes in the region during the 1970s and 1980s, as economic resentment against the south's comparative prosperity grew. It is more than possible that for the ringleaders of the localized northwest morris revival, their historical sentiment had been reinforced by the very sources they consulted for reconstructive purposes. Around one hundred years earlier, a more articulate northern identity had begun to gain a profile. This found expression in newspaper articles; short stories, poetry, and books written in Lancashire dialect; published local reminiscences; and local histories. It was often this very same material that late-twentieth-century morris dancers were drawing upon to resource their revivals. A detailed analysis of the expression of northwest identity within the Folk Revival must await future consideration, but suffice it here to say that in the more extreme instances, an exclusive regional essentialism was espoused:

Personally, I don't like people in places like Devon or somewhere dancing Northwest morris, it just doesn't seem right. How can a Southerner for instance *be* something he isn't? You are a product of where you live, and your own area is ingrained in you, as part of your character. So someone from Devon, say dancing Lancashire morris dances is not really going to put the dance across with anything near the same conviction as a lad who *is* a Lancashire morris dancer. One is a representation while the other is authentic.

[It's] not a hobby or owt [anything] like that, it's much stronger than a hobby, it's part of Northwest England, [a] British way of life. To have your own local traditions is good and you've got to keep them going, otherwise we'd all be the same, wouldn't we?

Assertions of longevity in the area were manifest in the choice of team names to correspond with those of the past, such as Preston Royal Morris and the Horwich Prize Medal Morris. The original teams bearing these names had long ceased to function, and the revival personnel had few links with the dancers, beyond residence in the locality and obvious personal contact in seeking out the old dancers.

Distinctiveness is essential to the creation and maintenance of identity, but this emphasis also accords with Sharp's characterization of traditional morris as being continuously rooted in one place. In 1910 he had written: "Our experience proves that each village where morris dancing survives has its own tradition, its own dances and its own special methods of performance, all of which reflect no doubt the peculiar temperament and artistic sense of the community." Although primarily concerned with the example of Cotswold morris, Sharp's declaration continued to exert a huge, shaping influence on the Folk Revival, including the neo-traditionalists of northwest morris dancing.

The assertions of separate identity for northwest morris were nevertheless still rooted in the values of the first national revival. As Georgina Boyes has concluded, addressing here the term "the Revival" to the larger framework of the mid-twentieth revival of folk performances: "for all its apparent innovation and variety, the Revival was hidebound by historical theory. Determinedly producing a policy of authenticity, it became a more effective vehicle for Sharp's views than the English Folk Dance Society of the 1920s."

Less directly, antagonistic commentary on women's morris further signaled older attitudes that drew upon an othering of gender that followed classic nineteenth-century divides. It was one that was often tied to an authenticity of traditional masculinist working-class culture. Authentic morris dancing was acknowledged as the former preserve of the lower classes, and thus certain values associated with traditional working-class culture were espoused as desirable for reproduction within the Revival. In this respect, of course, pointing to the Tradition was a useful means of legitimating contemporary practice.

Male dancers in the overwhelmingly middle-class morris revival of the twentieth century were often nervous about dancing in public for fear of charges of effeminacy and homosexuality. This strong sense of a working-class male body as the only authentic vehicle for the performance of northwest morris in the revival was often manifested in a comparative emphasis on heaviness, discipline, and power in the dancing. Sometimes the historical record was willfully obscured with respect to the gender of previous performers, most notably in the instance of the Garstang Morris team, which was nationally known in the revival for its anti-female stance and for its emphasis upon "masculinity" in the dancing.

In 1996, the chief collector of their dances, the former wife of the team's leader, revealed that the repertoire had originally been founded upon her aunt's childhood morris dancing. Such revelations were not made at the height of the team's fame. Where there was acceptance by other revival teams of female morris dancers on the grounds of historical precedence, there often tended to be a glossing over of the fact that from the late 1890s children and very young women had often been participants. If a men's team's traditional credentials were challenged on the grounds that the former dancers were female, a typical response might draw from a line of thinking popular among some members of the Morris Ring: that women had only acted as conduits of the tradition until such a time as when men could rightfully reclaim what was their legitimate heritage.

It was such thinking on the interrelations of past, gender, and place under the rubric of tradition that I was almost continuously to encounter when pursuing my doctoral research. And, in several respects, it was to permeate my own understanding.

INTERPRETING THE PASTS OF OTHERS (AND SELVES)

In returning to past research in 2001, physically, intellectually, and emotionally, I discovered and rediscovered past selves, forcing me to reflect upon the conditions that had led me to construct others in order to carry out my research. During my doctoral research, I had remained convinced that my conceptions and values were distinct from those of the revivalists. It was axiomatic during that time that Tradition and Revival were dichotomous, although such a polarization was already beginning to be called into question in North American literature in anthropology and folkloristics. Among purists within the English Folk Revival, however, such a division continued. If I entertained any such doubts about clear boundaries between the characteristics of traditional and revival teams, I could at least point to two clearly distinguishing criteria: the dancers' respective attitudes toward the past and their use of historical sources. There appeared to be a sharp contrast between the older, established Britannia Coco-Nut Dancers and the revived northwest morris teams.

From my ethnographic research of the late 1970s and early 1980s, it was evident that the Britannia Coco-Nut Dancers, and indeed most of their local community, were not engaged in uncovering source material to write history. Such archival pursuits were for outsiders, "university types," and students, who were often regarded as synonymous with members of the Folk Revival by some of the older Coco-Nut Dancers. Only one of the Coco-Nut Dancers I interviewed had experienced formal education beyond sixteen years in contrast to a sizable number of revivalist dancers. The Coco-Nut Dancers, though, had no compulsion to demonstrate their traditionality—not only had the EFDSS provided such authentication in the 1920s, but local oral memory could testify to the nineteenth century and reputedly beyond.40 The revivalist morris dancers possessed no such public affirmation. My ethnographic research revealed that the Britannia Coco-Nut Dancers placed a high premium upon the transmission of kinetic knowledge through local human bodies.

It's something that, you know, has been handed down and handed down by word of mouth and practical help in learning the steps. It's not something you can just go and pick a book up, read about, go and do it. Impossible. It's got to be—it's that sort of dance that it's got to be handed down from man to man.

Such bodily continuity was much respected and coveted by many revivalists.

In circumstances where immediate kinetic transmission was not possible, revivalists necessarily had recourse to other forms of documentation, highlighting anthropologist Paul Connerton's distinction between incorporating and inscribing practices in the transmission of memory.

Written records and photographs of former local morris dancing were interpreted in local and national folk magazine articles, contributing to wider knowledge of traditional practices and announcing a team's revival/arrival with historical credentials. Members of the Britannia Coco-Nut Dancers, on the other hand, were not at all interested in creating historiography nor, for the most part, in consuming it. Some individual members did possess an archive of the team's activities and articles written about them, but the sources for history and their own historiography were rarely discussed and almost never on display. They knew who they were, and so did the local community; their national significance was annually affirmed by huge visiting audiences on their local day of dancing. Thus, it appeared that the writings of revivalist morris teams, setting out their own historical sources, positioned them further in opposition to the traditional team.

I distinguished myself from the revivalists in that my own historical inquiry into northwest morris teams and the past and present of the selected case study was more "sociological" in orientation. My agenda included details such as the age of the performers, their social status, occupation, and gender, the composition of the audience, as well as the constituent features of performance such as costume, music, instrumentation, repertoire, and contexts of performance. Inspired by the anthropological wave sweeping British social history and by the structural analysis of dance forms based on linguistic analogies, my approach to the records of the past was necessarily different from that of contemporary revivalists. I wanted to investigate what the Tradition was *really* like in order to understand the society that gave rise to these dances and what were the social, political, economic, and cultural factors that led to its transformation from a community-based adult male performance in the early 1800s to a predominantly competitive display by children, often of both sexes, that had developed with no relation to the Folk Revival by the 1920s.

It might be argued that the activities of nonspecialist historians of dance, as in the case of revivalist morris dancers, can be ignored by the academic: it is unlikely that amateur historians' representations will enter into professional discourse since, for most, publication in academic journals and in conference proceedings is not their intention. Similarly, the reverse may be true. In the instance of the English folk dance revival in the last third of the twentieth century, however, such a strict division does not reflect the fluidity of interchange that existed between the personnel involved in academic study and in revival performance.

My self-appointed role was comparable to that of those historians who "seem happiest at work puncturing legends, proving the modernity of much of what passes for old, showing the artificiality of myth and its manipulable, plastic character."45 This indeed had been an abiding interest from my undergraduate studies of other ceremonial dance forms in England: an interest in the past as a resource for contemporary meaning, and a desire to de-mythologize the dominant theory of the origins of morris dancing. To my mind, though, the use of the past and belief in myths were what others did; as a trained academic, a professional, I considered myself to be outside this. From my position of power I might perceive the reality: the disjuncture between the professed past of ethnographic revelation and the authentic past of historicity. Systematic academic investigation might demonstrate that claims to ancient traditionality could not be substantiated after all.

My identification and scrutiny of historical records on the past of the Britannia CocoNut Dancers brought to light the strong possibility of a comparatively modern origin for this so-called ancient tradition. Such a discovery provoked a moral dilemma for me in terms of whether or not to publish my findings.46 In contrast, I felt less worried about revealing inconsistencies in the historical record and in the claims of revivalist dancers. Many of these revival dancers came from a similar social and educational background as mine, even if they had not been trained in folk life studies, history, or anthropology. Correcting, indeed dismissing, their use of history was, I considered, perfectly ethical; the revival dancers were not the subject of my investigation, and their beliefs were not hallowed as the Tradition. Their activities were tantamount to "invented traditions," symptoms of modernity and of a lesser order to the traditional.47 In this respect, these revival morris dancers, although equally employed in investigating the past and using similar sources to myself, were other to my academic self. The Britannia Coco-Nut Dancers were not only other to my academic self but were also other to the revivalist dancers. In my mind, they were the "real thing"—Tradition—demonstrable through bodily continuity with the local past and authenticated through written and oral records back into the nineteenth century.

By the 1970s in England, most purists and academic folklorists had come to equate "folk" somewhat pejoratively with revivalist activity. In an avalanche of criticism, serious researchers and purists had jettisoned the concept in favor of the term "traditional." During the 1970s and early 1980s in England, within the newly positioned academic study of folk life studies, this label was considered by many academics to be a more faithful appellation, distinguishing between those activities that were inspired by the revivalist movement and those that continued outside of its remit.

A new wave of university-trained folklorists within British universities also sought to distinguish their own work from that of past and present amateurs. In the debate, their fields of study were framed variously as popular, working-class, or vernacular customary practices, rather than as "folk" or "folklore." Such academics believed that legitimate and worthwhile academic interest lay in uncovering the reality of tradition, the past, and history. Similarly, any ethnographic inquiry was to focus on the "authentic." As testimony to this move toward professionalizing the study of folk performance, a series of academic conferences and published proceedings was launched that expressly examined traditional drama and dance.49 Designed to uncover the real history and practice of Tradition, these conferences, in fact, attracted numerous revival performers, who were also keen to learn more about the "real" Tradition.

By the mid-1980s, it seemed as though that thirst for historical knowledge of the Tradition had been assuaged among many revival morris dancers. Confidence in their own revival efforts had developed, boosted not least by the realization that some of these twentieth-century teams had been performing for longer on a regular basis than a number of the so-called traditional teams. This sense of self-worth among revivalist morris dancers found particular expression in an academic conference entitled "Contemporary Morris and Sword Dancing" in 1988.

If continuity of performance in one place was to be a major criterion of traditionality, then it was not surprising that the revival morris movement itself had now become an object of study, with many of the conference papers based upon personal experience and autobiography. The self-consciousness of the Revival, however, was evident in the emphasis upon self-documentation; unlike morris teams of the past, which had left scanty traces, revivalist morris dancers were keen to record their present activities with the intention of leaving fulsome records for posterity. The revival teams employed techniques of scholarly collection. In addition to minutes, photographs, journals, newspaper cuttings, and videotapes, data on the composition of teams were collected through distribution of questionnaires.

Increasingly, comparatively new teams in the Northwest and elsewhere claimed traditionality. The Revival had become the Tradition, it was claimed, and deserved academic analysis. Of interest to me, though, was the continuing use of this concept of Tradition as a legitimizing force in the argument. Through my increasing interest in anthropological theory, I could no longer justify, as in my previous research, valorizing one group of dancers over another as traditional. What became fascinating were the grounds of that valorization, and thus I shifted ground toward a meta-commentary on the discourse of morris dancing in northwest England.

In company with the anthropologically inclined ethnographer, today's historians and folklorists are interested in the uses to which understandings of the past are put, and in how representations, regardless of supposed verisimilitude, are constructed, by whom and in what contexts. As historians Raphael Samuel and Paul Thompson highlight, in parallel with more anthropological and cultural studies perspectives, significance lies not in "the reality content in our documents rather [it lies in] what they may tell us about the symbolism categories through which reality is perceived."

Their statement obviously applies to all oral and archival testimonies, regardless of their date. Not only should the symbolic realities of testimonies of the researched be interrogated but also those—often less discernible—of the researcher. Over the years, I had come to view the revivalist northwest morris dancers not as impostors nor as poor historians but as fascinating in their own right. During my doctoral research, I had come to position them as other on three counts: first, as other to historical and ethnographic records of traditional dancing; second, as other to me (on the basis of the uses to which they put historical sources); and third, as other to me on the basis that I was not a morris dancer. By the late 1990s, however, this latter distinction had also dissolved.

REVISITING ETHNOGRAPHY AND HISTORY: PERSONAL PERSPECTIVES

In revisiting northwest morris teams in 2001–2, as a northerner by origin now living in the south, I came with the different academic persona of an established dance scholar, and with several years of participation as a Cotswold morris dancer. Any pretence at viewing the Folk Revival from a nonparticipant outsider position was over.

As I now joined in practices of mixed and female morris teams, my body experienced what I had only rarely felt but often witnessed twenty years before. I remembered the boredom of watching many similar dances with little to interest me, so repetitive were the spatial patterns and arm and leg movements. Present participation tallied with my memory of joining in a very occasional practice in the 1970s before politics shut down my access and before I had stopped associating too closely with the revival morris teams. I admitted to myself in 2001 that the physical and mental boredom had served as a further distancing device, contrasting and elevating the more choreographically varied dances of the Britannia Coco-Nut Dancers.

What I did not remember, however, were the sustained aerobic demands of the northwest morris dancing. I longed for the rise and fall of the contrasting dynamics of Cotswold morris, its opportunities to rest within the dance, the attention needed to remember steps, and how to control the handkerchiefs to make patterns in the air. There was no such individualism apparent in northwest morris, and my lungs, knees, and upper arms ached as I executed the seemingly relentless high skipping; my feet pounded into the floor, my arms fixed exactly in position, as I performed as a drilled member of a team. Participation in both styles had now given me greater understanding of contrasting dynamics.

It also provided a base for understanding discussions of how the dancers perceived regional identity, not just as a repertoire, but as a way of moving, both as an individual and within a group. My recent past experience as a morris dancer now proved a useful ethnographic entry point, making up numbers when too few dancers had turned up to rehearse, as well as providing me with a useful and enjoyable methodological tool. On my return to the field in 2001–2, I discovered that a number of the teams had since faded away. The northwest morris revival appeared to have been a phenomenon linked to a particular generation, who, having now grown older, were either physically challenged by the dance style or had moved on to other activities. There was still a strong sense of regional identity professed among the continuing teams I interviewed, but time had softened the ferocity.

Among those dancers who had joined in the 1990s, such passion for tradition, authenticity, and keeping the dances for only those in the Northwest was comparatively weak. Other reasons beyond a satisfaction of performing something old were now articulated as dominant, and it was mostly those dancers who had joined the team in the heyday of chauvinism who still professed historical and regional commitment. More recent recruits had little to say about the past, even when they were older members of the team in age.

Dancing alongside a near seventy-year-old woman, I reflected on the change with regard to age: previously it had been valued as an indicator of Tradition; now it seemed to be a testimony to the new virtues of maintaining youth and fitness. These dancers had joined because they had seen, not the living continuity of local Tradition, but people of a similar age to themselves, having a good time. It was a group activity for keeping fit. Indeed, for most of the recruits of the 1970s and 1980s, physical enjoyment and camaraderie most likely always did outweigh the rhetoric of the Tradition. It had always been the case that extreme views tended to have been held by those with vested interests in the recovery of the Tradition.

I returned to the field as a published expert on the history of northwest morris dancing, uncertain of how much of my own profile as a previous organizer of conferences on Traditional Dance was known. Little, it would seem, as many of the dancers I talked to had not attended such events, either because they had become morris dancers much later or else were not those personally driven to spearhead the setting up of the team. The crossover between practitioners and academics interested in traditional dance and music, so noticeable in the 1970s and 1980s, was no longer discernible. The collecting and research into the past had been completed; what mattered more to dancers was the present, looking forward to sociable events and meeting up with other morris dancers at folk festivals and weekends of dance.

In this final stage of my inquiry, though, a further manifestation of otherness was to be revealed, a historical self that I had forgotten. By the mid-1980s, I became known among the revival movement as a historian of northwest morris dancing. During this time, I received a letter requesting help from a recently constituted team whose leaders had moved from the south of England. Although the dancers had formerly performed a variety of different regional forms of morris, they were now located in Cheshire, a county in northwest England, and wanted to perform only morris dances from the locality. On rereading copies of our correspondence, I am surprised that they ever replied to my boorish letter in which I corrected their logo of a clog-shod morris dancer in stereotypical Lancashire as opposed to Cheshire working-class dress, and insisted that most Cheshire morris could only be accurately danced in shoes, not clogs, and then only reenacted by children as the true original performers according to the historical record. There mirrored back to me in these documents was not the objective scholar I had believed myself to be, but the self-righteous academic historian and the partisan ethnographer. Not only had I become totally bound by the directive of the Tradition, associating with those teams who operated such a policy, but a deeply felt anti-southern prejudice was also revealed. I had evidently taken it upon myself to protect the culture of "northern identity."

CONCLUSION

Undertaking reflexive ethnography in the present and reflecting critically upon the ethnographic records of one's past throw into relief the various selves and others that are created in order to carry out social investigation, whether or not evident to the researcher at the time of study. By shifting the focus of interest in my later fieldwork from the exclusive Tradition to an undifferentiated cast of northwest morris dancers, I realized that the exercise of otherness had almost blinded me to that which I shared with the dancers of the Revival. The demands of my scholarly task prompted the construction of my academic self against a field of amateur researchers and occasioned preferential evaluation and treatment of some people over others. My pursuit of authenticity, in the senses of setting the historical record straight and of paying more attention to the opinions and practices of so-called traditional dancers, positioned the latter as culturally more significant than their revivalist peers. Such privileging of individuals is a symptom of the notion of the "tradition bearer," an inheritance from classic folk studies methodology whereby some people's knowledge of older practices is valued more than others by the researcher.55 The perceived authenticity of the practice is thus transferred to the authenticity of the person.

During the 1970s and 1980s, I had believed myself to be operating within a modernized folk life studies perspective but had failed to realize that the concept of Tradition had quietly transferred across from nineteenth-century studies to my own doctoral studies, escaping critical scrutiny. I had also believed myself to be relatively unbiased, pursuing the purity of academic rigor to uncover an authenticity of historicity. My northern upbringing, however, had resurfaced, erupting in a passionate defense of that which I clearly held to be an aspect of my own identity under threat.

The exact premise upon which any parameters for inquiry rest will rarely be fully discernible and will inevitably be enmeshed between the prejudices of the discipline(s) within which the research is conducted and those of the researcher's biography. This is particularly the case when working among past and present cultural traditions in dance practices of one's own country. Critical recognition of the fluctuating and situational dimensions of constructed selves and others in relation to the research aims and objectives is vital when conducting dance ethnography at home. Undoubtedly, as recent dance scholarship has demonstrated, the insights afforded as a result of collapsing the boundaries of self and other, of participating fully in the dance practices, and of resisting the classic anthropological demand to make the familiar strange are crucial correctives to a legacy of positivism and colonialism that has created hierarchies of knowledge and power.

The acceptance of a more public personal voice in ethnographic and historical writing since my doctoral days has widened debate and understanding of epistemological concerns in ethnographic and historical scholarship. The authority and authenticity of researcher and findings may be challenged, arguably resulting in a greater democratization of knowledge transfer, and the voice of the native researcher is gaining a welcome profile. Yet we must not automatically suppose that the voice of the native researcher necessarily guarantees an authenticity of knowledge in and of itself. Other historical and contemporary politics may well be operating, hidden in scholarly paradigms and in the history of the researcher herself, as this chapter has tried to demonstrate. And for the fuller revelation of that, we may have to look not only at the past and present but, assisted by the benefit of hindsight, await its unveiling in the future.

10

Famous Dances

India can boast of an innumerable number of folk dances, each dance forming a specialty of a particular region or tribe. Each form will have its own specialty & grace, along with a set pattern of costumes & make-up.

The classical dance forms which have developed, have set rules that have been followed traditionally over the years. On the basic model, various gurus incorporate their own imaginative innovations, leading to various schools within a particular dance form. Apart from the gracious hand & leg postures & movements, the dancers have to acquire the skill of portraying various emotions faithfully in each expression on their face & each fluid movement of their hand, legs & in fact their whole body. Every part conveys some meaning in their graceful motion.

The various dance forms have also developed a particular form of make-up for the performance, which is a skill by itself. Several dance schools today, incorporate costume designing & make-up as special section of the curriculum. The costumes for all forms are elaborate & rich, but each form & style have their own traditional patterns set down. Jewels for the dancers are also specially created to suit their purpose. Flowers adorn their hair & in the case of portrayal of Gods, their necks as garlands. The hall is also richly decorated with flowers. Application of mehendi in various styles is also an essential part of the make-up in most forms.

DANCE FORMS OF INDIA

Bharata Natyam

Bharatanatyam is the most popular of Indian dances and belongs to the South

Indian state of Tamilnadu. Its antiquity is well established. In the past it was practised ad performed in the temples by a class of dancers known as the devadasis. It was a part of the religious rituals and has a long and hoary past. The kings and the princely courts patronised the temples, as well as the various traditions sustaining the dance form.

The salient features of Bharatanatyam are movements conceived in space mostly either along straight lines or triangles. In terms of geometrical designs, the dancer appears to weave a series of triangles besides several geometrical patterns.

In nritta (pure dance) to the chosen time cycle and a raga (melody), a dancer executes patterns that reveal the architectonic beauty of the form with a series of dance units called jathis or teermanams. The torso is used as a unit, the legs are in a semi-plie form and the stance achieves the basic posture called araimandi. The nritta numbers include Alarippu, Jatiswaram and Tillana, which are abstract items not conveying and specific meaning except that of joyous abandon with the dancer creating variegated forms of staggering visual beauty.

In nritya, a dancer performs to a poem, creating a parallel kinetic poetry in movement, registering subtle expressions on the face and the entire body reacts to the emotions, evoking sentiments in the spectator for relish - the rasa. The numbers are varnam, which has expressions as well as pure dance; padams, javalis and shlokas. The accompanying music is classical Carnatic. The themes are from Indian mythology, the epics and the Puranas.

Chakiarkoothu

This dance form is believed to have been introduced to Kerala by the early Aryan immigrants & is performed only by the members of the Chakiar caste. A highly orthodox type of entertainment, it can be staged inside temples only & witnessed by the Hindus of the higher castes. The theatre is known as Koothambalam. The story is recited in a quasi-dramatic style with emphasis on eloquent declarations with appropriately suggestive facial expressions & hand gestures. The only accompaniments are the cymbals & the drum known as the mizhavu, made of copper with a narrow mouth on which is stretched a piece of parchment.

Chhau

With origins shrouded in mystery, the Chhau dancer communicates inner emotions and themes through cadences of body flexions, movements and kinetic suggestions.

The word Chhau is interpreted differently by scholars. 'Shadow', 'Disguise' and 'Image' are the most common interpretations due to the extensive use of masks in this dance form. The martial movements of Chhau have led to another interpretation of the word as meaning 'to attack stealthily' or 'to hunt'.

Three styles of Chhau exist born from the three different regions of Seraikella (Bihar), Purulia (West Bengal), and Mayurbhanj (Orissa). Martial movements, strong rhythmic statements and dynamic use of space are characteristic of Chhau.

Seraikella Chhau flourished under royal patronage. Its vigorous martial character made it suitable only for male dancers. The princes were not only patrons but also dancers, teachers and mask-making experts. The Seraikella masks are similar to those used in the Noh dance of Japan and the Wayang Wong of Java.

Purulia Chhau uses masks which is a highly developed craft in the region. The barren land with its tribal inhabitants and multi-layered influences of Vedic literature, Hinduism and martial folk-lore have all combined to shape the Purulia Chhau dances which have only one message - the triumph of good over evil.

Mayurbhanj Chhau has highly developed movements, no masks and a more chiselled vocabulary than the other two Chhau styles. Like Seraikella Chhau, it had also thrived under royal patronage and is considered a link between the earthy Indian dance movements and the flying, springing elevations of Western dance.

Unlike other Indian Classical dance forms, vocal music in Chhau hardly exists! Instrumental music and a variety of drums like the Dhol, Dhumba, Nagara, Dhansa and Chadchadi provide the accompaniment. Combining folk, tribal and martial traditions and yet covering the three aspects of Nritta, Nritya and Natya as well as the Tandava and Lasya aspects of classical dance, the Chhau dances are complex combinations of Folk and Classical motifs.

Kathak

Prevalent in the North as a classical dance form, Kathak has a long history. Nurtured in the holy precincts of the Hindu temples, Kathak has over the centuries attained refinement and enriched itself with various hues and embellishments. Kathak means a story teller and it developed as a dance form in which a solo dancer tells and interprets stories from mythology.

In nritya, the expressional numbers called gats are danced by delicate glances of the eye and by using the art of mime. Themes from life are taken like enacting simple chores of carrying water from the well or walking gracefully, covering a face with a veil and looking through it in a tantalising manner at the lover. Also, to the lyrics, expressions are shown evoking the rasa or emotion in the spectators, who, if the musical traditions are shared along with the songs, enjoy it by expressing their appreciation with a round of applause.

The themes of Krishna, Radha, Shiva, Parvati and mythological characters find a prominent place in the Kathak dancer's repertoire. Nowadays, experiments are being carried out with group choreography exploring the dance form. Both men and women perform Kathak which is also used to present dance dramas of historical tales and contemporary events.

Kathakali

Kathakali means a story play or a dance drama. Katha means story. Belonging to the South-Western coastal state of Kerala, Kathakali is primarily a dance drama form and is extremely colourful with billowing costumes, flowing scarves, ornaments and crowns. The dancers use a specific type of symbolic makeup to portray various roles which are character-types rather than individual characters. Various qualities, human, godlike, demonic, etc., are all represented through fantastic make-up and costumes.

The world of Kathakali is peopled by noble heroes and demons locked in battle, with truth winning over untruth, good over evil. The stories from the two epics, the Mahabharata and the Ramayana, as well as the Puranas constitute the themes of the Kathakali dance dramas.

The macro and micro movements of the face, the movements of the eyebrows, the eyeballs, the cheeks, the nose and the chin are minutely worked out and various emotions are registered in a flash by a Kathakali actor-dancer. Often men play the female roles, though of late women have taken to Kathakali.

The pure dance element in Kathakali is limited to kalasams, decorative dance movements alternating with an expressional passage where the actor impersonates a character, miming to the liberetto sung by the musician. A cylindrical drum called chenda, a drum called maddalam held horizontally, cymbals and a gong form the musical accompaniment, and two vocalists render the songs. Using typical music known as Sopanam, Kathakali creates a world of its own.

The most striking feature of Kathakali is its overwhelming dramatic quality. But its characters never speak. It is danced to the musical compositions, involving dialogues, narration and continuity. It employs the lexicon of a highly developed hand-gesture language which enhances the facial expressions and unfolds the text of the drama.

Koodiyattam

Practised and preserved by the Chakyar community in Kerala, Koodiyattam is the oldest surviving link with ancient Sanskrit theatre. A precursor of Kathakali drama, Koodiyattam has several conventions which reflect the aesthetic conventions of the Natyashastra. The stylised mode of acting, the same character playing different roles, the use of the spoken word akin to chanting, stories within stories, flash backs, improvisations, eye expressions (netrabhinaya), an extensive gesture vocabulary or 'hastas', body movements (angika abhinaya) and facial expressions (mukhajabhinaya), the use of Sanskrit by the main character and Malayalam by the court jester or vidushaka who comments, satirizes and ridicules the protagonists... these are the salient features of Koodiyattam.

Performances are traditionally held in the Koothambalam which are special theatres attached to temples. The Sanskrit play selected for the performance usually takes over several days. Female dancers called Nangiars deliver the invocatory songs and also participate. The use of the tirashila or curtain, different colours for the face to depict characters and elaborate ornaments are all similar to Kathakali. The mizhavu is a special drum used as an accompaniment for Koodiyattam performances.

The repertoire consists of Sanskrit dramas like Ascharyachudamani of Shaktibadra, Subhadradhananjeyan of Kulasekara Varman, Abhisekha Nataka and Swapnavasavadatta of Bhasa, Kalyana Saugandhikam of Mahendra Vikrama and Bhagavadajjukiyam of Bodhayana which are the popular favourites. With disciplined and dedicated performers like Ammanur Madhava Chakyar, Kocchukuttan Chakyar and Kitangur Kuttappan Chakyar, this ancient classical form has a growing legion of students and afficionados in India and elsewhere.

Krishnattam

It is intended for presentation on eight successive nights to unfold the entire story of Lord Krishna, the style is almost akin to Kathakali.

Kuchipudi

Kuchipudi, like Kathakali is also a dance-drama tradition and derives its name from the vilage of Kuchipudi in the Southern State of Andra Pradesh. In recent years, it has evolved as a solo dance for the concert platform and is performed by women, though like Kathakali it was formerly the preserve of men. The female roles were enacted by men and even today, the tradition boasts of gifted male dancers enacting female roles with such consummate artistry that hardly anyone would notice them as male dancers.

The movements in Kuchipudi are quicksilver and scintillating, rounded and fleet-footed. Performed to classical Carnatic music, it shares many common elements with Bharatanatyam. In its solo exxposition Kuchipudi nritta numbers include jatiswaram and tillana whereas in nritya it has several lyrical compositions reflecting the desire of a devotee to merge with God - symbolically the union of the soul with the super soul.

The songs are mimed with alluring expressions, swift looks and fleeting emotions evoking the rasa. A special number in the Kuchipudi repertoire is called tarangam, in which a dancer balances herself on the rim of a brass plate and executes steps to the beat of a drum. At times she places a pot full of water on her head and dances on the brass plate. The song accompanying this number is from the well known Krishna Leela Tarangini, a text which recounts the life and events of Lord Krishna.

In expressional numbers a dancer sometimes chooses to enact the role of Satyabhama, the proud and self-assured queen of Lord Krishna, from the dance-drama Bhama Kalapam. She goes through various stages of love. When in separation from Lord Krishna, she recalls the happy days of union and pines for him. At last they are reunited when she sends him a letter. One more number from the Kuchipudi repertoire that deserves mention is Krishna Shabdam, in which a milkmaid invites Krishna for a rendezvous in myriads of ways giving full scope for the dancer to display the charms of a woman.

Manipuri

Manipuri dances originate from the North Eastern state of Manipur and derives its name from its native state. Intensely devotional in mood, the Manipuri dances are a part of the daily life of the Manipuri people. Essentially presented as a group dance with gorgeous, colourful costumes and gentle, swaying petal-soft movements, Manipuri dances create a hypnotic impact. The dances are influenced by the religious movement of Vaishnavism, the worship of Lord Vishnu, and have flowered in exquisite Rasalila performances, the favourite dance in a circle by Krishna with his milkmaids. Various types of Rasalilas are performed on special occasions and festivals.

Besides Rasalilas, there are other dances called Natasankirtana, in which a group of men play cymbals and dance in a circle or in two rows singing praises of God. In Pung Cholom, the dancers play upon pung, the drum, and dance while playing the intricate time cycles, executing somersaults and breathtaking acrobatic feats. In group dances like Lai Haraoba, the merry-making for the gods, the dancers perform various steps and weave patterns, involving various choreographic compositions. From the corpus of Manipuri dances, one sees on the contemporary stage solo, duet and group performances. The music is typical of the region and is influenced by the kirtan school of Bengal due to the influence of Vaishnavism.

Rasalila, Lai Haraoba, Choloms, Pung Cholom, Natasankirtana, Khubak Ishai and other Manipuri dances share both nritta and nritya aspects and are edited judiciously for the concert platform to suit the urban audience. However, to enjoy Manipuri, one should see the dances in their natural setting. Gossamer veils, cylindrical mirrored skirts and ornaments dazzle the audiences with their colourful costumes which create a dream-like effect.

Mohiniattam

Mohini Attam as a dance form has developed in Kerala. Performed by women it has graceful, gentle bobbing movements. Mohini means an enchantress and a dancer with enchanting movements, dressed in a typical white saree with gold border, hair gathered in a bun on one side and with golden jewellery epitomises the image of a beautiful maiden. Apparently it resembles the Bharatanatyam dance form but is quite distinct in its execution of movements, usage of hand gestures and its stark, simple costume.

Mohini Attam has enjoyed a revival in recent times and is the most popular dance form among the young aspirants in Kerala. It has a format which follows the Bharatanatyam form and the repertoire has common names. In nritta a number called Cholukattu consists of pure dance movements at the end of which is tagged a poem that is in praise of a deity and also narrates the story of the Ramayana in a nutshell. The mnemonic syllables are sung instead of being uttered by the musician. Another item of pure dance is Tillana which follows the musical mode of Bharatanatyam with classical Carnatic music. However, of late, kerala's Sopana music is being employed for Mohini Attam and the repertoire has also been enlarged with the choreography maintaining the typical movements of this graceful style.

In nritya, the padams are mimed with facial expressions and hand gestures and the themes are drawn from mythology. The nayika or heroine longs for union with her beloved. A confidante goes and conveys the message to the lover and the nayika describes the pangs of separation. A varnam follows the structure of a Bharatanatyam varnam dwelling upon the narration, impersonation and alternating with pure dance. Though the dance units in Mohini Attam are limited, the quintessential grace and the measured movements are its distinct features.

Odissi

Odissi has been revived in the past fifty years and can be considered as the oldest classical Indian dance on the basis of archival evidence. The form belongs to the East Indian state of Orissa. Odissi has a close association with the temples and its striking feature is its intimate relationship with temple sculpture. Tribhanga, the three-body bend characterises this dance form. It has a vast range of sculptural body movements which gives one the illusion of the sculptures coming to life.

In nritta the numbers consist of batu nritya, pallavi and mokhya. In batu nritya the dancer strikes poses holding various instruments like veena, flute, cymbals and drums and the choreography of this number reveals the imagination of the choreographer-gurus. Pallavi means to elaborate, and a dancer performs pure dance to a chosen time cycle and a musical raga (melody). Various body postures similar to temple sculptures are woven in this number. In mokhya, before the dance concludes, a dancer employs various dance units creating arresting visuals. In nritya, the songs from the celebrated Gita Govinda of poet Jayadeva written in the 12th century A.D., are used by dancers for expressional numbers.

The exquisite Sanskrit poetry and the sculptural movements to the typical Odissi music almost cast a spell on the spectators. Songs of other Oriya poets are also danced with subtle expressions, replete with emotions. In its revival period Odissi has received enthusiastic support from the young exponents and often one finds Bharatanatyam dancers also mastering the Odissi technique and performing both the dance forms though while doing so, they maintain the clear-cut differences in the execution of the movements. In recent years, group choreographic presentations and dance dramas are also attempted in order to bring out the full glory and sculptural wealth of Odissi which is truly a visually fascinating performance style.

Ottan Thullal

It is performed solo & because of its ready mass appeal, it is also known as the poor man's Kathakali. Kunjan Nambiar evolved it & brought out the social conditions of his time, the distinctions of class & the weakness & whims of the rich & the great. The dialogue is in simple Malayalam & therefore ensures mass appeal.

Yaksha Gana

This belongs to Karnataka & has a rural origin. It is an admixture of dance & drama. Its heart lies in Gana meaning music. It is about 400 years old. The language is Kannada & the themes are based on Hindu Epics. The costumes are almost akin to the Kathakali ones & the style seems to have drawn inspiration from Kathakali. As prescribed in the Natya Sastra, it has the Suthra Dhara (conductor) & the vidushaka (the Jester).

hitambu Nritham is the ritual art form in North Kerala that is more than 700 years old. It is mainly performed by Namboodiris of this part of Kerala. Late Vethiramana Sreedharan Namboodiri is known to be the "Father of Thitambu Nritham."

Luckily this ritual art form has not died out with his withdrawal from the stage. Experts in this field like Matamana Sankaran Embranthiri and his disciple Brahmasree Puthumana Govindan Namboodiri are carrying on the great tradition in the north.

The dancer, in the traditional style after performing the usual rituals, comes out of the sanctorum, and standing under the flag, holds aloft the replica weighing about 10kg - 30kg on his head and starts the divine dance. One Namboodiri to bear the thitambu, seven players on percussion instruments, and two persons to carry lamps - in all ten persons are needed to present this.

The dance begins with 'Kotti Urayikkal' (drumming to make the dancer possessed). As the dancer comes out carrying the replica of the idol on his head, the Maaraar makes the characteristic drumming when rituals are performed. The word 'Thitambu' suggests the direct manifestation of the deity. This is placed over a decorated turban known as Ushnipeetam. Idols being carried on top of elephants during festivals as also replicas beings held on shoulders while dancing to the rhythm of percussion instruments are a common sight in South and Central Kerala. But, dancing with the replicas on the heads is a unique feature in the North. The origin of Thitambu Nritham cannot be easily traced. Replicas called 'chattam' are made of bamboo or wood within which a beautiful frame with intricate designs is created.

Foot work is most important in this dance and this is executed to the rhythm of the drums. Each circumlocution is regulated by a different Thaalam (Thakilati, Atantha, Chempata and Panchari). Thitambu Nritham has undergone some changes in accordance with the trend of the times. Though the basic ones (Thaalavattom) remain the same, there are some changes made in drumming (thaalam). Innovation also adds to the novelty and variety of Thitambu Nritham.

Gestures in Bharata Natyam

Abhinaya is a Sanskrit term meaning (abhi -'towards'; ni-'to carry'). Thus it means reaching a performance to the audience. The main aspect of dance, the four-fold abhinayas are Angika (Expression through body), Vachika (Expression through speech), Aharya (Expression through ornaments) and Satvika (the refinement of the soul). Angika Abinaya is the use of gestures. There are slight variations in the numbers of gestures mentioned in the Natyasastra & Abhinayadarpana, but most of them have common names & definitions. Head Natyasastra mentions thirteen gestures Abhinayadarpana mentions nine gestures Eyes (No common names in the 2 works) Natyasastra mentions three main classes gestures (The first two classes are further divided into eight varieties each & the the third class has twenty varieties.) Abhinayadarpana mentions 8 gestures Neck (No common names in the 2 works) Natyasastra mentions four gestures Abhinayadarpana mentions nine gestures Hands (Both works mention 3 classes. There are several gestures with common names, but the no. of gestures in each class varies) Single-hand gestures: twenty-two gestures with common names Natyasastra Single-hand gestures: twenty-four Combined-hand gestures: thirteen Nrtta-hastas: twenty-seven Abhinayadarpana Single-hand gestures: twenty-eight Combined-hand gestures: twenty-three Nrtta-hastas: thirteen

DANCE JEWELLERY

Temple Jewellery - these jewels were originally made of gold set with rubies & pearls - used by the devadasis or temple dancers. Today, jewellery made of other metals with gold finish is available & is widely used by dancers. Traditional patterns such as mango, peacocks, anna patchi, gopurams are used.

CLASSICAL DANCE FESTIVALS OF INDIA

Place: Baripada (Mayurbanj Dist.), Kakatpur (Puri Dist.), Orissa

Date: April

The 'Chaitra Parba' or 'Chhau Festival' commences from the 10th/11th April every year and continues for three days concluding on 'Mahabishuba Sankranti Day' at Baripada. Celebrated in honour of Lord Shiva and Surya, the Sun God.

Dharani Kalotsav

Place: Kochi

Date: Nov 1st week

Dharani Kalotsav is organised by Society Dharani and held at Kerala Fine Arts

Hall. In December 1999 Shayamala Surendran formed the Society Dharani for bringing eminent artists to perform and give lecture demonstrations in Kochi.

Ekamra Utsav

Place: Mukteswar temple, Orissa

Date: January / February

Ekamra Utsav - A lively downtown 15 days festival at Bhubaneswar in early January, Ekamra Utsav is a life time experience for the vacationers. The highlight of the festivities is Mukteswar Dance Festival held on the courtyards of this famed temple where the eminent exponents of Odissi dance enliven the stage with their magical performances. Besides the dance performances, the visitors to Ekamra Utsav are treated to an expo of traditional art and craft, a flower show, a multicultural food court, a heritage walk and the attractive discounts offered by the leading shopping centres to the tourists complement the festival mood.

Elephanta Festival

Place: Elephanta island, Maharashtra

Date: mid February

To commemorate the living heritage of Indian dance, sculpture and art, Maharashtra Tourism Development Corporation (MTDC) in association with Tata Consultancy Services (TCS) has organized the Elephanta Festival. The Elephanta Festival is a tribute to classical performers and an initiative to popularize Indian classical dance and heritage art forms. A renowned world heritage site, Elephanta forms a stunning backdrop for India's leading artists as they enthrall you with their music and dance recitals. TCS in partnership with MTDC is delighted to be associated with the Elephanta festival.

The festival features eminent artistes, showcasing a traditional welcome with the catchy tunes of 'Koli' fisher folks, the aesthetically erected stage, bright lights, delicious ethnic food and the marvelously illuminated Maheshmurti cave. The festival also hosts a number of ethnic food stalls which highlight the traditional foods of the locality. First started in 1989, this festival is organized by MTDC, in Association with Tata Consultancy Services.

Ellora-Ajanta Festival

Place: Soneri Mahal, Aurangabad

Date: November / December

The Ellora Ajanta Aurangabad festival is organized by Aurangabad Festival Committee under the chairmanship of the Divisional Commissioner Aurangabad in association with MTDC. The Festival is held at the Soneri Mahal, a grand historical Haveli in Aurangabad. Apart from the cultural entertainment of the highest order - a mix of classical and folk dancing, instrumental, vocals and milajula mushaira, there are stalls exhibiting the artistry of the craftsmen from across the state, along with activities like Rangoli, painting, mehendi, cookery, essays, bhajans, games & competitions.

The venue was shifted from the Kailash temple at Ellora in 2002 & the name changed from Ellora festival to Ellora-Ajanta festival. Previously held at the enchanting Ellora caves the festival has now shifted its venue to the magnificent Soneri Mahal. Built in the 17th century, this Mahal was built by Pahadsing a Orchha chieftainis and is an architectural marvel of Aurangabad. The Ellora Ajanta Aurangabad Festival aimed to put the historical and pictorial sites in and around Aurangabad in the spotlight, some of them being Ellora, Daulatabad, Bibi-ka-Maqbara, Panchakki (A watermill), Lonar, Ajanta and Shirdi.

Ganga Mahotsav

Place: Varanasi, UP

Date: November

GANGA MAHOTSAV, a five-day cultural tourism fiesta is organized by the Government of Uttar Pradesh on the banks of the river Ganges in Varanasi. This festival is celebrated to promote Varanasi as the cultural capital of India and the Ganga as India's vital lifeline. The festival is a crowd puller and both foreign and Indian tourists make a beeline to the heritage ghats - symbols of eternal India - to experience music and dance.

Gunghroo Festival

Place: Different cities in Madhya Pradesh

Date: November

In order to provide platform to young and talented artists of different styles of Classical dance Academy has arganised Gunghroo Festival. This festival is on since 1984. This programme since last few years is been arganised every year in one of the cities successfully. This is a very unusual festival on defferent styles of classical dances of India.

Ustad Alauddin Khan Music and Art Academy organises various festivals to promote music & dance - "Alauddin Khan Vyakhayan mala", "Utteradhikar", "Gunghroo", "Durlabh Vadya Vinod", "Dhrupad Festival", "Chakradhar Festival", " Kumar Gandharva Festival - Dances","Ameer Khan Festival- Indore", "Alauddin Khan Festival-Mehar".

Hampi Utsav

Place: Hampi

Date: November

A three-day mega cultural festival of dance, music and drama, folk forms is celebrated, with stages set at various places in Hampi. Other attractins are the colourful procession by the folk artistes, dressed in their traditional attire, illumination of the rocky terrain and the fireworks.

Kalidas festival

Place: Nagpur

Date:

The Festival endeavors to bring back memories of the golden period of the Vidarbha region. It was here that Mahakavi Kalidas penned some of his greatest literary works, Kumaarasambhava, Meghaduuta, Ritusamhaara, etc.

The Kalidas festival is organized in association with the District Collectorate Office of Nagpur & features some of the greatest exponents of music, dance and drama from all over the country. It is held to showcase Nagpur, the Orange City, Maharashtra's second capital.

Kalinga Mahotsav

Place: Peace Pagoda at Dhauli

Date: February

A festival of Martial Dances at Dhauli, this festival commemorates the victory of Peace over War where renowned dancers perform harmonising the vigour of martial arts with sublime dance forms with their swords, spears and shields. This annual thrilling display of dances and music takes place at the foothill of the famous Peace Pagoda at Dhauli, where Emperor Ashoka is believed to have fought the last battle before his metamorphosis into an apostle of nonviolence and peace.

Kathak Mahotsav

Place: Khamani Auditoriumm, New Delhi

Date: February

Kathak Mahotsav is an annual festival held by Kathak Kendra. (instituted in memory of Maharaj Kalka and Maharaj Bindadin of Lucknow). Kathak Kendra is a unit of the autonomous Sangeet Natak Akademi - National Academy of music and dance.

Khajuraho Dance Festival

Place: Khajuraho, Madhya Pradesh

Date: February / March

Held every year from 25th February to 2nd March, Khajuraho Dance Festival takes place at the open-air auditorium in front of the Chitragupta Temple dedicated to the Sun God and the Vishwanatha Temple dedicated to Lord Shiva. They are situated in the Western Group of temples, which is the largest, well maintained and most easily accessible temple group of Khajuraho. Started regularly since 2002, this weeklong festival has already become legendary with its outlandish classical dance performances presented in a dreamlike setting of splendidly illuminated temples. Khajuraho temples present sculptures depicting various skills and arts of courtly love including dance and music in stone and what venue can be more befitting to hold the cultural festival highlighting the various classical dances of India!

Some of the best artists and performers that have marked themselves in their fields come from the various states of India to participate in the festival and the performances including some of the best known dance styles such as the intricate footwork of Kathak, highly stylized and sophisticated Bharathanatyam, soft lyrical temple dance of Odissi, the dance dramas of Kuchipudi, Manipuri, the dance of rare and ancient civilization and Kathakali stage fights with elaborate masks. Recently, modern Indian dances have also found their place in the Khajuraho Dance festival. Along with the dance performances one can also see a number of craftsmen trading off their indigenous arts and crafts to the visitors.

Konark Dance Festival

Place: Konark Natya Mandap, Arka Vihar, Konark

Date: 19th to 23rd February every year

The Konark dance festival is organized by eminent Odissi guru Gangadhar Pradhan's Orissa Dance Academy in association with the Eastern Zonal Cultural Centre, Kolkata at Konark Natya Mandap in Konark. As the sun sets, the open air auditorium gains life in the form of musical beats and rhythmic movements under the star lit sky. With the poem in stone as the backdrop, the festival proves to be a true cultural feast. A celebration of Odissi, Bharathnatyam, Manipuri, Kathak and Chau Dances; the festival truly comes as a lavish feast for the eyes and ears. The sound of Ghungroo bells, flute and Pakhauj add on to the festive mood.

A crafts mela is also put up during the Konark Dance festival. Serving a wide array of delectable cuisines and a variety of handicrafts, this mela adds more fun to the festival thus making it a perfect venue for a family get together on a holiday or a joyous experience to the tourists.

Kutiyattam Festival

Place: Ammanur Chakyar Madhom, Irinjalakuda, Kerala

Date: January

Since 1988, the annual Kutiyattam Mahotsavam (12 days) of Ammannur Chachu Chakyar Smaraka Gurukulam is held at Natanakairali and has played an important role in moulding a new generation of actors in the Kutiyattam Theatre Tradition. The oldest surviving classical Sanskrit theatre tradition of India, Kutiyattam, has a unique representation of Sanskrit plays and a highly stylized and complex theatre language. Recently UNESCO declared Kutiyattam as a "Masterpiece of the Oral and Intangible Heritage of Humanity". Irinjalakuda has been the home of the Ammannur Chakyars since several centuries.

Lai Haroba

Lai Haroba is the most important pre-Hindu ritual festival of Manipur. Lai Haroba means entertainment of the gods. There are nearly 400 shrines of different animistic deities and this festival, held in their honor, lasts from a week to a fortnight each spring with the advent of monsoons. The rituals of the Lai Haroba are conducted by the Maibis, priestess-oracles. Maibis are chosen by fate when they exhibit certain psychic signs and fall into trances. Though they may be men or women, they dress as women when they become Maibis. They are then trained in the dances and rituals of the Lai Haroba Festival and learn to prophesy the future through trances. Each evening of this festival begins with several hours of ritual dances by the Maibis, followed by dances offered by other members of the Meitei or Manipuri community.

Mamallapuram Dance Festival

Place: Mamallapuram (Mahabalipuram), near Chennai, Tamilnadu

Date: Dec, Jan, Feb - Every Saturday

This festival is held every year during Dec-Jan in Mamallapuram, Tamil Nadu, organised by Department of Tourism, Govt. of Tamilnadu.

Mamallapuram, once the ancient port of the Pallavas is renowned for Pallava culture and art. Exponents of Bharatanatyam, Kuchipudi, Kathak, Odissi, Mohini Attam and Kathakali perform against the magnificent backdrop of the Pallava rock sculptures. Apart from the classical performances, one can also see artists performing numerous folk dances.

Modhera Dance Festival

Place: Sun Temple, Modhera, Gujarat

Date: January

The Sun Temple is the site of an annual festival of Indian classical dances organized by the Tourism Corporation of Gujarat.

Natyanjali Dance Festival

Place: Chidambaram, Tamilnadu

Date: February 4th week - March 1st week

Starts from the day of Mahashivaratri, for 5 days. Chidambaram is situated along the coast of the Bay of Bengal, 75 kms south of Pondicherry. Lord Nataraja, according to the Hindu mythology is a cosmic dancer. He is called the Lord of dances. This is an opportunity for all dancers, from all India, to perform and to pay their tribute to Lord Nataraja.The Natyanjali festival, which brings all the prominent dancers of India, together on the same platform, opens on the auspicious occasion of Mahasivaratri, in the month of February.

It is performed at the 'Prakara' of the temple, and the dancers, full of intense bliss and devotion, with their evocative abhinaya, offer their dance to the great divinity, Lord Nataraja.

The festival is jointly organised by The Department of Tourism, Government of Tamil Nadu, The Ministry Of Tourism, Government of India and The Natyanjali Trust, Chidambaram. It is designed to promote a universal message of 'Unity in Diversity' conveyed in the universal language of music and dance.

New Festival

Place: Chennai

Date: December

The Park's New Festival is hosted by Prakriti Foundation (started in 2007). A five day festival held in the first week of December in Chennai, showcases new and emerging work in the field of dance, music and theatre for Chennai audience. Earlier Prakriti Foundation & Arngham Trust co-hosted the Other Festival. This festival was held for 9 years from 1998- 2006.

Nishagandhi Festival

Place: Nishagandhi Open Air Auditorium, Kanakakunnu Palace grounds, Thiruvananthapuram, Kerala

Date: January

It includes a food festival and craft mela on the adjoining Sooryakanthi grounds.

In 2005, the festival was held in April

In 2007 & 2008, it was held from Jan 20-26

Pachmarhi Festival

Place: Bhopal, Madhya Pradesh

Date: November / December

The annual six-day Pachmarhi Festival is organized at Pachmarhi, the Verdant Queen of Satpura featuring cultural programmes, art performances and quisine. Stalls are put up for display and sale of the products of skilled artisans sponsored by the Handloom and Handicrafts Development Corporation and food stalls offer a variety of delicacies including Indori Chat, ice creams, cold drinks, South Indian dishes and Chinese food. The display and sale of carpets, saris, dress material, durries, bamboo crafts and woolens produced by self help groups besides bari, papad, pickles, sauces etc would be added attraction. Cultural evenings are organized every day during the festival featuring artists of national and international repute.

Pattadakal Dance Festival - Chalukya Utsav

Place: Pattadakal, North Karnataka

Date: January / February

Every year during the first quarter (January or February) Pattadakal celebrates the annual dance festival also called the Chalukya Utsava. Apart from Pattadakal the venues includes the nearby ancient sites Badami and Aihole too. This three days extravaganza of dance and music attracts hordes of art lovers. The majestic temple backdrops and the performance by renowned artists brings alive the magic of the bygone era.

Puri Beach Festival

Place: Puri, Orissa

Date: November

The Puri Beach Festival is organised by Hotel & Restaurant Association of Orissa (HRAO) in November. The Festival showcases a number of attractive events to attract large number of tourists from far and near.

The 2004 festival (the 10th year) took place from 23rd to 27th November 2004.

Rajgir Mahotsav

Place: Rajgir, Bihar

Date: October

Department of Tourism, Bihar holds a colourful festival of dance and music, Rajgir Mahotsav at Rajgir in Bihar.

Sharadotsav

Place: Bangalore (Ravindra Kalakshetra)

Date:

Sharadotsav, the annual Bharatanatyam festival is conducted by Sri Guruvayurappan Bhajan Samaj Trust featuring various artistes of national and international repute. Dancer Ranjani Ganesan organizes the festival.

Shreekshetra Utsav (The Puri Festival)

Place: Puri, Orissa

Date:

Puri represents the rich traditions and culture of its people manifested in its various festivals celebrated throughout the year. The two weeks long extravaganza of art and culture Shreekshetra Utsav is an authentic showcase of everything that's Orissa, offering handloom, cuisine, dance, music and its famed sand art.

Soorya classical music and dance festival

Place: Thiruvananthapuram

Date: 1st to 10th of October

The Soorya classical music and dance festival is conducted for ten days every year in Thiruvananthapuram, the capital of Kerala.It starts from 1st October and concludes on the 10th of October. The festival is organized by Soorya Stage and Film Society, one of the largest cultural societies in Asia. Founded by Soorya Krishnamoorthy, the society organises many programs including Dance and Music festivals, film festivals, theatre, painting, photography, lectures and talks, sound and light shows etc.

The Dance and Music festival presents different forms of dance like Kathak, Odissi, Manipuri, Bharathanatyam, Kathakali, Kuchipudi and Mohiniyattam as well as classical music renditions, instrumental music, jugal bandhis, etc by popular artists. Renowned dancers and musicians from all over India participate in this festival. Dancers such as Padma Subramaniam, Alarmel Valli, Chitra Viswesvaran, Lakshmi Gopalaswami, Rajendra-Nirupama and musicians such as Ustads Allah Rakha, Amjad Ali Khan, Bismillah Khan, Zakir Husain, Balamuralikrishna, Bhimsen Joshi are a few among the famous artistes who have performed here.

Another dance and music festival 'Parampara' is also held by Soorya in November every year to spot young talents. This festival is also held in Thiruvananthapuram, where artists pay tribute to their Gurus.

Vasantahabba

Place: Hessaraghatta, Bangalore Rural District, Karnataka

Date: first Saturday of February, from dusk to dawn

Vasantahabba (Spring Festival) is an all-night festival of dance and music organized by Nrityagram every year.

Thirteen years after the first Vasantahabba, it is now considered the 'Woodstock' of classical dance and music in India. Living legends and leading artists congregate together, under one sky, to make Vasantahabba what it is - an unmissable treat!

The history of Vasantahabba is remarkable. From an audience of 3,000 in 1990, there were over 40,000 in 2003! The festival has been covered on the web and on television networks from around the world. And millions have witnessed the event LIVE on Doordarshan, the public broadcasting station of India.

Entry to Vasantahabba is FREE.

Past performers include Dr. Chitti Babu, Louis Banks, Beliappa & Dollu Kunita, Dr. B. Bhanumati, Pt. Vishwamohan Bhatt, Pt. Hari Prasad Chaurasia, Shri Kadri Gopalnath, Gundecha Brothers, Ustad Zakir Hussain, Dr. Doraiswamy Iyengar, Pt. Jasraj, Pt. Bhimsen Joshi, Ustad Amjad Ali Khan, Ganesh Kumaresh, Shankar Mahadevan, Guru Kelucharan Mahapatra, , Pt. Birju Maharaj, Aditi Mangaldas, Rajan Sajan Misra, Shubha Mudgal, Taufiq Qureshi, Smt. Malini Rajurkar, Guru Jayaram & Vanashree Rao, Raja-Radha Reddy, Smt. Veena Sahasrebuddhe, Leela Samson, Malavika Sarukkai, Aruna Sayeeram, Shashank, Pt. Shiv Kumar Sharma, Daksha Sheth, Smt. Bharati Shivaji, Talvin Singh, Ranjabati Sircar, Sivamani, Dr. L. Subramaniam, Begum Parveen Sultana, Alarmel Valli, Pt. Vikku Vinayakram, Nasir & Nazir Warsi, amongst others.

Daman Festival

The West Zone Cultural Centre, Udaipur and District Administration Daman organized the festival from December 19 to 21, 2007 at Daman. The NEZCC participated in the festival by sending a Manipuri Raas team consisting of 16 members from Manipur.

Bhagyachandra National Festival

A four day Bhagyachandra National Festival was organized by North East Zone Cultural Centre, Dimapur, Eastern Zonal Cultural Centre, Kolkata and Department of Art & Culture, Government of Manipur from November 27 to 30, 2007 at Imphal Manipur.

Folk songs and dance festival of Sikkim

A one day Folk Songs & Dance Festival was organized by North East Zone Cultural Centre, Dimapur and Cultural Affairs & Heritage Department, Government of Sikkim at Pakyong, Sikkim on July 7, 2007. Altogether 195 artistes from different parts of the State representing different communities/tribes of Sikkim participated in the festival. The presentation of folk songs and dances by the artistes in full traditional attire during the programme was a composite display of the beautiful culture of Sikkim.

Lokrang - National folk dance festival

2007: The festival was organized by WZCC, Udaipur & Jawahar Kala Kendra at Jawahar Kala Kendra, Jawahar Lal Nehru Marg, Jaipur on October 27 & 28, 2007. The

NEZCC participated in the festival by sending Lai Haraoba, Pung Cholom & Dhol Cholom and Hazagiri consisting of 20 and 15 member respectively from Manipur and Tripura.

2008 : The NEZCC participated in this prestigious festival by organizing folk dance troupes from the State of Arunachal Pradesh, Meghalaya, Mizoram, Nagaland and Sikkim. The troupes from Northeastern States presented colourful and vibrant traditional art forms of the region at different venues. The Khampti tribe from Arunachal Pradesh presented the Kaa - Kong Tokai (Cock fight) dance, and the Hajong tribe of Meghalaya presented a folk song and dance, the Mizoram troupe presents the "Sarlamkai/Solakia" "warrior" dance and the Mungyanta (Harvest dance) was performed by the women folk from Nagaland. The Maruni dance the oldest and most popular dance of the Nepalese from Sikkimwas also performed. Altogether 75 artistes participated in the event.

Manipur Raas Festival

The festival was organized by Sree Sree Radha Madab Sanskriti Samanwaya Committee, Agartala from November 21 to 25, 2007 at Agartala, Tripura. The NEZCC (The North East Zone Cultural Centre) Co-sponsored the programme.

National Classical Dance festival

A two day National Classical Dance festival was organized by the North East Zone Cultural Centre (NEZCC), Dimapur in collaboration with Department of Information, Cultural Affairs & Tourism, Government of Tripura on August 27 & 28, 2007 at Rabindra Shatabarshiki Bhawan, Agartala. The Classical dance festival was organized with the view to promote the Classical art forms in North East States and to provide opportunity to the artistes from the region. The remarkable classical dance participated from EZCC, Kokata, SCZCC, Nagur, Manipur, Assam and Tripura.

North East Folk dance festival

2007 : A one day North East Folk dance festival was organized by NEZCC in collaboration with the Department of Art & Culture, Government of Meghalaya on December 06, 2007 at New Nongstoin, Meghalaya. The following folk troupes from Manipur, Tripura, Nagaland and Meghalaya performed in the festival viz: Pungcholom, Lai Haraoba and Thang - ta from Manipur, Hozagiri dance from Tripura, Chicken dance was presented by Chakhesang Zuve Cultural Troupe, Dimapur, Nagaland and Lepcha dance, Sikkim besides other local troupes from Meghalaya who presented the Drum and Lahoo dance.

2008 : A two day North East Folk Dance Festival was organized by North East Zone Cultural Centre in collaboration with Department of Art & Culture, Government of Arunachal Pradesh on January 14 & 15, 2008 at Parasuram Kund, Arunachal Pradesh.

Prakriti - A festival of tribal arts

The NEZCC participated in the three – day Festival of Tribal Arts, "PRAKRITI", organized by the Ministries of Culture and Tribal Affairs in association with the Zonal Cultural Centres and Sangeet Natak Akademi from December 5 to 7, 2007 at New Delhi. The NEZCC participated in the festival alongwith three cultural troupes from the Northeastern States consisting of 18 members each from the State of Arunachal Pradesh, Meghalaya and Nagaland and presented the Lion & Peacock dance, Lahoo dance and Khupielili dance.

Shipgram Utsav

The Shilpgram Utsav was organized by West Zone Cultural Centre, Udaipur from December 21 to 30, 2007 at Shilpgram, Udaipur. The NEZCC participated in the Utsav by sending the following 5 folk dance troupes - Maibi Laichung Jagoi, Manipur, Singhi Chham, Dimasa Kachari, Nagaland, Bagrumba & Bordoishikla, Assam, Dhol Dholok Cholom, Manipur.

Natya The Essence of Hyndhava - Dharma

We find the instinct to dance in the savages as in the cultured. When dance transcends the physical, it becomes art giving pleasure to all. Dance is a sacred art cherished and preserved in our country for more than 2000 years. Dancing in India is not merely a spontaneous emotion or idea translated into movement but a long thought out and carefully fashioned ritual that needs concentrated study and constant effort.

Mythological Significance of Dance

The ideals of India through ages have retained a remarkable continuity clearly recognising between the concept of activity, the relationship between the concept of God & Man. The Upanishads quote "DEVAM BHUTVA DEVAM YAJET' - 'become a God to worship God'. This signifies the basic idea, to identify oneself with truth, before offering prayers to God. Various methods of attaining this sanctity have been propounded in the Vedas and Upanishads and the most sanctified way of worship is Sangitha.

Gitam Vadyam Tatha Nrityam Trayam Sangitam Uchyate

Dance or Nritya is the one in which all these aspects of creation are unified, that is Geetham-the sound, Vadyam-the rhythm or time and Nrittam-the movement. Brahma says, For the welfare of the generations to come I create the fifth veda. Therefore natya is the essence of all the vedas. The knowledge of the world from Rig Veda, music from Sama Veda, expression from Yajur Veda and rasa or enjoyment from Atharvana Veda. Bharata says, There is no wisdom nor knowledge, no art, no craft, no device or action that is not to be found in Natya and in ancient India, Natyam was a synonym for dance, drama and music.

The term BHA-RA-THA

The name Bharata Natyam is actually a general term for all Indian dances but has become synonymous with the South Indian dance which was previously known as Sadir/ Chinnamelam or Dasiattam. There are a few attributes to the Bha-ra-tha.

1. That the sage Bharatha created it.
2. That the word is the Anagram from the first letters of Bhava, Raga and Tala.
3. That which banishes distress. BHARAM TARAYATI ITI BHARATHA.
4. The dance of India or Bharata Desa.

The purpose of Dance

Apart from spirituality or spiritual quality of dance there is a definite purpose in dance. The purpose is to educate the illiterates, to enlighten the literate and entertain the enlightened ones. According to gradations of the mind, Uttama (the great one), Madhyama (ordinary) and Adhama (the lesser one), Natya generates morality and an awareness of well being. It instructs and gives motivation to achieve perfection in every action. It relaxes the mind of sick persons, distressed ones, tired souls, bereaved family members and also the Tapaswi (sages) after their meditation. Natya gives dharmopadesa (the path of righteousness) to happy ones, instructs the way to praise the worthy and also to live long. Natya sharpens the mind, increases the intellect. As such Natya gives all things needed for the well being of the people.

Dance is also considered to be a Yagna (sacrifice). The effect of conducting a dance performance is shared by the audience, the sponsor and the dancer. It is said, any auspicious occasion like child birth, marriage, rituals, festivals and celebrations must either begin with a dance performance or conclude with it. It has the effect of performing a hundred yagnas.

Salient Features of Dance

Any visual activity has a good impact on the mind of man. Dance is the imitation of our own action, reaction and conviction presented in sophisticated gesticulation, exploiting the body mind and soul. These three aspects are represented in the form of Nritta, Nritya and Natya.

Nritta

Nritta is pure dance or rhythmic movement of the body. There are several intricacies of Nritta like the defined positions starting with a 'Samapada' position. There are innumerable combinations of adavus (the basic dance steps), the variation of foot movements.

Nritya

Nritya is the application of physical movement sin conjunction with the mind, a combination of rhythm and mind. To express one needs a language. The traditions have evolved a perfect system of gestures. The basic alphabets of this gestural language begin with the single handed gestures and move onto double handed gestures. These alphabets form words and then make sentences. Expression comes from the mind and is shown through the face and eyes.

Natya

Natya is dramatic representation of stories from mythology. The concept of dance actually originated in the form of dance dramas and later gained importance as a solo performance. Even here the dramatic representation is prominent. The solo dancer portrays different characters while narrating stories.

All aspects of artistic merits are conjured up in Natya. There is music for the musician, dance for dance lovers and drama for dramatists, beautiful line and picturesque poses for the painters and the sculptor and poetry for the poet. Bharatha describes four kinds of dramatic presentations known as Chaturvrithi in Natyasastra. They are Bharathi (expression through speech), Sathwathi (expression achieved through thinking and feeling), Kaisiki (the Lyrical, subtle movement for ladies) and Arabhati (an acrobatic, forceful movement to represent war, duels, etc.)

This is the only system of art which exploits the body, the mind and the sentiments fully and brings an absolute co-ordination between all senses. Without this absolute co-ordination it is not possible to convey the purpose of dance to the spectators. The prime aspect is literary contribution. The emotions are universal and common to all human beings. these emotions are classified into eight categories namely Sringara, Karuna, Veera, Roudra, Hasya, Bhayanaka, Bibhatsa, Abdhuta and the ninth one called Shanta or tranquility.

This quotation from the Vishnudharmottara Purana sums up the greatness of the art form.

"To worship God by Natya is to fulfill all desire and to that one is unfolded the path of salvation. The Dance gives prestige and longevity and destroys all misery. The art gives guidance to the dull witted and increases the good fortune of humanity"

RASA

The Rasas are nothing but human feelings and emotions. These are of course universal, known to Man and Art perhaps since culture began, but in the Indian cultural tradition that they have been analysed, codified and commented upon, threadbare. The chapter on Rasa in Bharata's Natyasastra, has been the mainstay of all traditional literature, dance and theatre arts in India.

There is no actual counterpart to Rasa in the English language. The nearest in meaning, in this context, is human feelings or emotions. There are nine classified by Bharata, who says that Brahma enunciated only eight, and the ninth, Shantha was his contribution. Today, Navarasa is a common terminology and it has been so for quite some time, though some eminent scholars and famous authors like Kalidasa (in Malavikagnimitram) mention only eight. Their contention is that Santham does not evoke any Rasa or enjoyment and consequently is a static, motionless state of mind.

The Definition of Rasa:

There has always been controversies about its definition. Even today, there are people who confuse Rasa with Bhava and mistake one for he other. On a literal level, Rasa means that which is being tasted or enjoyed. Hence the word Rsika is employed to denote connoisseurs. Now, the question might be asked whether Rasa comes from Bhava or Bhava from Rasa. Bhava means, that which becomes (bh00, bhav, i.e., to become), so Bhava becomes Rasa. But Rasa does not become Bhava. There is also this complementary effect on the dancer or actor.

It is said that Sringara, Rowdra, Veera and Bibhatsa are the main Rasas and the others Hasya, Karuna, Adbhuta and Bhaya are derived from the former four. That means that from Sringara comes Hasya; from Rowdra comes Karuna; from Veera comes Adbhuta and from Bibhatsa comes Bhaya. Certain colours have been specified for the artistic representation of these Rasas, codified so to speak, for use in the performing arts. Green is used for Sringara, red for Rowdra, golden yellow for Veera, blue for Bibhatsa, white for Hasya, grey for Karuna, black for Bhaya, yellow for Adbhuta.

For every one of these Rasas, there is a Sthayi Bhava, (the permanent state of mind), Lakshana (the definition), and Vibhava (the fundamental determinant) and Uddeepana Vibhava (the excitant determinant). Then follow Anubhava (the consequences), Sattvika Bhava (the involuntary) that is, that which springs from the involvement of the mind, and Vyabhichari Bhava or sanchari Bhava (tranitory or passing state of mind)

ELABORATION OF THE RASAS

Sringaram

The common concept is that Sringara Rasa refers to love between man and woman and its consequences. A much deeper sense is actually conveyed by this term. The meaning of this term, Sringara is beauty, Soundarya. That is why Sringara Lahari is also known as soundarya Lahari.

Beauty is that which attracts the mind or appeals to a particular penchant of the mind. That is love; love is not just Rati the amorous attitude. There can be love between a child and its mother, between friends, between a teacher and disciples and of course love towards God. The beauty in Man is love and this love is what distinguishes Man and makes him supreme in all creation. Hence, love is beauty, that is, Sringara is truth and naturally it is considered to be the king of the Rasas; not because it is seductive, passionate or amorous love, though the general belief is so.

Thus Sringara rasa can be created by many different kinds of methods. 'Kuru Yadunandana' from 'Geetagovindam' represents the Sambhoga Sringara. This can be depicted by the meeting between the male and the female, their attitudes to love varying from shy to bold. 'Krishna nee begane baro' can be shown as Vatsalya, the bond between a mother and child; or Bhakthi, the tie between a devotee and God. Amorous interpretation of this would be inappropriate.

While exhibiting, acting or dancing the basic idea of a theme, the study of various theories and literary allusions help the performer to elaborate it properly and give the required strength of mood and atmosphere for the audience, enabling it to get the most out of it. Of course, there are various kinds of Sringara - Sambhoga Sringara, Vipralambha Sringara etc., but these need independent treatment for themselves.

Roudram

Rowdra can be expressed by violent jumps, striking the floor forcefully with the feet. Anger is one of the more easily communicable emotions. Audiences can easily identify this feeling. To evoke such a feeling, the performer endulges in violent actions. Roudram is characteristic of wicked characters, like Rakshasas, true, but it does not mean that good characters should not show Roudram even for a moment. Though their basic nature is not cruel, they can have a momentary fir of anger.

Bad characters , on the other hand, show their inherent quality of Roudram in their normal speech, action and even in the manifestation of their love. When such a character is shown the audience should immediately savour the taste of it, even by the figure, costume and make-up.

Veeram

The next important Rasa is Veera. This quality of heroism is attributed only to great, benevolent and chivalrous men. Enthusiasm and valour is in the natue of such heroes. When one thinks of such a hero, one imagines a handsome valiant, beautifully attired, pleasing to look at and on entry, he should give the impression of leadership and heroism. The stature itself should create the Veera rasa. Otherwise, its opposite will result, Hasya. The very gait itself can differentiate between men, the heroes and fools.

Veera Rasa is generally associated with Sringara, because a hero's basic qualities are love and good nature. A veera, a hero that is, comes across a heroine and the ensuing relationship between them gives room for various other bhavas and rasas. Thus Sringara and Veera have been the dominant rasas in the most popular of tales from our Puranas, History, Literature, Folk Tales and even real life. hence these Rasas can be called the root of most creativity in all fine arts, and more so in literature, music and dance. There are various shades of heroes, Dhirodatta, Dhirodhhata, Dhiralalitha and Dhirashanta are some of them, their names denoting the qualities predominant in them.

Beebhatsa

Beebhatsa rasa is employed only in very brief stretches as no one likes to experience this rasa, disgust, for very long, whether reading a book or seeing something on stage.

There is not much to describe in this rasa, except to say that it is creted when things like vomit, bad ocour are properly depicted. A good artiste can communicate this area easily and a bad one might create it inadvertently. The other Rasas, Hasya, Karuna, Adbhuta and Bhaya are also sparingly used in specific instances. It must be remembered that these are the lesser rasas.

Shantam

There is a controversy whether this Rasa is to be included in the list of Rasas at all. That apart, this rasa has a great significance since it is here that every thing begins and ends. This denotes a frame of mind, blissful, free from tension, content and near salvation. This quality is personified by great sages like Buddha, Sankaracharya etc., Reading or hearing about them elevates the human mind to a higher realm of thought, of tranquil repose. Seeing such a saintly character of simple attire and serene demeanour, naturally ccompanied by a simple and elevating music, fills the audience with a feeling of purity and piety. This can be noticed quite often in the auditorium, when such a scene comes to pass in a drama, ballet, harikatha, musical discourse or ven a vocal concert.

One way of showing this area of rasa would be to show what it would be without it. A good example would be Thyagaraja's 'Santhamuleka Sowkhyamuledu'. It must be noted that to throw proper light on Shantha, the elaboratic must be about what it would be without it.

The Concept of the Male Dancer

Indian dance is very popular today. In popular parlance, it is the in-thing. There are different classical Indian Dances, the most famous of which are Bharatanatyam, Kathakali, Odissi, Kathak, Manipuri and Kuchipudi. These dances arouse public enthusiasm and consequently such performances now draw knowledgeable and highly sophisticated audiences, compared to those of past decades.

Amidst all this renaissance of interest in Dance somehow a wrong notion has crept into the minds of our people that dancing is meant only for women. The historical and socio-cultural factors that led to this misconception are many. It is a fact that for many decades, dance has been a near monopoly of women, be it in the South or the North. Nowadays the male dancer is a rare phenomenon and it happens that a section of the public looks down upon him. Men may become dance teachers, they may provide nattuvangam and musical accompaniment and do everything else needed to make it possible for women to dance, but if they themselves don ankle bells and start to dance, they are put down as effeminate upstarts in an exclusively female domain.

The traditional, meaning hereditary, dance teachers, usually refuse to teach men; and the less said about women teachers in this regard the better. This is very surprising since the very concept of Dance is masculine in origin. Nataraja, meaning the king of performers, the patron deity of dancers is male and according to Indian scripture, the originator of Dance.

Parallels from nature also, can be drawn showing that the male is more oriented towards the movements that appear dance-like to us. The dance of the peacock, the gait of the male swan or the stance of a lion.

The writer of Natya Sastra and all its great commentators have been men. So have been the foremost masters and composers of this medium of dance.

In folk and tribal dancing, the performers are generally men while women are mostly excluded from magical and ritual dancing. Thus the present social prejudice against the male dancer is entirely without basis. It is interesting to note that the Natya Sastra, the ancient Indian science of dramaturgy views dance as a male prerogative. The stylistic elements of its techniques are described under 'Tandavalakshana', the male overtones of which term are obvious. 'Lalitha Nrithyam', the soft and gentle type of dance is only a part of 'Kaisiki Vritti' one of the four dramatic presentations described in texts (the others Arabhati, Satvathi and Bharathi).

It is believed that Parvathi, the consort of Nataraja Siva, introduced the 'Lasya' or the delicate-feminine mode into Dance. Yet as compared with her consort Nataraja, her dance finds an insignificant place in literature, over-shadowed, as it were, by the extreme and all-pervasive vigour of Nataraja's 'Tandava'. Apart from this divine couple there are quite a few personages from our mythology who are associated with the art of dancing in one way or the other and among these, invariably men outnumber women. Krishna, the frolic-some stealer of hearts is a dancer. Arjuna was conscripted by Indra to judge the better amongst the celestial dancers, Rambha and Urvasi. And while in exile, Arjuna taught dance as Brihannala to Uttara. Kamadeva, Ganesha, Anjaneya and even Ravana were all supposed to be masters of music and dance. Bharata and his hundred illustrious sons who propagated this art form throughout our country can also be cited as evidence from the Itihasas.

According to the more substantial evidence from literature, men have been predominantly associated with dance from ancient times. Bharata, the author of Natyasastra, Nandikeswara the author of Abhinayadarpana, Dhananjaya who wrote Dasarupaka, and many other writers and commentators, including Dattila and Kohala alluded to by Nandikeswara in the introduction of his oft referred treatise, were men.

So was Jaya Senapathi, of Nrittaratnavali and Ilango Adigal, the author of Silappadikaram (Tamil literary work) which devotes a chapter exclusively to an erudite discussion of music and dance as it existed then.

The heritage of Indian Dance embraces several forms which can be broadly classified as classical, folk and tribal. Apart from the major classical styles, there are at least a dozen other forms so highly developed that they deserve to be ranked along with the principal styles mentioned earlier. An interesting feature of these diverse styles is that, most of them were originally intended for men alone. It is only recently that women have been taking part in them. Looking back again to scriptures, Dance originally existed as dance dramas. Kathakali, Bhagavathamela, Kuchipudi, Krishnattam, etc., were all presentations of drama through the medium of dance. With this vast back-ground supporting the existence and virtually the pre-eminence of the male dancer, it is highly regrettable that so many misconceptions continue today. There are some people who hold that dancing should be delicate and graceful, even if a man is the performer. Some teachers go to the extent of coercing their male students to imitate their female counterparts in the departments of dress, ornamentation and presentation.

The cumulative effect of these misconceptions of the public and the mis-direction of the teachers is such that very few men are taking to dance, fewer still making the grade to become professionals. This apart, there is immense social and parental pressure on boys to become doctors and engineers so that a lucrative career is assured. With all this psychological stigma, social approbation and economic sanctions, it is not surprising that dance is fast becoming more oriented towards the fair sex. On the other hand, this is something akin to damning with faint praise, if a boy is delicately featured and minces to match, he is considered a fit candidate for dance lessons.

Unless these trends are reversed by educating public opinion, the dignity and prestige of this magnificent art form will be lessened, probably for ever, by excluding the male element from it. Let us hope it will not come to pass.

KATHAKALI - ORIGIN & BACKGROUND

Origin of Kathakali

Sometime in the 17th century A.D., one of the Zamorin Rajas of Calicut composed a lyrical poem meant for a dance called Krishna Natakam. It came to be enacted in the great Krishna Temple of Guruvayur, then under the control of the kings of Calicut, under the name of "Krishnattam". A contemporary of his, further South, belonging to the Royal family of Kattarakara, required this play to be enacted in his palace but the Zamorin refused to oblige him. Tradition has it that the prince of Kottarakara composed several plays on the theme of the Epic Ramayana, calling them "Ramanattam", which were staged as a challenge to the Zamorin of Calicut.

Later another great royal composer, the Raja of Kottayam, composed several other beautiful dance-dramas taking the themes from the epic Mahabaratha. Since these were on Sri Krishna, the name was no longer applicable and the general title "Kathakali" meaning dance drama evolved. Since the time of these two royal composers, several other beautiful plays have been written by other kings, chieftans and members of the great noble families who could afford to maintain Kathakali troupes of their own.

Out of the temple

As in all classical plays of Kerala, Kathakali had its origin in temples. Even now 'Kodiyattam' and 'Krishnattam' are not performed outside temples, but 'Kathakali' while it continued and still continues to be performed in temples, is also performed outside. Its great popularity is due to the fact that it is not confined to the precincts of the temples. Kathakali can be staged anywhere - in a rural setting, under a tree, in the courtyard of a house, or in any place convenient to the public - wherever a number of people can sit and watch the play enacted. A raised platform is not necessary. The actors, the singers and the drummers require only a minimum of 100sq. feet of flat space on a level ground. A temporary thatched roofing over this so called stage is also prepared.

The state of affairs

In the earlier part of this century there was a sudden cultural awakening throughout India with the momentum given by the freedom movement. Of course it was Rabindranath Tagore who really sowed the seed for cultural renaissance. Smt. Rukmini Devi revived the art of 'Sadir or Dasiatam' now known as Bharatanatyam, Poet Vallathol Narayana Menon revived the art of Kathakali with the establishment of his Kerala Kalamandalam - (the school for Kathakali) - and Kathakali regained its lost prestige and a lot of development took place. Now there are several academies for teaching Kathakali in and outside Kerala. As in the case of other art forms the patronage also shifted from temple to clubs and cultural organisations. It must be noted that considerable improvement has been achieved in the presentation of the dance drama, Kathakali. Since technically and theoretically Kathakali has its roots in Natyasastra traditions, certain innovations and modifications were not successful and they did not fit in well to match the loftiness of this unique dance style. But the music for Kathakali has tremendously improved and now it almost follows the Karnatic style of singing leaving behind its original folk character.

The Drama & its Historical Background

Kathakali is an indegenous, classical dance-drama from Kerala in the south west of India. Kerala, situated as it is on the coast of the Arabian sea, claims ancient contact with countries like Egypt, Syria, Rome and Greece and to certain extent, these contacts are reflected in the art, literature and society of that area. It is said that even Kathakali shows traces of the influence of other countries. Kathakali is made up of two words. 'Katha' in Sanskrit means story and 'Kali' a Dravidian word meaning play. The very name is indicative of its Aryan-Dravidian character.

Early Influences

The earliest to be noted in this form is the ritualistic influence. In Kerala, the earliest form of dance are connected with the rituals of the temples (known by the names of Kaliyattam, Tirayattam and Theyyam). The origin of the costume worn by the Kathakali dancers is to be traced to these time-old ritual dances. Though the crowns and other ornaments and costumes worn by Kathakali actors are highly sophisticated and artistic, the prototypes were comparatively crude, although, in their own way, very ornamental.

Another influence which can be traced is the martial art. The Nayars of Kerala were warriors by profession and were trained in a very rigorous system of martial exercises which are still used in the training of Kathakali. To these, the overwhelming influence of the tradition of presentation of Sanskrit plays was added and a new art form came into being, called Koodiyattam. Gesture and facial expression formed the main vehicles of this acting technique. For all purposes, Koodiyattam may be taken to be as the ancestor of Kathakali.

Kathakali - Classical Technique

The technique in Kathakali is highly classical and the audience have some knowledge of the idiom of the play. The actors do not speak at all. The only speech comes from the singers and the songs tell the story and are very often in dialogue form. The words, sentiments, the emotions, all these are expressed by the actors through body movement, stylized hand gestures (called Pastas or Murders) and through facial expressions.

Hand Gestures

The hand gestures are stylized and each one of these gestures has a meaning. These 'Hashes' as they are called, have the common characteristics of all forms deriving from the Natty Sister of Brahma. Kathakali has adapted these and developed its own code, and the entire vocabulary of the spoken language. In Kathakali, these gestures are dynamic in movement, while in many other dance forms they are static. Number, tense, mood and all the shades of grammatical niceties can be conveyed through gestures.

The Speaking Drums of Kathakali

It is very strange - the same drum speaks differently on different occasions - whether it be a temple festival of the 'Thirauattam' (a folk ritual) or Velichappadan (Oracle) or the Onathar (a folk dance indicating the arrival of Mahabali during Onam day) or a cinema pamphlet's distribution. The people of Kerala can distinguish the different beats of the same drum in those different situations. And the same drum, 'Chenda', speaks a different note for a Kathakali event and that is how people get notice of a Kathakali performance.

The hustle and bustle of the busy evening is broken by the strains of the 'Chenda' heard even at a distance of 4 to 5 miles, announcing the performance of Kathakali that night somewhere, and the people are drawn towards the sound of the speaking drums, Chenda and Maddalam. Chenda and maddalam are high precision classical instruments which need rigorous training for several years to master the art, and the intricacies are even greater than the Tavil or Mridangam. For each occasion, the refrain of beats is distinct. To play Chenda and Maddalam for a Kathakali performance requires an entirely different training, to evoke the requisite speaking quality of the drum.

The combination of Chenda, Maddalam and Elattalam is a feast of marvelous sound with penetrating and reverberating beats, which only the classically tuned ears can take, like any other classical forms of art. The richness of Kathakali commences with the vibration of these mystical drums and carries splendour from the finger tips of the player to the attentive ears of the spectators.

Making of a Kathakali actor

Generally to become a Kathakali actor one has to undergo a very strenuous and rigorous course of physical training, including separate exercise of muscles, eye-balls, eye-brows, eye-lids, lips, neck, shoulder, etc., and must have a through knowledge of literature, Sanskrit and Malayalam and deep awareness of the Puranas and Ithihasas (epics and mythologies). he must also have the dexterity of an artist (painter) to know the combinations of colour and lining to draw the intricate designs on the face, plus a face itself that would match the imaginative make-up. One in whom all these are combined only can make a mark in Kathakali.

Also there is no question of doing 'Arangetram' in six months or one year or even three years. The only standard for 'Arangetram' in Kathakali is real proficiency in the art with all perquisite knowledge. The tradition still persists that no cheap popularity is attained by publicity or high influence. One has to come up only by virtue of merit.

Kathakali - Costume & Make-up

The costumes are very elaborate and fall into basic types. The make up is equally elaborate. While being made up, the actors lie on their backs as the make up men work on their faces. The facial makeup is designed in such a way as to indicate the intrinsic nature of each and every character. Pacha, Kathi, Thadi, Kari, Minukku and Theppu are the different types of make-up followed in Kathakali which are determined according to the basic qualities of the character portrayed. The underlying purpose is to create in the minds of the audience an atmosphere of the supernatural.

As all the stories depicted in Kathakali relate to mythological characters and as the natural stage is nothing more than a few square feet, lit by a single coconut oil fed lap, the entire get up is designed to generate an atmosphere to suit the story. The loud instrument used, the make-up and costumes employed, the painting of the faces, the display of the 'Chutti' as part of the facial make-up, are only the instruments used to achieve this objective. Irrespective of the individual who puts on the costume of a character like Nala, the audiences sees only Nala. The individual artiste is fully submerged by the elaborate make-up. It is, however, true that the outstanding talents of an individual artiste cannot be contained within the formal frame-work of a standard costume. In course of time, the individual does make an impression on the audience, but on a basis quite different from other histrionic arts. The costumes are thus intended to make the play as impersonal as possible.

Pacha

Mythological characters are classified into different categories. The first in the order of precedence is the Dhirodatta, the noble hearted, upright hero. The make-up known as Pacha (Green) is allotted to such characters. Examples are the Gods of the elements, noble kings like Nala, Yudhishtra, Rukmangada, Arjuna and Bhimsena. Even Daksha is given Pacha, although he ultimately turns out to be arrogant and wayward. All characters who do Pacha also wear Kiritas (Headgear). But when it comes to characters like Vishnu, Krishna or Rama (the incarnation) hear gear is changed to what is called Mudi. This costume also has now come to be referred to as 'Mudi'. For both Mudi and Pacha, the facial make-up is the same. krishna wears a dark jacket as distinct from the purple or red jackets of Pacha.

Kathi

Kathi, another prominent costume of kathakali is devoted to heroes who are not too particular about the means they use to gain their needs. The costume in general is similar to Pacha, except that in the make-up, a knife-shaped pattern is drawn on either cheek in red pigment. In addition, a small ball is fixed to the tip of the nose and another one in the fore-head. kathi represents restlessness easily swayed towards wickedness and is the costume of characters like Ravana, Kamsa and Duryodhana. Kathi can be said to denote a combination of royalty and evil. Kings of demons like Ravana, or demons among kings and villains are depicted in Kathi. Whereas 'Pacha' characters do not open their mouths or create any noise 'Kathi' characters are permitted to make weird noises appropriate to the occasion or to the emotion expressed.

Thadi (Beard)

The costume that represents Thamoguna (wickedness) is Thadi. Thadi means beard. There are red, black and white thadis, each depicting a distinct type of wickedness. Red thadi has the face painted in frightening dark portions and wears an impressive red beard.

The head gear is round in shape and much larger in size than those worn by Kathi. Red thadi is usually given to extremely wicked characters like Rakshasas or despicable men like Dussasana. Examples of Rakshasas are Bakasura and Jatasura. The concept of the red thadi is only of the destructive evil force with little or no thinking faculty. The costume has, therefore, been extended to portray roles like Srichakra and Veerabhadra. Srichakra is the all powerful weapon of Vishnu. Annihilation without thought is its motto. So also Veerabhadra who is born out of the fire of Siva, the Destroyer, is nothing but an agency for destruction and blind obedience.

A further extension of thadi is its application to monkey kings like Vali and Sugriva. Here again, the human contempt for the unthinking monkey has influenced this decision. There is no doubt, a slight modification in the white make-up pattern, but it is noticed only by careful observation. White Thadi or white beard is a further refinement of the Thadi group of characters. A good example is Hanuman, the monkey God. The intricate patterns drawn on the face with red, black and white, suggests a monkey face almost similar to the baboons of african forests. Hanuman, the monkey God of the epic Ramayana merit special mention. The crown is known as Vattamudi, a ceremonial military hat-like headgear and a white beard. The make-up is different from the ones usually given to the monkeys. Hanuman occupies a very special place in Hindu mythology. So also in Kathakali. Hanuman is also permitted to make weird noises appropriate to the occasion.

The black Thadi or black beard is a costume given to a character like Kali in 'Nalacharitra'. The character is as evil as the red Thadi but has the subtle distinction of denoting a schemer as well. The make-up is the same as red Thadi, the beard alone being black in colour.

Kari (Black)

The 'Kari' is an all black costume. The face is painted in black; the jackets and skirts are blacker still. The headgear is primitive. The costume is used for depicting the lowest of primitive human beings both men and women. The noises they produce can almost amount to howling. Characters portrayed in this costume are demonesses and evil beings of the 'under world'.

Chutti

The 'Chutti' or white make-up plays a very important role in Kathakali make-up. In the olden days, the chutti was laid, layer after layer with a mixture of rice paste and lime. It used to take about three to four hours to get an actor's 'Chutti' done. Today, the base is laid with a paste and the rest made of paper. The purpose of the 'Chutti' is to raise the contours of the face so that the area of aesthetic expression is clearly marked out. It also helps to draw the eyes of the audience to the actor's facial expression.

Minukku

The make-up used for gentle characters is 'Minukku'. It consists of a mere painting of the face with yellowish orange pigment. There is no white chutty make-up and no elaborate clothing as in other characters. Women, sages and Brahmanas appear in 'Minukku'. Other characters who appear in Minukku are charioteers and messengers.

The Mask conception in Kathakali

The Chau dance of Bihar and the Balinese dance are mask dances, but they hardly bear any resemblance to Kathakali, which is known for its exaggerated mime and dramatic exposition. Still there are many who mistake the Kathakali make-up as masks. The painted face and the white frames made on the face (chutti) certainly give the dubious appearance of a mask, but they are not, and they are drawn and painted on the face each day employing a different artist, who is again specialised in this art of Kathakali make-up. The rich colours are obtained from special indigenous stones ground in coconut oil and mixed in the right proportions to get the right shades. The mixing of these colours and grinding of the stones another art, which again needs sense of proportion and precision. A wrong proportion could give a wrong chemical reaction, which could affect even the face and eyes of the actor.

The Red Eyes

People are often puzzled and fascinated by the red eyes of the Kathakali performers and they wonder how it is done. Making the eyes red has two objectives. One is to equate the colour combination on the face; if one watches a kathakali painted face without the eyes being red, you will realise how dead the face looks with pale eyes. Therefore against the green or black background for the face, the eyes must have a red base to stand out vividly.

Secondly, if the eyes are left free while all the other parts of the face are chemically treated, it is bound to affect the eyes with the warmth emitted by these paints. So the eyes must also be treated to equalise the chemical reaction. To make the eyes red, a tiny bit of a herb (chundappoo) is laid in the lower eye lid. It is very dangerous if it goes into the upper eye lid.

'Rasaprakarana' or (Raavikalpam) chapter in Natyasastra enunciates the various colours attached to various moods and sentiments. Though there is not much in common between this approach and the pattern followed in Kathakali, it has a definite bearing on the colour schemes ascribed to various sentiments.

DANCE INSTITUTIONS

Kalakshetra

Kalakshetra literally means (Kala - Arts, Kshetra - Field or Holy place) a Holy place of Arts. This Centre was started in1936 in order that India may once again revive and develop its ancient culture and set a standard of true Art in its new life after its freedom. It seeks to build up the character of the young through the Art and create a true Centre of International Understanding through the one universal language - Art.

In the words of Dr. Annie Besant -

"Art is an attempt to bring down within the vision of ordinary mortals some of the Divine Beauty of which the artist catches glimpses, strives to transalate these into colours, sounds, forms, words, by creating pictures, melodies, sculptures, poems and other literature."

"Beauty diversified into the arts is the true refiner and uplifter of humanity. It is the instrument of culture, the broadener of the heart, the purifying fire which burns all prejudices, all pettiness, a coarseness. Without it, true democracy is impossible, equality of social intercourse an empty dream."

"Art is the international language in which mind can speak to mind, heart to heart, where lips are dumb. The arts need no transalations, they speak the universal mother-tongue. Centuries do not age them, Custom does not stale them. Boundaries do not exist for them. Their message is for every country, for every tongue. Art will permeate the whole atmosphere of the New Civilisation which is on the threshold."

At the College of Fine Arts, music, dancing, painting and crafts are taught to students of both sexes from India and from other parts of the world. A "gurukula" atmosphere prevails within the campus and students are encouraged to lead simple lives. Throughout the year, special cultural programmes are arranged for the benefit of the students, so that they may learn to appreciate true art and the ancient culture of india.

From its inception, the College's faculty has included teachers of repute. To name just a few, Tiger Varadacharya, Veena Krishnamacharya, Mysore Vasudevacharya, Karaikudi Sambasiva Ayyar, Budalur Krishnamurti Sastri, M.D. Ramanathan and

Papanasam Sivan in music, in addition to Rukmini devi herself, Pandanallur Meenakshisundaram Pillai and Mylapore Gowri Ammal in Bharata Natyam and Chandu Pannikar in Kathakali.

The curriculam of the dance students includes classes on dance theory which is based on the work Abhinaya Darpana, and selected portions of other ancient texts on art and literature. The traditional form of dance in all its purity and dignity is the trademark of Kalakshetra. Music is a subsidiary for all dance students. They are encouraged to learn vocal music.

The art of Indian make-up, traditional costumes and theatre craft are learnt gradually by the advanced and post graduate students through participation in the various Kalakshetra productions and in their preparation.

PRODUCTION AND PERFORMANCES

Among Kalakshetra's major activities is the one relating to production and presentation of dance-dramas and the like. Apart from solo Bharata Natya recitals and such items as Kummi and Kolattam (folk dances), a considerable part of Rukmini Devi's work in Kalakshetra pertains to new productions. This work is indeed its unique contribution to art.

These performances serve several purposes:

1. They are part of Kalakshetra's effort to make available to the public the best of Indian classical arts.
2. They are intended as an essential training for the students and teachers, who become thoroughly familiar with preparing for and participating in public performances which, though performed by amateurs, are kept as far as possible to professional standards.

SHREE BHARATALAYA

Modest Beginnings...

Shree Bharatalaya came into being in 1970 following an initiative jointly taken by K.Soundararaja Iyengar, Sudharani Raghupathy & Madurai N. Krishnan.

The classes were started in a covered space available within the family compound on Luz Church Road in Mylapore.

It was truly a modest beginning. But the concepts & the ideas that would make Shree Bharatalaya not only a pre-eminent but also a unique institution of learning were developed & introduced even then. The aim would be to go beyond providing instruction in dance & music to assisting broader human development, so that Shree Bharatalaya's graduates would be not only competent dancers or musicians but cultured individuals as well. Visits to places of architectural & sculptural interest like temples, museums etc., would be used to serve the larger purpose.

With this aim in mind, students would be selected after careful tests to ascertain their potential & aptitude. Only those showing interest in pursuing a general education(in regular schools & colleges) would be taken in as students.

There would be no guarantee of an arangetram or rangapravesam. Art should be pursued for art's sake.

The emphasis would be on quality rather than quantity. The number of students at any time would be limited.

Thus: In addition to compositions of the Tanjavur Quartet & others which form the core of the Thanjavur tradition of Bharatanatyam, the students learn to sing & perform virtually all the compositions for dance created by Madurai N.Krishnan. In addition to dance & music, students would be taught Sanskrit & Telugu languages. Furthermore, they would be encouraged to learn all aspects of presenting a dance programme, like stage-craft & makeup, costume designing & production,and self-adornment prior to performances. They would be given guidance as well in regard to aesthetics & artistic values. Senior students would be taught nattuvangam also. Thus the students would learn the art of music & dance in their entirety rather than the performance aspects alone, & learn them in the wider context of the arts in general.

All the students learn to perform special exercises based on the Martha Graham technique. These exercises, taught by Sudharani Raghupathy herself, are aimed at making the dancers' bodies more responsive & flexible, & at creating an understanding of the therapeutic value of dance itself.

Training in Kalakshetra

"Whatever we are today, it is because of Rukmini Devi and Guru Chandu Panicker."

Were it not for providence in the form of Guru Chandu Panicker, Dhananjayan would have been working in some monotonous job in Kerala. Chandu Panicker taught Kathakali and Sarada Hoffman and N S Jayalakshmi taught Bharatanaatyam. The training imparted at Kalakshetra was painstakingly precise and the dance dramas produced there taught the students set designing, discipline and administrative acumen. The Dhananjayans have served as performing artistes and teachers in the Dance and Academic Faculty in Kalakshetra.

As a scholarship student at Kalakshetra, Dhananjayan learnt Kathakali, Bharatanaatyam, mridangam and music. Shanta trained in Bharatanaatyam and music apart from other subjects for nearly a decade. Dhananjayan also displayed an interest in academics. Even as they evolved into world-renowned professional artists and then into teachers, Dhananjayan continued to shape his artistic experience with academic learning. Shanta matured in dancing and outshone other girls. With Rukmini Devi as mentor and Chandu Panickar as Guru, Shanta and Dhananjayan blossomed into outstanding dancers. Shanta enacted the female lead opposite Dhananjayan in many Kalakshetra compositions. They were paired opposite each other as Rama and Sita or Chitralekha and Aniruddha etc. Dhananjayan played the role of Arjuna when 93-year-old Chandu Panickar played the role of the Brahmin in 'Santhanagopalan' in the premises of the Subramanya Temple in Payyanur.

Dhananjayan made his feelings clear to Shanta when he was 18, but she kept him in suspense. He thought his lower economic status was the hurdle, when Shanta left Kalakshetra after her post graduation in 1962 and taught dance in Malaysia. She started receiving proposals for marriage, which she turned down. When her parents were convinced that Shanta's interest in marrying Dhananjayan was genuine, they gave their blessings and Shanta returned to India. They tied the knot in 1966 at the Guruvayoor temple in Kerala. Maybe each would have independently carved a niche in the dance world, but together they represented a force, which would take the world of dance by storm.

The Duo

In the late 60s, aristocrats, who could spend to have their own children perform, dominated the dance scene in Madras. The caliber of the Dhananjayans was such that they stole the thunder with their novel ideas that they brought to their presentations via unique repertoire that they developed. The vitality of dance, the costumes, the attraction of merging of the male and female dance principles in specially conceived duets, were all part of the charisma of their performances. It was no wonder that they started to receive invitations from both within the country and from abroad. They have traveled all over the world to all major cultural centers to present their art.

To the Dhananjayans, the realization of their art is both a philosophy and a religion. From a modest start to establishing their own dance academy, it has been a story of deep commitment, fervor and dedication. Bharata Kalanjali has emerged as a full-fledged academy of dance and music with a repertory fashioned out of its own students and graduates.

Partners on and off stage, the Dhananjayans perform with a rare togetherness, born of years as a dancing couple.

Shanta is his perfect partner in life as well as in art. Lack of conflicts in dance is a result of the mutual understanding, which has grown over the years. Dhananjayan is past 60 now, but he and Shanta still continue to enthrall audiences all over the world.

Despite dancing together for 50 years, the Dhananjayans complement each other beautifully in their personal life and manage to keep routine and boredom at bay by working on varied themes, involving themselves in different projects, collaborations and workshops apart from being totally involved in guiding their students' recitals.

Dividing their time between Bharata Kalanjali in Chennai and Bhaaskara in Kerala, keeps them busy year round. The varied activities, which take up so much time and energy, keep their spirits vitalized and their outlook fresh.

Dhananjayan has served as the honorary founder secretary of ABHAI (Association of Bharatanaatyam Artistes of India) and completed 2 terms as its president. He has authored a book on Bharatanaatyam apart from contributing numerous articles on dance and social issues. His book 'A Dancer On Dance' strives to create an awareness of dance and its related problems to contemporary society. He is a guide and counselor to numerous dance organizations.

The 15th Natya Kala Conference titled "PURUSH: The male in dance" was convened by Dhananjayan in December 1995. He has always voiced his concern about the plight of the male dancer in India. Whenever he is on a public platform, he is known to speak out on what ails Indian dance and culture today and has a reputation for being forthright in his views.

"I am a politics graduate, so I take up many issues with political overtones. As far back as the mid 1960's, that many years ago, I advocated bringing about Tamizh as the medium of education in schools but the govt. turned it down."

"In 1969, I wrote to the then Prime Minister Indira Gandhi, that the first thing she should do is issue ID cards for Indian citizens. It was not implemented but I got a letter from the PM's office that the letter was received and passed on to the concerned dept. I also wrote to demonetize the 100Rs note. I would like to think that in some small way I contributed, because later, Indira Gandhi took action in nationalizing the banks and so on."

"I write frequently to the papers on public issues. I have even written on the Cauvery issue. Some get published, some don't. Nothing will get changed overnight. But my contention is to keep on writing, because, sometime somewhere, awareness will be created in the minds of at least a few people."

"By choice and by chance, I have become the spokesperson for the dance community on a variety of issues. Maybe that's why I am labeled as a controversial person, though no one can specify what is exactly controversial about me."

The Dhananjayans do a lot of shows free of charge for charitable causes. However, they are particular that organisers collect at least a particular / respectable sum to make the effort worthwhile.

They have 2 sons. The elder son Sanjay lives in the USA while the younger son Satyajit who's a good dancer is carving out a niche for himself as a photographer. The people and the press often describe the Dhananjayans as institutions by themselves. The success of this unique couple has not deterred their humility, simplicity and humane-ness, which probably make them greater dancers.

South India is full of various traditional and classical dances. Since the ancient period, various dance and music festivals and competitions had been organised. Some of them are discussed below:

Chennai Dance and Music Festival

Every year from the mid December to mid-January, the Chennai Dance and Music Festival is organised in Chennai. This is organised mainly to celebrate the classical music and dances of South India. Many renowned artistes from all over the state and the country participate in this festival. This takes place in many places of the Chennai city like in the auditoriums, well-known temple premises and heritage bungalows. This festival is well known as the 'Margazhi'.

In 1927, this festival of dance and music started for the first time to celebrate the anniversary of the Madras Music Academy. Several organisations, which used to organise art festivals in different parts of the city, then adopted it.

According to the Hindus and South Indian classical music, the Tamil month of Margazhi is a sacred month and devotional in nature. Therefore, it has been a traditional form of worshipping in this month from time immemorial. Many Indian people leaving outside the country gather here in Chennai during the festival to attend it and take a glimpse of our rich cultural heritage. The performances of this festival include vocal and instrumental music, solo and group dance. The festival is a great platform for the upcoming artistes to display their talent.

Chidambaram Dance Festival

The Chidambaram Dance Festival is organised in the holy city of Chidambaram, which is situated about 245 km from Chennai. The dancing bronze image of Nataraja can be seen in the ancient Nataraja temple and Chidambaram is well known for this temple.

The Natyanjali festival of Chidambaram is dedicated to Lord Siva. Every year during the month of February or March, the dance festival is held in the temple premises. This festival runs for five days during the auspicious occasion of Maha Sivaratri. During the festival, top dancers from all over the country gather here to dance in the temple premise to pay their tribute to Lord Nataraja. The Department of Tourism and the Government of Tamil Nadu jointly organise this Natyanjali festival of Chidambaram.

Through this dance festival a universal message of 'Unity in Diversity' is promoted all over the world by the language of music and dance. According to many dancers, it is a blessing to be able to perform in this temple, the pillars of which are carved with the images Lord Nataraja in 108 poses of Bharatanatyam.

Mamallapuram Dance Festival

The Mamallapuram Dance Festival is organised every year from early January to the first week of February at the venue of Arjuna's Penance. Mamallapuram is a coastal town along the Coromandel. It is situated 58km away from Chennai. It used to be a port town during the rule of Pallavas. The town is famous for the rathas or monolithic temples and cave temples created by the Pallava rulers. Now, it is recognised as one of the World Heritage Sites by the UNESCO.

The Mamallapuram Dance Festival is organised by the Department of Tourism, Government of Tamil Nadu. The great performers of classical dances like Bharatanatyam, Kuchipudi, Kathak, and Kathakali assemble here and present their dance in an open-air stage against the backdrop of the Pallava rock sculptures.

Nishigandhi Dance Festival

The Nishagandhi dance festival is organised in the Nishagandhi open-air theatre in the Kanakakunnu Palace compound. This dance festival is organised every year February 21st to 27th. The Tourism Development Corporation of the state organised the function and entry is free of cost.

The Kanakakunnu Palace is situated at Thiruvananthapuram, the capital of Kerala. It is located in the southernmost region of India. This palace used to stage many cultural meets and programmes.

In the Nishagandhi dance festival, famous dancers from all over India perform Bharatanatyam, Mohiniyattam, Kathak, Odissi, modern ballet and other folk forms. Several artists and experts visit here to attend the festival. It gives a fascinating glimpse of India's rich dance heritage.

Pattadakkal Dance Festival

The Pattadakkal Dance Festival is organised every year to celebrate the temples of Pattadakkal. The Government of Karnataka organises the festival. Many well known dancers from all over the country come to perform in this festival. This Nrithyotsava is accompanied by a craft mela.

The village Pattadakkal is located 20 kms from Badami in Karnataka. It is situated on the left bank of the Malaprabha River. Pattadakkal is a World Heritage Centre and has 10 major temples representing both north and south Indian architectural traditions. Most of these temples are dedicated to Lord Siva. It used to be the second capital of the Chalukyan kings. Virupaksha and the Mallikarjuna temples are the largest temples of Pattadakkal.

Mabali

Mabali or Mahabali, also known as Bali is a great asura on whom the Onam festival is celebrated.

Mahabali is said to have reigned in South India, before Lord Ram and his empire extended from the Vindhyas in the north to the south. He was one of the great disciples of Lord Vishnu and is believed to have sacrificed his whole kingdom for the Lord.

Shivaratri

Shiva Ratri is one of the most auspicious Vratas for the devotees of lord shiva. The Hindu Puranas explain the grand significance of this Vrata.

Skandha Puranam describes about four Shivaratris. The first one is Nitya Shivaratri or daily Shivaratri which is observed every night. The second one is Masa Shivaratri which is observed in the Krishna Paksha Chaturdashi of every month (fourteenth Monday on the diminishing phase of moon). The third one is Magha Pratham Adi Shivaratri, which is observed for the first thirteen days starting from the Prathama Tithi in the month of Magha. The fourth one is the most important which is observed on the Krishna Paksha Chaturdashi of Magha month (mid February to mid March). The Lord is worshipped all throughout the night and this Vrata is observed in a widespread manner. It is called Mahashivaratri.

In the day of MahaShivaratri , the devotee wakes up early in the morning and meditates on auspicious Shiva Lingam, which is decorated with number of garlands. The Maha Shiva Lingam is the formless symbol of the holy god. The follower takes bath and stays clean. He/she worships lord Shiva in the all four jamas of night (four equal time interval of night). The Linga worshipping is explicitly mentioned for this Vratam as this time god wants to show his grace for the benefit of 'Pashus' and appeared in a formless form, whose true outcome is Maha Shiva Lingam.

There are many legends entwined with the MahaShivaratri. Brahma and Vishnu fought between themselves to determine who was the greatest. To stop them Lord Shiva appeared between them as a pillar of fire. The gods were not able to find the starting and end of that pillar. When Brahma and Vishnu repented their mistake and prayed to Lord Shiva to forgive their sin then Lord Shiva appeared before them and blessed them in the night of Maha Shivaratri. After that follower of lord Shiva started observing the vrata of Shiva Ratri by performing Abhisheka and chanting other holy deeds.

During the Samudra Manthan by gods and demon a poison came up which was so toxic that it had the ability to wipe out the whole creation. So Vishnu advised the Gods to pray to Lord Shiva. Lord Shiva was pleased by the prayer and drank the poison to hold it in his neck. His throat became blue due to the poison and hence he was known as 'Nilakantha', who was the protector of the world. ShivaRatri is also observed to remember the story.

In another story, during Pralaya or deluge, the whole world was facing destruction. Parvati prayed to Lord Shiva to save the Jivas(the living souls), who were living in space as particles of gold dust in a lump of wax. Lord Shiva granted the prayer of Parvati and the Jivas became active again.

Parvati named the night for worshipping Maheshvara or Shiva as the great night for the worship of Iswara or Maha Shiva. After the deluge stopped and creation was complete, Parvati asked Shiva which rituals pleased him most. Lord answered the fourteenth night of new moon in the month of Magha , was his most favorite day. Parvati spreaded the words among her friends and whole creation started observing the Shiva Ratri.

Another legend says that in a Shiva temple on a Maha ShivaRatri day the lamp kept on the alter was very dim. That time a mouse that was running after the prey touched the flame and due to heat it removed its head very quickly. In this process the mouse kindled the lamp brightly and the alter was well illuminated. Lord Shiva was very pleased with the mouse. He blessed him and made it Mahabali, the renowned Asura king.

The story of king Chitrabhanu is also very interesting. In the Shanti Parva of Mahabharata, Bhisma while lying on the bed of arrows gave reference to this story.The King Chitrabhanu of the Ikshvaku Dynasty, ruled over the whole of Jambudvipa, was observing fasting on the day of MahaShivaRatri with his wife. The sage Astravakra come to visit him and wanted to know the reason. The King explained that he has a gift to remember his previous birth.

On his previous birth he was a hunter in Varanasi named Suswara who used to earn his living by killing and selling birds and animals. One day while roaming through the forest for his prey, he could not kill a single animal. He had let a deer to live after seeing the deer's sad family. Overtaken by the darkness of night and unable to return home, the hunter climbed a tree nearby, which was a Bael tree. He could not sleep throughout the night as he was thinking about his fasting wife and children. He did not eat or drink anything and the water leaked drop by drop from his canteen. The hunter engaged himself in plucking the Bael leaves and dropping them onto the ground.

The next day when the hunter returned home he bought some food for his family. But the moment he was about to break his fast, a stranger came to him, begging for the food. He served the food first to the stranger and then took his own part. At the time of death the hunter saw two messengers of Lord Shiva, who took his soul to the abode of Shiva. The hunter came to know he was blessed as unknowingly he has worshipped Shiva. There was a Shiva Lingam under the Bael tree, which he climbed and he washed the Lingam with water from his canteen and dropped the Bael leaves. Unknowingly he was fasting all day and all night. Thus he got the divine bliss of Lord Shiva, living in his abode for a long time and was reborn as a King.

Mamankam, Ancient festival of Kerala

Mamankam was a festival organized in every twelve years when the tenure of a king expires. In this festival the king used to undertake self-sacrifice and in his place another is crowned as the king for the next twelve years.

Mamankam was one of the ancient festivals of Kerala which was connected with the winning of a kinship. These accounts take us deep into the shadows of the sacred wood, for they suggest the presence among the ancient Dravidian rulers in prehistoric Kerala of the institution of sacrificial kingship. As per the legend of Kerala, Parasurama, the sixth incarnation or avatar of Lord Vishnu, planted the sixty four joint families of Brahmins as the seeds of Keralan villages, and provided them institutions and laws to govern themselves, But, very similar to the modern Malayalis, the Brahmins were unable to agree, and their republic declined into chaos. Then, Parasurama advised them to bring someone from out of the country to govern them and thus started a line of monarchs known as the Perumals whose tenure of rule was set for twelve years.

There was a tale linked to the festival of Mamankam, of the twelve-year reign of the lord of Quilacare (a dependency of the kingdom of Quilon) and of the ritual suicide that brought his rule to an end. In the province of Quilacare there is a gentile house of prayer in which there is an idol, which they hold of great account, and every twelve years they celebrate a great feast to it, whither the gentiles go as to a Jubilee. This temple possesses many lands and much revenue. It is a very great affair.

The province has a king over it, which has no more than 12 years to reign from Jubilee to Jubilee. His manner of leaving is in this wise, that is to say: when the 12 years are completed, on the day of this feast, there assemble together innumerable people and much money is spent in giving food to Brahmin. The king has a wooden scaffolding made, spread over with silken hangings: and on that day he goes to bathe at a tank with great ceremonies and sound of music, after which he comes to the idol and prays to it and mounts to the scaffolding, and there, before all the people, he takes some very sharp knives, and begins to cut off his nose, and then his ears and his lips, and all his members, and as much flesh off himself as he can, and he throws it away very hurriedly, until so much of his blood is spilled that he begins to faint, and then he cuts his throat himself. And he performs this sacrifice to the idol, and whoever desires to rule other twelve years and to undertake this martyrdom for love of the idol, has to be present looking on at this: and from that place they raise him up as a king.

It is probable that already by the 16th century the real ruler of Quilacare did not die, and that only a proxy carried out this gruesome self-immolation, for in The Golden Bough Sir James Frazer quotes an account of certain princes of Malabar who delegated their powers in a part of their domain to a substitute who would accept on their behalf the ritual sacrifice. This institution was called Thavettiparothiam or authority obtained by decapitation. It was an office tenable for five years, during which its bearer was invested with supreme despotic powers within his jurisdiction. On the expiry of five years the head of the man was cut off and thrown up in the air amongst a large concourse of villagers, each of whom vied with the other in trying to catch it on its course down. He who succeeded was nominated to the post for the next five years.

Another aspect of the ritual sacrifice appeared in the feast of Mamankam which was last held in the year 1755, by the Zamorin of Kalikod (Calicut) in the holy town of Tirunavayi in Malabar. As the festival was then carried out, the king offered himself for assassination by whoever dared attempt it. The successful assassin (there are no known instances of such success) would rule in his place. The ceremony was regarded as confirming the status of the Zamorin as the suzerain of all northern Kerala. It was said that he had usurped the right to hold the festival, and hence the right of suzerainty, from the Rajas of Valluvand, and it was these rulers who always sent their chavers, or suicide fighters, to attempt the killing of the Zamorin.

A ceremony is followed by the Samorin, that a Jubilee is proclaimed throughout his dominions at the end of twelve years and the tent is pitched for him in a spacious plain, and a great feast is celebrated for ten or twelve days with mirth and jollity, guns firing night and day, so that at the end of the feast any four of the guests who have a mind to gain a crown by a desperate action in fighting their way through thirty or forty thousand of his guards, and kill the Samorin in his tent, he that kills succeeds to him in his empire.

In Anno 1695 one of these jubilees happened when the tent was pitched near Ponnany, a seaport of about fifteen leagues to the southward of Calicut. There were but three men that would venture on that desperate action who fell on with sword and target, among the guards, and after they had killed and wounded many were themselves killed. One of the Desperadoes had a nephew of fifteen or sixteen years of age that kept close to his uncle in the attack on the guard, and when he saw him fall, the youth got through the guards into the tent and made a stroke at His Majesty's head and had certainly dispatched him, if a large brass lamp that was burning over his head, had not marred the blow; but before he could make another he was killed by the guards, and it is believed that same Samorin reigns yet.

All the accounts of the feast of Mamankam present it as a festival of great antiquity, dating to the time before the Chera empire disintegrated in the early twelfth century, and all indicate the former existence of a custom of sacrificial kingship, actually observed by early Dravidian rulers, but long transformed, by a series of evasions, into a ceremonial in which either a substitute victim suffered or the ruler presented himself for a combat which only by an extraordinary accident could end in his death. After the Aryanization of Kerala, religious dedication was accepted as another kind of substitute for the physical sacrifice of the king on the termination of his customary period of office for twelve years. At least two Chera kings renounced their temporal power and took up the life of the religious renunciate. One was the Vaishnavite devotional poet, Kulasekhara Alwar, who ruled Kerala in the eighth century and a later renunciate king who became the most famous ruler of Kerala was Cheraman Perumal, and it is believed that he gave up his throne in 825 and went on a pilgrimage from which he did not return.

Holi

Holi symbolizes dawn, light, life and a surge of energy. Holi, a festival, which begins at night, suggests destruction of evil and a hope of good. In the beginning it was celebrated as festival of fertility and harvest but today it is also celebrated in the commemoration of some Hindu legends. Since it symbolizes rebirth. Holi is celebrated in the month of March or in the month of Phalgun (Hindu calendar) or Masi (mid-Feb to mid-March). Holi is also called Kamadahana (destruction of passionate desires). It lasts for two or five days in different parts of the country. It is even celebrated for sixteen days at few places. A fire, Holika, is lit at night nearly in he night; and people offer coconuts and flowers to the Holika.

The origin of Holi is not specific, though many mythological legends are described for its celebration. It is older than the current legends explained for its origin. Holika was Hiranyakashyapu's evil sister, who was immune to fire and she had gained this power, after a long penance. So he told her to use the same for killing his son Prahlad, by sitting on a pyre with Prahlad on her lap. But, instead Prahlad came out of the fire alive and scar free, but in the due process Holika was burnt to death, since her powers lost their effect before Pralhad 's faith. Thus, this day is celebrated to commemorate the good's victory over evil (Holika).

Another narrative of the love of Lord Krishna and Radha is prevalent. Lord Krishna often told his mother, Yashodha, about Radha who unlike him was fair in complexion. So one day, his mother told him to try some colour on her, to see a change in her complexion. Thus, Krishna took different colours and coloured Radha and the Gopis. Radha and Gopis were reluctant to play with colours but they enjoyed it. This instance thus, became an occassion of merry-making every year, where Krishna continued this festival in Vrindavan, Gokul, Nandgaon, Barsana. Thus, this celebration introduced colours to Holi. It is this mischievous spirit of courtship that enters this festival and Holi, thus honours the divine love of Radha and Krishna.

In Tamil Nadu, people honour the sacrifice of Kama Dev (God of Love). Parvati wanted to marry Lord Shiva. But since Lord Shiva was in his penance, he didn't even look at her. The marriage of Lord Shiva and Parvati was necessary. Hence, in order for their marriage all the Devas and Dootas decided to take the help of Manmatha (Kama Deva), in order to arouse a feeling of love for Parvati in Shiva's heart. He was aware of Shiva's third eye which emits out fire and was ready to give his life for a good cause.

Thus, in order to disrupt his penance, Kama Dev shot five of his arrows of love at Lord Shiva's heart at the moment when he was looking at Parvati with his half-open eyes. This interrupted Shiva's penance and he being furious opened his third eye and instantaneously Kama Dev was burned to ashes. Lord Shiva smeared his forehead with Kama Deva's ashes and disappeared. At the request of Rati (Kama Deva's wife), Kama Deva was brought back to life but in a form visible only to Rati and Shiva. This incident of burning off Kama Dev is called kamadahana or Holi in Tamil Nadu. The posture of God burning kama is called kama dahana murthi (Shiva's murthy facing south) and is one of the 25 maheshvara murthis.

Fire marks the beginning of Holi. Earlier it was celebrated all over India for five days. Holi is just not about light, colours and sweets; it is also about wishes, love, friendship. The customs and traditions to lit Holika and the celebration of Holi vary slightly in some parts of the country. One can call Holi by any name he wants but the spirit of Holi can never change. It is called Latthmar holi in Barsana, Nandgaon, Mathura; Dulandi holi in Haryana; Ranpanchami or Shimga or Shimgo in Maharashtra and Goa; Basanti Poornima or Vasant Poornima in Shantiniketan; Dol Poornima, Dol Jatra in West Bengal and Orissa; Hola Mohalla in Punjab; Phagu Poornima or Phagwa in Bihar; Kaman Pandigai in Tamil Nadu.

During Holi, in some states, there is a custom in the undivided Hindu families that the women of the families beat their brother-in-law with her sari rolled up into a rope. This is done in a mock rage as the brother-in-law tries to douse her in colour. In the evening, he brings her sweetmeats. It is also tradition, at few other places, to invite son-in-laws for meals. They are presented with Pyalas - a crisp note of any denomination from rupees five to five hundred along with a glass of a drink. The mother of the married girls gives them Kothli or travel-money in laws or the eldest lady in the family. At few places, mothers give their daughters new dresses. Sweets are an inseparable part of any festival. During the day of Holi boys enjoy Bhang, since it gives one a feel of ecstacy. Thandai from Gujarat is a sweet drink made from milk is also a favourite of the people.

After a boisterous activity, people feast on vegetarian or non-vegetarian meals. But the quiet evenings are marked by visits of relatives and friends. Here, sweets are exchanged which demonstrate a sharing attitude. People all over India like Puranpoli, a very favoured dish from Maharashtra. Other sweets such as gujiya, mathri, petha, malpua, dahi badas, bara, gulgula, phulourie, bigany, mango or tamarind chutney, potato ball, prasad, channa, ghoja, mahambhoog, kheer or sweet rice are also prepared at Holy gatherings in temples. Celebration of Holi differs in various parts. Thus, we see different moods of Holi- the aggressive mood in Nandgaon and Barsana and the serene in West Bengal. There is much adrenaline flow in Punjab during Holi.

11

A Brief History of Classical Dance from South India

Various successive south Indian dynasties, from the Pallavas and Cholas (6th to 9th, and 10th to 14th centuries) to the Andhra kings of Andhra and Tamilnad, and the Maratha rulers of Tanjore (who reigned into the 19th century), contributed some measure of patronage to this dance art. And another line of dance history in the courts can be traced from "Kashmir to Malwa and Sourashtra and then to Karnataka, Andhra and Tamilnad." (Raghavan, 1958).

In the ninth and tenth centur7ies, South India witnessed a sudden spurt of temple building which brought with it a comparable increase of interest in the temple arts. The class of musicians and dancers known as devadasis ("servants of god") enjoyed high status and prosperity at this time and were encouraged in their art (Dasi-attam). "There is hardly a Chola temple and Chola inscription which does not refer to the temple dancers, some of the more distinguished among them even being mentioned by name." (Raghavan). A Tanjore inscription commissioned in 1004 A.D. by the Chola king Rajaraja refers to four hundred devadasis who were attached to the Great Temple, received free living quarters on four neighboring streets, and were allowed tax-free land out of the temple endowment. (de Zoete)

The next well-documented period of dance history is far more recent. In the first half of the 19th century the dance tradition was revitalized and defined anew through the contributions of four talented brothers (known today as the Tanjore Quartet): Chinniah, Sivanandam, Ponniah and Vadivelu. By coordinating their diverse talents, the four managed to organize all the basic dance movements of pure dance into a progressive series of lessons [adavu chapters]. Each adavu (basic unit of motion) was taught in systematic order and then combined with others to produce choreographed sequences based upon the rhythmic contour of a musical composition. (Krishnamoorthy Pillai) In addition the brothers composed new music specifically for the dance, and introduced a different sequence of items which integrated the various aspects of dance and music into a carefully coordinated, aesthetically sound progression. This infusion of creative energy marks the early 19th century as one of the most innovative periods in the history of Indian dance.

Barely fifty years later, however, an unfortunate combination of social and historical circumstances threatened to extinguish the very life of the tradition. During the millenium which had elapsed since the Chola Dynasty the artistic reputation of the temple dancers (devadasis) had gradually become associated with their skills as courtesans. More and more frequently the exalted and respected dance became enlisted into the service of professional, secular pursuits, "an amusement, an entertainment at its best, and an instrument of indiscipline, temptation and vice at its worst." (Vatsyayan, 1968) Throughout the 19th century the clash between Indian social practices and Western reforms under the British produced some interesting (and some tragic) results. Indian families of wealth and status were encouraged by their British counterparts to allow young women the opporutinity of a liberal education. Yet "one of the great objections urged against the education of respectable Indian girls was that they might be mistaken for dancing girls, who alone of their sex could read, write, sing and play a musical instrument." (de Zoete)

Many devadasis may have been bright and able artists, but by the end of the 19th century they were no longer respected members of the Indian social community. It took the combined zeal of Christian missionaries and morality-conscious Hindus to finally tip the balance against devadasis. It must be admitted that many prostitutes on the fringe of the devadasis community had taken up "nautch-dancing", an impoverished and conspicuously sexual version of the classical dance, to attract business. And the reform minded zealots who led the anti-nautch campaign were hardly disposed to make fine distinctions between one form of the accursed dance, and another. "It was beyond the conception of the Victorian Christian to imagine that faith could be expressed through so immodest and voluptuous a medium as the 'nautch dance'."(Singha)

Few realized that the authentic lineage of classical dance, while temporarily shamed and driven underground during this unseemly commotion, was being preserved among certain artistically distinguished families. Several of the great teachers (nattuvanars), some quite old, who carried the knowledge and substance of the art in their heads, "lived neglected lives in remote villages." (Singha) This was a difficult time for such people, and were it not for the courageous and persistent efforts of a handful of supporters, the art might well have been totally suppressed.

Three artists stand out in sharp relief for their efforts in restoring the classical dance to its traditional place of honor in India.UDAY SHANKAR'S great contribution to Indian dance was his international experience and perspective, coupled with a vigorously independent style. Another well known Indian dance personality to come under the influence of internationalism was RUKMINI DEVI, founder of the Kalashetra International Arts Center in Tiruvanmiyur, Madras. Showing an early and stubborn sense of cultural independence she espoused Theosophy and married Dr. George Arundale, while still the young daughter of a highly respected Brahmin family in Tanjore. But it was her scandalous decision to take up classical dance (and her intellectually disciplined dedication to the art) which focused public attention on the possibility that the dance might contain something of interest and value in the lives of 'respectable' people. As an accomplished dancer and well-travelled lecturer, Rukmini Devi has made dramatic contributions to the revival of Indian classical dance, and continues to supply the profession with numerous dancers and musicians who receive their training at Kalakshetra.

At the height of the anti-nautch crusade in 1925, a young dancer of seven named BALASARASWATI was presented for the first time at the Ammanakshi Amman temple in Kanchipuram. The several leading exponents of music and dance who were present that evening are said to have been deeply moved by the technical assurance and natural expressive range exhibited in this child's performance. In the years that followed, Balasaraswati lived a regimen of dance and music, lessons and practise, which left her virtually no time for play or leisure but helped shape her into the greatest classical dancer of her time.

"Balasaraswati made the public Bharata Natyam conscious, not by conscious efforts as a torch-bearer or a reformer but by the beauty and eloquence of her dancing. It was left to others to fight prejudices and stupidity, do research, delve into the past. But Balasaraswati made us aware of the living miracle of Bharata Natyam to be seen and to be enraptured."(Menon)

The long political campaign for Indian independence, and its final realization in 1947, inspired great interest among Indians in the cultural history of their country. Literature, the plastic arts, music—but above all, classical dancing—were enshrined as the living embodiment of a thriving cultural heritage which could be traced back over two thousand years of continuous development. Along with all this recognition came a need to endow the classical dance of Tamilnad and Andhra with a suitable name.

Several names had been used in the past: popular terms such as sadir and dasi-attam were proposed, as well as the literary terms adal and kuttu, and the names which had enjoyed some currency in music and dance circles, cinna melam and Bharatam; nautch was the only term everyone seemed to agree upon—negatively. Eventually the term Bharata Natyam (the dance of Bharata) took hold, and the solo tradition of South Indian classical dance is currently known by this name.

"The new name...invested (the dance) with the requisite status which was needed in the circumstances of its revival, and served to underline its classical moorings. The name at once established the form in a historical continuity which went up to Mohenjo-daro and the Rgveda. An understanding of the art in such a space-time has its own value for appreciation, criticism and improvement of the art." (Raghavan, 1958)

DANCES OF TAMIL NADU

Tamil Nadu, the south Indian state of India, has been the focal point of culture, art and tradition, since ancient times. The various kingdoms that ruled Tamil Nadu, added on the charm of this beautiful land. They build exquisite temples and encouraged the development of culture in the state. The folk music and dances are a part of Tamil cultural ethos. Dances of vibrant Tamil Nadu are inspired by the temples build by the Chola, Pallava and other dynasties. The dances of this state are very popular across the country and the world. The most prominent dance of Tamil Nadu is the gracious dance form of Bharata Natyam. Other popular folk dance forms are Mayil Attam, Bommalattam or Puppet Show, Kummi, Kai Silambu Attam and many others.

Bharata Natyam, A Popular Dance Form

The famous Bharata Natyam, originates from the state of Tamil Nadu in South India and is one of the oldest and most popular dance styles in India. The word 'Bharata Natyam' is a combination of many various attributes, that complete the dance form. These attributes are :- Bharata Natyam = Bhava (expression) + Raga (musical mode) + Tala (rhythm) Natyam (dance).

Bharata Natyam is directly derived from the devotional dances performed in the temples of South India from the tenth century to the middle of this century. This form of dance has been carried by 'nattuvanars' and ritualistic dancers called devadasis, in the temples of south India.

Bharata Natyam is like a poetry in motion. It's history has been written in the Natya Sastra by the great sage Bharata. It is a highly traditional and stylized dance form, which has been immortalized in successive generations, by the great graceful dancers and by the renowned sculptors who have demonstrated the perfection of Bharata's technique on the exotic temples of Tamil Nadu.

Bharatanatyam is a blend of the abstract and the emotional and is derived from its fusion of two prime elements, nritta (pure dance or dance without interpretive meaning) & nritya (expressive dance). This lovely dance form has derived much of its intense, dramatic impact from the juxtaposition and contrast with which both nritta and nritya are utilized. Nritta consists adavus, which are the basic dance units of Bharatanatyam. Each adavu contains 3 essential elements, a basic standing position (sthanaka), movement of the legs & feet (chari) and decorative hand gestures (nritta-hasta).

Folk Dances, The Essence of Tamil Nadu

Mayil Attam

This beautiful folk dance is performed by girls dressed as peacocks, decorated with peacock feathers and a glittering head-dress complete with a beak. This beak can be opened and closed with the help of a thread tied to it, and manipulated from within dress.

Bommalattam or Puppet Show

Bommalattum or the puppet shows are held in almost every village of Tamil Nadu during festivals and fairs and for that matter in every village of India. The puppets used for these shows are made of cloth, wood, leather, etc. They are controlled by strings or wires. The persons stand behind a screen and the puppets are held in front. The stories told in the puppet shows are from Ved-puranas, history and folklore. These puppets shows are very amusing and interests both adults and children.

Kummi

Kummi is among the most important and famous ancient dance forms of village dances of Tamil Nadu. It originated when there were no musical instrument. The participants form a circle and clap their hands to match to the rhythm. This dance form is performed by women. Kummi is of many varieties, such as, Poonthatti Kummi, Deepa Kummi, Kulavai Kummi, Kadir Kummi and Mulaipari Kummi etc are the well-known ones.

This famous dance is usually performed during temple festivals, Pongal, the harvest festival and during family functions like celebrating the coming of age (onset of puberty) of the girl-child etc. The first line of the song is sung by the leading lady, which the others repeat.

Kai Silambu Attam

Famous Kai Silambu Attam is mainly performed in temples during Navaratri festival. The dancers wear ankle-bells and hold anklets or silambu in their hands, which makes a rhythmic noise when shaken. The dance is performed to praise all female deities, specially to praise the powerful angry goddess - Kali or Durga.

DANCES OF KARNATAKA

Kunitha - A Ritual Dance

The ritualistic dances of Karnataka are known as Kunitha. One of such ritualistic dances is the Dollu Kunitha. It is a popular dance form of Karnataka, accompanied by the beats of decorated drums and singing. This dance form is mainly performed by the men of the shepherd community known as the Kuruba community. The Dollu Kunitha is characterized by vigorous drum beats, quick movements and synchronized group formations. Another dance form of Karnataka is the Puja Kunitha. In this dance form the dancers carry a wooden structure having a deity on their heads.

Other dance form - Devare Thatte Kunitha, Yellammana Kunitha, Suggi Kunitha are named after the deity or the symbol or instruments which are balanced on the head or held in the hand of the dancer. The Pata Kunitha, the Gorava Kunitha and the Kamsale are some of the other common ritualistic dances.

Classical Dances

Among the classical dances of India, the Mysore style of Bharatanatyam, is the oldest and most popular dance form. It is widely performed here. Other mainstream classical dances here include Kuchipudi and Kathak.

Folk Dances

Krishna Parijatha

Krishna Parijatha is a popular folk theater art form of North Karnataka. It is an amalgamation of Yakshagana and Byalatta, portraying stories or incidents from the great epic Mahabharata.

Bhootha Aradhane

This dance form is widely performed in the coastal areas of Karnataka. The Bhootha Aradhane or devil worship, includes a procession of idols depicting 'bhoothas". This procession is characterized by the beating of drums and bursting of firecrackers. After the end of the procession, the idols are placed on a plinth. Then, a dancer personifying a devil dances around the plinth with sword and jingling bells. The dancer dances vigorously at one point of time and then slows down, signifying that he is now a divine person.

Nagamandala

This ritualistic dance form is performed by the people of south Karnataka. It is done to tranquilize the serpent spirit and is an extravagant affair held throughout the night. The dancers called the Vaidyas are dressed as nagakannika. They dance all night long around a huge figure, drawn on the sacred ground with natural colors, in a pandal specially erected in front of the shrine. This ritualistic dance is generally performed between December to April.

Dance Drama

Yakshagana

Yakshagana is a dance drama performed in the coastal areas of Karnataka. This unique dance form is a perfect blend of dance, music, songs, scholarly dialogues and colorful costumes. Yakshagana mesmerizes each and everyone in the audience with its enchanting music and colorful performances.

The word Yakshagana litreally means celestial music. This dance drama is also performed throughout the night, usually after the winter crop has been reaped.

Odissi Dance of Orissa

The sculptures in Brahmeswara temples and in Konark Sun temple dancing hall depicts the art of traditional dances of Orissa. Odissi dance - the traditional dance form of Orissa owes its birth to the temple dance performed by the devadasis. In mid of 20th century the entire Odissi dance form was revived with the support of the Abhinaya Chandrika and was given a new look. Orissa also enjoys a rich tradition of tribal and folk dances as well. Chhau is a martial dance form derived from of Orissa's age-old tradition. Danda Nata dance performed for a longer duration has acrobatic sequences, which are quite thrilling. Ranapa — dances includes balancing of talented dancers on bamboo stilts, which is a great source of attractions among the natives.

Odissi dance, the soul of Orissa State is the highly galvanized, rapturous form of dance. Possibly the oldest classical dance form, one must sit through a performance to experience its sheer lyrical grace.

Orissa treasures some of the most world-renowned temples, each carved out of stones and rocks, displaying the people's religious faith. These temples are the 'magnum opus' showcasing the skills of master craftsmen, sculptures and architects which, later on became the center of art and culture. It was here that Odissi Dance — one of India's enchanting dance-forms took birth. In ancient times the Odissi dance was performed by the Devadasis (the temple dancers) in the temples of Orissa on the occasions of holy ceremony and rituals.

Charming Odissi Dance

It is a well entrenched and systematized classical dance form of India, where the methodology, the characteristics, its style and stages, are almost indescribable. Today Odissi dance is considered as a dance of love, ecstasy and deep passion, divine all combined together.

Folk Dances of Orissa

Ghumra Dance

The special feature of 'Ghumra' Dance is musical instrument — a kind of drum that produces a deep musical sound. The dancer ties ghumra - the drum round his neck and plays it all the while dancing. The player sings and dances to its tune at social functions like marriages or any religious festival.

There are also competitions that are held among the groups. Each group consists of about twenty people and the dance goes on the whole night. It is the most lively form of dance that attractions attention of tourist.

Chhau Dance

Chhau Dance is one of the most important tribal dances of Orissa. The basic postures and styles of this dance favor the postures of a fighter in a traditional fight. It is also known as Phari Khanda Khela — the game of sword and shield or Rookmar Nacha - the dance of offence and defense.

Chhau dance is mainly drawn from the episodes of Ramayana , Mahabharata and Krishna - the great legends of India. Most of the dance sequence represents the fight of 'Abhimanyu' with the 'Sapta Rathis', the killing of 'Mahishasura', 'Shiva Tandav', 'Kirat Arjuna', etc. There are also significant tribal themes like 'Sabara Toka', 'Kala Chakra', 'Sabara Sabaruni'. The themes of Chhau are thus legendary, mellowed with grace displaying the story of opera which is at times co-related to visual poetry.

Naga Folk Dance

In this dance the dancer dresses like a worrier and wears a special dress. He carries a shield of the hide of the rhinoceros, a sword, a gun, a horn used as a whistle, an iron shield, bow and arrows, tiger skin, and a bell. The bows have the face of a tiger that looks magnificent. His crown is embellished with splendid peacock feathers, ware a bead string around his neck, a mirror and a string of beads on his wrist, small bell attached to the thigh. He applied a yellow powder to his entire body and marks his forehead with vermilion. He wears an artificial beard and moustache. A complete appearance of a dancer gives a brutish look. The most interesting part of the dance is that it doesn't have any song, it is just a gesture, face expressions and the music that rules the entire show.

The other forms of folk dance like 'Humo', 'Bauli', 'Jhulki', 'Jamudali', 'Mayalajar', 'Gunjikata', 'Rasarkeli' and 'Puchi' are prevalent among the Oriyas and natives of Orissa.

12

The Great Dance: The Myth of the Metaphysical

INTRODUCTION

Every society has its own mythology of being, a way of understanding and sharing experiences that would otherwise remain untold. The validity of such tales is not as important as the means of expression. In this vein, many ethnographic films attempt to find a negotiated means of representing cultural myths in a manner that is authentic. This authenticity, however, is localised in the negotiated meaning between the subject, the filmmaker, and the audience (Woodward, 1997:2). This implies a certain degree of conversion from one cultural to another; a mythical transformation of meaning that seeks to bridge the gap between the "other" and us. This transcendence is never neutral in its ability to assign agency, instead, there are cultural signifiers that are in operation that no only create difference, but assign power and knowledge.

The representation of the Bushman has been mythologised through film. The commodification of the Bushman image is embedded with the discourse of film and its ability to re-present reality, this results in the spectator's understanding being rooted in the filmmakers ability to convert cultural practices onto celluloid. It is this process, from the empirical to artistic form, that allows for intervention of the part of the filmmaker. An intervention that seeks to assert the Western tradition that the visual is synonymous with knowledge (Fabian in Gordon, 2002).

This essay will critically discuss the representation of !Xo Bushman mythology in The Great Dance: A Hunter's Tale. This representation is will be analysed in terms of how documentary discourse functions in the film to represent the metaphysical world-view of the Bushman and their myth of transformation and being. This will be achieved by anaylsing how the stylistic conventions employed in the film act as a nexus between Western understanding and Bushman mythology.

SYNOPSIS

The Great Dance is an ethnographic documentary that explores the Bushman traditional hunting practices as it relates to their cultural belief of harmony with nature. An ethnogrpahic film is one that attempts to "explain or describe some aspects of another culture to members of the film maker's own culture" (Nichols, 1981:238) It depicts the lives of the !Xo people of the Kalahari as we follow them on the mythical and spiritual journey of hunting. The hunt, in the documentary, is understood to be like dancing, whereby the is a sense of unison between hunter/dancer and the natural world. The documentary attempts to depict the !Xo people's hunter-gather lifestyle and the provisions they make in order to survive. Their traditions and beliefs are show to be influenced by the Western world and modernity to the extent that the film concludes by stating that the !Xo's hunting rights have been revoked by governmental organisations.

The film is highly stylised and it uses various cinematic techniques to portray the bushman as mythical beings that are at one with the world. Through the eyes of the hunter the film seeks to reveal a world that would not have been visible to Western eyes, a world seemingly lost in its traditions that are becoming increasingly affected by Western rationale and policy. However, the aim of the film, primarily, is not to invoke sympathy but instead invoke a sense of celebration of the metaphysical ways of the !Xo and their traditions. This, however, is not without contradiction, as the film itself provides an unnatural vantage point into their lives from which Western metaphysical understandings of the world are rehashed through the magic of technology.

MYTHOLOGIES AND SOCIETY

Myths are a part of human existence; they serve as epistemological markers inferred from personal experiences of the world that are expressed collectively. Claude Levi-Strauss, an influential anthropologist, argues that myths "express unconscious wishes which are somehow inconsistent with conscious experience" (in Cook & Bernink, 1999:328), the use of the word "inconsistent" is favored over the common belief of myths being false. Falseness is an idea invoked from the modernist paradigm, in which empiricalism is favored as a source of meaning over the symbolic exchange of meaning found in myths. However, myths contain their own degree of 'truth' embedded in the cultural used to express them. These myths find truth in their ability to provide people with a view of the world and a set of values that can be as important as any scientifically verifiable fact. This interpretative model of myth is the source of cultural understanding as well as the core of many religious held beliefs about 'being-in-the-world' and our transcendental capacity to connect to that which can not be perceived or measured. The collective understanding of this metaphysical presence in the world is expressed, rather than recorded, in symbolic systems that are as arbitrarily link to the physical world as the myths transported within them.

Myth: Characteristics and Function

According to Rollo May, a contemporary existential psychologist and theorist, myths are the vehicle for meaning and they serve a need of "making sense in senseless world" (in Hergenhahn, 2005:531). In this vein myths have four primary functions: (1) they provide a sense of identity, (2) a sense of community, (3) they support moral values, and (4) provide a means of dealing with the mysteries of creation (ibid). These are functions that cannot be understood in terms of Western empiricalism and rationale; instead myths are humankind's engagement with one another on a symbolic level that functions as a means of establishing a sense of past, present and future. May comments on this in his paper The Cry for Myth (in Hergenhahn, 2005:532):

> We awake after a sleep of many centuries to find ourselves in a new and irrefutable sense of myth of humankind. We find ourselves in a new world community; we cannot destroy the parts without destroying the whole...Perhaps it will again be possible to study man scientifically and still see him as whole.

May poetically highlights the progression of man as a social being, defined not by the understanding of deconstructed fragments of being, but instead as man in his totality and wholeness. Myths form part of our collective consciousness (to use Jung's term; Hergenhahn, 2005: 511) that cannot be reduced to pre-modern tenets of human existence, progression, in this sense, would deny the process of becoming.

Percy Cohen identifies five characteristics of myths as they pretain to their historical functions and position within society: a myth is a narrative of events; the narrative has a sacred quality; the sacred communication is made in symbolic form; at least some of the events and objects which occur in the myth neither occur nor exist in the world other than that of myth itself; and the narrative refers in dramatic form to origins or transformations (Cohen, 1969:1). The medium through which myths are conveyed takes the form of narrative; this story structure involves characters, settings, themes, morals, and traditional ways of understanding the world.

The 'sacred' nature of these stories lies in their poetic form through which a nexus is created that merges past, present and future. This can only be achieved though symbolic interaction, a process that places its emphasis not on the boundaries of the symbolic form (e.g. language, paintings, images, etc.) but in the thematic triggers that seeks to probe the collective unconscious of the cultural. Cohen highlights an interesting issue for contemporary society in his fourth characteristic. The meaning of myth lies not in the uses of objects and events that occur in myths, instead Cohen isolates meaning within the discourse of the myth. In this vein, the discourse functions as a means that naturalises the myth in its own form, this creates a distinction between the meaning inferred from myths and their longevity as mythical and magical stories of the past. This is interesting because the metaphysical referent, if such a term can be used, of myths is achieved through interpretation, an interpretation that is, as Nichols (1981:238) suggest, culturally determined. Therefore the mode of expression is only significant to the extent that such a referent can be expressed in terms of the culturally significant meaning attached to the series of images depicted on screen.

DOCUMENTARY DISCOURSE

John Grierson, a British filmmaker and producer, describes documentary as the "creative treatment of actuality" (Grierson in Plantinga, 1997:10), this because film, by nature, attempts to 're-present' events within the conventions of the medium. In this vein documentaries have been classified as "non-fiction", however this doesn't fully acknowledge the abstraction and organizing of filmic materials within a visual text. This classification undermines presents of a narrative within non-fiction, "narrative should not be seen as exclusively fictional but instead should be merely contrasted to other (non-narrative) ways of assembling and understanding data" (Branigan in Plantinga, 1997:84). And as Plantinga (1997:85) explains, the difference between fiction and non-fiction lies not in the filmic discourse, but the "stance taken toward the world it projects".

The notion of a "projected world" is useful is explaining the nature of visual image and its relationship to the physical. This projected world is only produced within the medium of film, a medium that incorporates its own means of production and discourse: "The discourse is the means by which the projected world or story events are communicated; its principle strategies, at the most abstract level, are selection, order, emphasis, and voice" (Plantinga, 1997:85). This description explains that the world of film involves an intervention by the filmmaker in some way or another, and it is this intervention, or engagement, that lends film to be regarded as a cultural product.

The distinction between fiction films and documentary has proven to be problematic. Although the documentary film is based on facts and actualities, the nature of film does, however, place limitations on objectivity and truth. The labeling of documentary as 'non-fiction' may be misleading in this sense because it leads us to discount documentaries fictive elements. Rosen (in Renov, 1993:3) states that the terrain of fiction and documentary inhabit one another. Consider how we percived a documentary film, the parameters of documentary are clearly identified as containing a clear beginning, middle, and an end. This classic structure presupposes some form of narrative structure, and it is this narravity that exists in documentary that serves as a means to represent events in such a manner as to formulate a particular portrayal of events.

Consider that in fiction films characters are presented to the viewer with certain attitudes, beliefs, opinions, and behaviors. The viewer internalizes these character dimensions to be naturalized within the films narrative and discourse. Although the viewer is aware that the events portrayed are, in fact, staged, there is a degree of suspension of disbelief on the part of the spectator (this is why viewers have emotional reactions to the events on screen).

The reason for this is that film offers a perspective on the world that is naturalized through the very encapsulated nature of the information on screen. Any inferences made outside what is depicted is made solely by the spectator. This is because film involves the manipulation of symbols and signs within the conventions of film, and the meaning attached to these symbols is culturally determined and embedded with the individual belonging to a specfic culture.

Documentary films have specific expectations around the validity of truth in documentary films because they present themselves as factually based, or epistemically sound. It is important to remember that although documentary films are based on 'truths', these truths still need to be portrayed thought the medium of film. The reading of truth is also culturally embedded as documentary films call upon the "regime of truth" specific to culture (Hall, 1997:49). In this vein, the ontological agency of film does not allow for the seamless conversion of facts-to-film. Instead what films offers is a visual array of images and sound that are received by the viewer, and it this reception that is culturally determined.

Myth and Discourse

The constructive nature of documentary discourse, as well as its narrative structure, positions it in the realm of myth. The projected world is a symbolic construction design to promote an argument about the nature of the events it depicts (Plantinga, 1997:85). If we consider film as contemporary medium through which meaning may be inferred, then the cinematic techniques implimented must serve to reveal this meaning. Although the 'truthfulness' of documentary is heighly contested, like myths, the visuality of the medium is secondary to the "knowingness" embedded with the discourse of the film. Like myths, documentary film make use of a transcendental sign system that creates a disavowal of perception in exchange for metaphysical meaning. This because the images presented are, in fact, absent as they only exist within the cinematic apparatus and are not localised in reality.

Documentary films are mythological because of their ability to infer meaning through a symbolic system that draws on the metaphysical connections made by the spectator. These connections are triggered by the image, however, knoweldge and meaning are not inherent in the representation. Instead, meaning is a negotiation between the medium, as a symbolic system, the image, and the spectator. This triad draws on our understanding and willingness to establish collective meaning through the stories and symbols utilised in film.

Micheal Renov states that one of the tendencies of documentary is to express (Renov, 1993:32), this expression is fundamentally a mythical process because it implies a transformational process that encourages the use of the medium as a expressive tool, rather than one of scientific inscription. The poetic qualities of a documentary film thus act as a trigger to draw attention to the meaning create by the image, and the belief of the image itself is truthful to the extent that the image functions as a means of expression by the filmmaker. Authenticity, in this sense, is not an objective and universal understanding of the phyiscal but instead a collective process though which fragments of subjective experiences are continually shared and re-created. This cyclic nature of meaning is a tenet of both myth and the documentary, insofar as to suggest that film is the contemporary myth-making machine, the 'truthfulness' of which, is only secondary to the meaning impose by the image.

The Paradox of Enthographic Documentary

When we consider documentary to be a 'myth-making machine' the ethnographic film become somewhat problematic in terms of the duality of representation at play.

Bill Nichols, one of the hallmark documentary theorists, states that ethnographic films "attempt to explain or describe some aspect of another culture to memebers of the filmmaker's own culture" (Nichols, 1981: 238). When we consider that a culture's understanding of the world, as well as their sense of identity, is embedded within their mythological transference of meaning, then the idea of the image, created by a member of another culture, becomes problematic. This is because the process of representation at play in film is subject to the symbolic conversion of the physical, as well as the interplay between absence and presence. If then we say that ethnographic film is a product of modernism and Western empiricalism, then the process through which the ethnographic film seeks to "explain or describe" cultural differences must be seen to present a fallacy embedded in the very cultural differences (i.e. norms, beliefs, world-view, practices, etc.) between the filmmaker and the subject.

If the ethnographic filmmaker is to consider a particular culture worth 'documenting', then the level of difference must be great enough to encourage such a decision. And because this usually translates into a difference of perceptions regarding the nature of reality, then contradiction of documenting a group for their difference becomes redundant to a degree. This is because the nature of the cinematic image does not allow for cross-cultural psycho-social inferences, accuring as a direct result of the meaning inferred from the symbolic systems used by a particular culture, instead the images acts as merely a tool of capturing otherness rather than understanding it.

This goes beyond mere authenticity because the focus of Western ethnographic films is to record a cultural that is of significant difference, rather than close proximity to that of the filmmaker (Renov, 1993:21). This translates into a division based upon development and Western progression. The metaphysical orientation and beliefs of the cultures being film must then be understood through the lens of modernism, hence the ethnogrpahic film presents a myth within a myth due to contradiction between what is culturally represented and they actual signified, and it is this inter-textuality of myth formation that creates a paradox between what is shown and experienced by the spectator and the actual myth upheld by the culture in question.

Otherness, Power, and the Enthographic Discourse

Hansen, Needham and Nichols (1991) make a claim for the thematic comparison between ethnographic film and pornography. The authors attempt to draw a simalarity between object-subject relationship presented in ethnographic film and subsequent power ascribed to viewer when bearing witness to the spectatacle of ethnographic film. This power is established though a pleasure principle that is embedded in the voyeristic and fetishistic nature of film (Nichols et al, 1991).

In ethnographic films power accurs as a result of others' "looked-at-ness" produced as a result of the gaze produced by the camera. The subjects of enthnographic films are in fact the "objects of desire and spectacle" (Hansen et al, 1991:207). The power of documentary discourse is derived from the representation of the other in such a manner as to invoke a sense of mastery over the image. Although this is already prescribed in the nature of the image itself, it is primarlily impacted on by filmmaker's own societial myths of power and pleasure.

This may involve stereotyping as a means of simultaneously creating otherness and sameness. The 'objects' of ethnographic film are established as "other" through their visual representation, whilst at the same time a sense of enduring similaritiy is created in the othering process. The result is the pleasure of cultural knowingness, this occurs primary through cinematic identification with the camera but also though the metaphorical role of the image in simplifying inter-cultural differences (Hansen, 1991:204).

BUSHMEN AND THE PHOTOGRPAHIC INTERVENTION

The concerns of the ethnographic film have largely been to record, reveal, and express the ways of another culture (Renov, 1993:21). Ethnographers have long been interested in the culture of Bushman as the primitive 'other'. However the results have produced a discourse of the Bushman through the eyes of colonialism and the Western desire for cultural knowledge. As Gordon (In Landu & Kaspin, 2002: 214) states: "The camera has provided a meeting place for science and fantasy, if only because the Western empirical tradition assumes that visualizing a society is synonymous for understanding it". This epistemological tenacity embedded in the image has served as the premise from which Western cultural understanding originates.

The Colonial Image and the Bushman

Issues of authenticity and objectivity have long hindered the 'capturing' the image of the Bushman, since the invention of the stereoscopic picture during the 1860's photographers found that colonial intervention was to be an influential factor in documenting these pre-modern natives. In 1909 Rudolf Poch made the first film on the Bushman, he found that "the physical nature of the Bushman was absolutely different from that of all low races he had previously seen" (Poch in Gordon, 2002:215). From Poch's statement we can already see the value judgment that modern filmmakers make that underpin their cultural investigations. A perception that undoubtly affects the documentation of the Bushman and their representation through visual media.

The result of such Western intervention is an image that serves to create a discourse of the Bushman that is something other than the Bushman themselves, a pseudo-image of stereotyping and colonial commodification. The Bushman's identity has become reduce to the series of images and films that have sought to capture these "native primitives" thought modernist paradigms of detractive comparison. This comparison results from "othering" the Bushman in such as way as to create a superiority continuum between the filmmakers and their subjects. It is this difference that is the reason that the Bushman have become an interesting culture to Western ethnographers, and it is improtant because difference "because it is essential to meaning" (Hall, 1997: 234). In this vein the image of the Bushman serves as a tool of Western self-fulfilling prophecy, resulting in a stream of stereotypical images that fail to capture the essence of these "tribes" in their totality. Bester and Buntman (1999:50) argue that it is this simplification of the Bushman's identity, constructed by colonial "others", that has resulted in the image reducing individuals and communities to easily consumable commodities.

The Myth of the Bushman

To commodify the Bushman through filmic and photographic intervention is to deny the very metaphysical orientation of these communities that spurred ethnographic interest in the first place. The mysticism of these pre-modern communities has resulted in a colonial gaze that places the Bushman at the center of the spectacle. The Bushman "hunt" has become one of the primary source of "entertainment-driven archetypes pivotal to the uninterrupted lifestyle and survival of the people called the 'Bushman'" (Bester & Buntman, 1999:52). This typifies the need of the Western image to create its own mythology of the Bushman through mythologising the symbols of the Bushman (bare-breastedness, the wearing of skins, a "click" language, etc.) and the visual codes that authorise this mythologisation (silhouettes at sunset, exaggerated body profiles, an emphasis on "natural" locations, distorted cinematic landscapes), (Bester & Buntman, 1999, 53). Through this mythologising process the Bushman's own sense of cultural identity and mythology is comprimised because the depiction of their culture is subject to the judgment imposed on them by the tools and apparatus of the modern Western mindset. Bester and Buntman (1999:57-58) comment on this myth as follows:

[The] photographic tradition, in popular, scientific, and academic discourses, has largely been informed and overshadowed by a myth of the "Bushman" as a unified, pre-colonial culture of "otherness," frozen in an ethnographic presents...While the convergence of documentary and aesthetic sensibility is not a problem in itself, the use of an aesthetic sensibility that merely entrenches Bushman(ia) is problematic.

What Bester and Buntman indicate is that the intention of ethnographic documentation is flawed, not in its theoretical purpose but in the nature of the image as it seeks to create a projected world in which the Bushman are presented. Therefore, the discourse of documentary presupposes a unequal power relations that creates a textual distance between the photographer and what is being photographed. In this vein the image of Bushman is subjectived to the signifying practices of the image of the culture in control of the production of the image.

BUSHMAN CANNED HUNTING: THE MYTH OF THE METAPHYSICAL

The Great Dance attempts to resolve the paradox of ethnographic film by utlising various cinematic techniques designed to reduce the void between cultures. The bushman are presented as a tribal society that recognise the world as a system of transformation that is interconnected to their own understanding of the nature and the universe. The emphasis on the metaphysical nature of being is considered, to an extent, to be lost by modern societies and their pragmatic values and sense of identity. In this vein, the film acts as a mythical machine through which pre-modern being-in-the-world notions are expressed within the narrative.

As mentioned, narratives are the channel through which myths come to be expressed and shared. The Great Dance presents a story of the !Xo Bushman and their ability to transend humanity in order to connected to the world in which they find themselves.

The myth of Transformation

The film presents the notion that the Bushman are able to understand the natural world to such a degree that they are inseperable from the enviournment they inhabit. This is achieved cinematically by imitating the hunter's metonymic process of becoming the animal they hunt. During the film the hunters are frequently juxtapositioned with shot of animals, this is paired with opitical effects that distort colour and perspective. The result is a clear sense that these Bushman undergo a transformation of spirit, whereby the distinction between animal and Bushman is blurred, in doing so the Bushman are seen to have a deep metaphysical understanding and connection to their world. Clelland-Stoke (in Tomaselli & Mclennan-Dodd, 2004:235) comments on this technique in the film:

> *Whereas a conventional continuity sequence may involve a shot of someone running, followed by a shot of her footprints that the audience would assume were hers by virtue of the juxtapositioning of the two shots, The Great Dance plays off these conventions and correlating audience assumptions to suggest that man and animal are the same. For example... A shot of a hunter drinking from the waterhole is followed by a shot of an animal's reflection in the water.*

This myth of transformation in the !Xo culture serves as a long standing sense of cultural identity, through which a sense of peace and oneness with nature. The depiction of this myth is somewhat subversive due to the films attempt to capture this culture phenomena, leading some authors to suggest that the film dehumanises the Bushman because there is not distinction between the !Xo and the animals they hunt (Tomaselli & Mclennan-Dodd in van Eeden & du Preez, 2004:236). This highlights the paradox of ethnogrpahic film as it fails to convey the metaphysical beliefs of a culture, instead ethnographic film can only make use of the films symbolic system in conveying such a belief. This results in an interpretation that represents the Bushman as primitive savages that lack the progressive knowledge achieved through modernism. This may be a rather cynical view of the Bushman's image, but it serves as a example of how cultural myths cannot be translated through film to reproduce the same cultural experience as that of the ethnographic subject.

Conversely, the lack of clear distinction between man and animal can be seen as a universalising agent of the Bushman myth. Rather then stressing the de-humanising of the Bushman, it is this one-ness with the world that highlights the modernism removal from a seemingly premodern mindset (hence the need to document the Bushman's culture as something other than that of the filmmaker), a factor that is lost in the ethnographic film by its mere form and disavowal from the mythology of such cultures.

Hunting the Hunter

Just as the !Xo Bushman undergo a mythical transformation of form in the films narrative, so does the film's commentary on the Bushman's placement in the contemporary world. The film progressively depicts the Bushman as becoming more and more influenced and affected by modernity. As Tomaselli & Mclennan-Dodd (in Eeden & du Preez, 2004:232) state: "The Great Dance interfaces them [the !Xo Bushman] in a direct engagement with modernity". In doing so the film presents a transformation of the Bushman from being natural entities in this surreal landscape to having their hunting rights revoked by the government. This transformation of the Bushman is presented as 'unnnatural' in this sense as the film sets up the Bushman as being one with his environment throughout the film.

Throughout the film the filmmakers attempt to create a 'man as animal' ideal, as discussed above. This places the Bushman as transcendental beings that are not bound by form. At one point in the film the Bushman's hunt is interrupted by the border of their hunting land from government property. The viewer is shown a Antelope running against the gate trying to break through, there is no juxtapositioned shot of the Bushman doing the same (as with the waterhole), instead such a comparison is implied as the film makes use of the Bushman-animal indexical relationship already firmly established. At this point in the film the spectator is suddenly shaken out of the myth of natural purity and instead we are led to consider the implications of such a barrier in terms of the viewer's relation to the Bushman.

If we consider the camera as a means of capturing a subject, as the Bushan appear as incomplete abstractions of their physical form, then surely the knowledge that what is captured is done so under a restrictive circumstances, reducing it to the equivilent of 'canned bushman hunting'. This strongly reminds us that the postion of power that the spectator holds is culturally determined, and the knoweldge of the Bushman's culture we unquestionably absorb is more a construction that we realise. It is this demythologising, achieved as a results of exposing the Bushmans myth of transformation of form through film, that could promote such remarks regarding the Bushman as an animal. It is Western modernism that has brought about this debunking of Bushman myth, because the Bushman are very much interested in retaining cultural traditions. The narrator goes to state that "new ways are not always better ways", this is in opposition to the modernist belief and faith in the new. In this vein the resultant image, in which the Bushman's own metaphysical beliefs are represented, triggers a sense of nostalgia for the Western Spectator, as we have been seemingly removed from our own metaphysical understandings of the world.

By presenting the viewer with an enclosed wilderness (as the Bushman are in fact inhabiting a clearly marked and divided terrain), the power of the discourse in promoting a sense of otherness is enhanced. This is because the process of "othering" involves the recognition of social difference as well as physical difference. The image presented on screen provides the iconic sense of difference (Iconic is the sense that the image draws attention to that which is not there). This results in the filmmaker presenting the Bushman in a position of powerlessness cause by a lack of cultural tenacity and landloss in the face of modernity; a perception brought about by a physical separation between 'them' and 'us' cause by ethnographic viewing practices.

We feel powerful as we chase the Bushman through the bushveld as they conduct their own hunt, we are the omnipresent colonialists closing in on them, exposing, revealing, and demythologising their way of life.

CONCLUSION

The ethnographic film has long been concerned with scientific validity of the culture being documented. These concerns stem from the constructivistic nature of film and the level of require intervention/engagement on the part of the filmmaker. The result is a representation of culture that is protrayed through the eyes of filmmaker's culture. The idea that we come to understand another's culture through our own understanding of the world is problematic. This is because the process of understanding the 'other' is hindered by the signifying practices embedded in images.

The Great Dance is an interesting ethnographic film becuause it attempts to interpret and transform the cultural myths and beliefs of the !Xo Bushman into a visual spectatcle. This visual spectatcle is design to create a point of indentification for Western audiences in order to promote the understanding of the Bushman's metaphysical ontology. However it is through this very process that the cultural integrity of the Bushman is simplified in order to create a complete sense of understanding and meaning with Western Audiences.

The Film also comments on the impact of modernity on the Bushman's own metaphysical beliefs. In doing so the film creates a sense of nostalgia for the Western spectator, an effect achieve by the very processes the filmmaker uses to convert the Bushman's metaphysical beliefs into a visual array of images. This presents a paradox of sorts, our own rehashed metaphysical sympathies are trigger, not by the Bushman's own way of life, but instead by the films ability to convert this lost sense of spirituality into a modern form (i.e. film). Thus, the Bushman is commodified in this sense because the ethnographic intent of the film revolves around the Bushman as the object, rather than the subject of cultural inquiry.

13

Other Forms of Dances

SWING

History

Swing dancing began during the Harlem Renaissance, a period of great cultural and intellectual achievement among African Americans in the 1920s and 1930s. The dances were generally performed to jazz music, another burgeoning art form of the time period. The Savoy Ballroom in Harlem was the birthplace of the Lindy Hop. In a sense the dance was the African American response to European social dances. However, while Latin American dances grew from a mix of Spanish colonial forms and African beats, swing was more like a mockery of Europe's sedate waltzes. Sure, the dance was performed with a partner, but the wild movements were a mix of tap, Charleston and free-form expression created as the inspiration struck. This improvisation had its roots in Africa. However, dancing with a partner was a foreign concept in African dance forms, so that is the enduring contribution of European dances to swing.

Swing dancing moved beyond the black community in the 1930s. It was viewed unfavorably by dance teachers, but they couldn't contain what was happening in local clubs. As swing dancing's fame grew and it spread across the United States, regional styles arose during the 40s and 50s.

Eventual variations of swing dancing included the original Lindy Hop, Balboa, Collegiate Shag, Carolina Shag, East Coast Swing and West Coast Swing. East Coast Swing is considered an American competitive ballroom dance and other styles of swing dance are sometimes noted as ballroom dances. Although each of these styles has its own distinctive steps, one of the hallmarks of the dance remains improvisation and free-spiritedness.

Despite being decades past the style's heyday, it still enjoys a resurgence from time to time. Even when the dance isn't currently in favor with trendsetters, college groups and swing dance nights at hipster clubs keep the spirit alive. While some dancers enjoy performing to nostalgic songs, you can find people swinging to everything from country to hip-hop. Modern dancers maintain many of the classic movements, but because of the form's openness to new ideas, you never know what innovative combination you might see on the dance floor.

Modern dancers enjoy both social dancing and performance. In addition to official DanceSport competitive dancing, local organizations also plan performances and competitions. Social dancing usually results in more restrained movements to prevent injury to themselves or other dancers. It may also be more repetitive as there isn't a need to pack a lot of moves in a short period of time. Dancers are more likely to do whatever feels most comfortable with the music, even if it means performing the same spin or pass multiple times.

WALTZ

History

The peasants of Bavaria, Tyrol, and Styria began dancing a dance called Walzer, a dance for couples, around 1750. LANDLER, also known as the Schleifer, a country dance in ¾ time, was popular in Bohemia, Austria, and Bavaria, and spread from the countryside to the suburbs of the city. While the eighteenth century upper classes continued to dance the minuet, bored noblemen slipped away to the balls of their servants.

Describing life in Vienna (dated at either 1776 or 1786), Don Curzio wrote, " The people were dancing mad [...] The ladies of Vienna are particularly celebrated for their grace and movements of waltzing of which they never tire." There is a waltz in the second act finale of the opera "Una Cosa Rara" written by Martin y Solar in 1786. Solar's waltz was marked Andante con moto, or "at a walking pace with motion", but the flow of the dance was sped-up in Vienna leading to the Geschwindwalzer, and the Galloppwalzer

In the transition from country to town, the hopping of the Ländler, a the dance known as Langaus, became a sliding step, and gliding rotation replaced stamping rotation.

In the 19th century the word primarily indicated that the dance was a turning one; one would "waltz" in the "Polka" to indicate rotating rather than going straight forward without turning.

The Viennese custom is to slightly anticipate the second beat, which conveys a faster, lighter rhythm, and also breaks of the phrase. The younger Strauss would sometimes break up the one-two-three of the melody with a one-two pattern in the accompaniment along with other rhythms, maintaining the ¾ time while causing the dancers to dance a two-step waltz. The metronome speed for a full bar varies between 60 and 70, with the waltzes of the first Strauss often played faster than those of his sons.

Shocking many when it was first introduced, the waltz became fashionable in Vienna around the 1780s, spreading to many other countries in the years to follow. It became fashionable in Regency period. The waltz, and especially its closed position, became the example for the creation of many other ballroom dances. Subsequently, new types of waltz have developed, including many folk and several ballroom dances.

FOXTROT

History

According to legend, he was unable to find single female dancer capable of performing the more difficult two-step. As a result, he added stagger steps (two trots), creating the basic Foxtrot rhythm of slow-slow-quick-quick. The dance was premiered in 1914, quickly catching the eye of the talented husband and wife duo Vernon and Irene castle who lent the dance its signature grace and style.

"Get Together; Fox trot", however, had been published in 1905.

W.C. Handy ("Father of the Blues") notes in his autobiography that Noble Sissle told a story that Handy's Memphis Blues was the inspiration for the Fox Trot., Jim Europe, the Castle's music director, would play slowly the Memphis Blues during breaks from the fast paced Castle Walk and One-step. The Castles were intrigued by the rhythm and Jim asked why they didn't create a slow dance to go with it. The Castles introduced the "Bunny Hug" in a magazine article. They went abroad and in mid-ocean sent a wireless to the magazine to change the "Bunny Hug" to the "Foxtrot

It was later standardized by Arthur Murray, in whose version it began to imitate the positions of Tango.

At its inception, the Foxtrot was originally danced to rag time. Today, the dance is customarily accompanied by the same Big band music to swing dance is also danced.

From the late teens through the 1940s, the foxtrot was certainly the most popular fast dance and the vast majority of records issued during these years were foxtrots. The waltz and tango, while popular, never overtook the foxtrot. (Even the popularity of the lindy hiphop in the 1940s didn't dent the foxtrot because the foxtrot could be danced to those lindy hop records, as well.)

When rock and roll first emerged in the early 1950s, record companies were uncertain as to what style of dance would be most applicable to the music. Famously, Decca records initially labeled its rock and roll releases as "Fox trots", most notably "Rock around the clock" by Bill Haley and His Comets. Since that recording, by some estimates, went on to sell more than 25 million copies, "Rock Around the Clock" is technically the biggest-selling "Foxtrot" of all time.

Over time, Foxtrot split into slow (Foxtrot) and quick (quickstep) versions. In the slow category, further distinctions exist between the International or English style of foxtrot and the continuity American style, both built around a slow-quick-quick rhythm at the slowest tempo, and the social American style using a slow-slow-quick-quick rhythm at a somewhat faster pace.

Basic step

The fox trot basic or "magic step." He steps forward, forward, side, close. The timing is slow, slow, quick, quick.

The woman's steps in the fox trot basic.

CHA-CHA

History

The dance teacher Pierre Zurcher Margolie ('Monsieur Pierre', who partnered with Doris_Lavelle) from London visited Cuba in 1952 to find out how and what Cubans were dancing at the time. He noted that this new dance had a split 4th beat, and to dance it one started on the second beat, not the first. He brought this dance idea to England and eventually created what is known now as Ballroom dance cha-

cha-cha. The validity of his analysis is well established for that time, and some forms of evidence exist today. First, there is in existence film of Orquesta Jorrin playing to a cha-cha-cha dance contest in Cuba; second, the rhythm of the Benny More classic Santa Isabel de las Lajas written and recorded at about the same time is quite clearly synchopated on the fourth beat. Also, note that the slower bolero-son ("rumba") was always danced on the second beat.

TANGO

History

American style tango's evolutionary path is derived from Argentina to U.S., when it was popularized by silent film star Rudolph_Valentino in1921, who demonstrated a highly stylized form of Argentine tango "The Four Horsemen of the Apocalypse (film)". As a result, the Hollywood style steps mixed in with other social dance steps of the times began this branch away from the Argentine style. Meanwhile, the tango was also making its own inroads into Europe.

Following the English standardization of their version of Tango, Arthur Murray, a ballroom dance instructor in the U.S., tried his own hand at standardizing the ballroom dances for instruction in his chain of social dance schools. Consequently, his tango syllabus incorporated steps with Argentine, Hollywood and socially popular influences and techniques. This looser social style was referred to as American style by the English.

Argentine tango made its way to Europe and gained popularity particularly in Paris. As the European dancers enjoyed the music and passion of the dance, they began to inject their own culture, style and technique. In an effort to teach a standardized version of the tango, the English eventually codified their own version of tango for instruction in dance schools and for performance in competitions in 1922. The resulting style was referred to as English style, but eventually took on the name International style, as this became the competitive ballroom version practiced around the world.

Eventually, championships in the international style tango were organized all over Europe with numerous participating countries. Adjudicators were able to judge against a standardized syllabus and book of techniques, thereby creating a more objective means of picking the champions, even though artistic interpretation remains an important element of competition.

Initially, the English dominated the International style tango, but eventually, technicians from other backgrounds, most notably the Italians, have chipped away at the English standard and created a dynamic style that continues to raise the competitive bar.

L.A. WALKS DANCE

History

It originally came from Texas, U.S.A. it uses country dance steps with its style using forward, backward, sideward right and left. L. A. walk attained its popularity among ballroom enthusiast because a partner is not needed.

LA CRUMBA

History

It originally came from Cuba. It uses quick steps that everyone can dance. LA Crumba attained its popularity along with other ballroom dances like salsa, samba, rumba, mambo, jive, and quick step.

BOOGIE

History

It is a jazz piano style characterized by sustained rolling eight beats to the bar off in the hand, a fast rhythmically intense version of blues guitar. It was played as dance, music in honky-tonks or as entertainment given by apartment tenants. The style did not reach wide popularity until the mid-1930 when it was promoted by the jazz record producer, John Hammond, after hearing a recording of"Honky Tonk Train Blues"/ he sought out its composer, Mead Lux Lewis, who was working in a Chicago car wash. Lewis made many records for Hammond as Pine Smith an Ammons did. They formed a boogie-woogie trio and played in Carnegie Hall at the height of the craze of the late 1930.

QUICK STEP

History

The Quickstep evolved in the 1920s from a combination of the Foxtrot, Charleston, Shag, Peabody, and One step. This dance is English in origin and was standardized in 1927. The Quickstep now is quite separate from the Foxtrot. Unlike the modern

Foxtrot, the man often closes his feet, and Syncopated step are regular occurrences as was the case in early Foxtrot. In some ways, the dance patterns are close to the waltz, but are danced to 4/4 time rather than 3/4 time.

This dance gradually evolved into a very dynamic one with a lot of movement on the dance floor, with many advanced patterns including hops, runs, quick steps with a lot of momentum, and rotation. The tempo of Quickstep dance is rather brisk as it was developed to ragtime era jazz music which is very fast paced compared to other dance music.

By the end of the 20th century the speed of Quickstep as done by advanced dancers has increased even more, due to the extensive use of steps eight note durations. While in older times quickstep patterns were counted with "quick" (one beat) and "slow" (two beats) steps, many advanced patterns today are cued with split beats, such as "quick-and-quick-and-quick-quick-slow".

Man's steps

Step1. Stand in closed dance position on your left foot with your right foot free, facing back to diagonal center.

Step2. Count one, two (say "slow"--two beats); rotate slightly to the left and take a step back onto your right foot, knee bent.

Step3. Count three (say "quick"--one beat); step to the side on the ball of your left foot.

Step4. Count four (say "quick"); bring your right foot to your left and change weight to the ball of your right foot. Both legs should be fairly straight, with the knees slightly flexed. At this point, you should be facing the wall.

Step5. Count five, six (say "slow"); step forward and slightly to the side on your left foot, stepping on the ball of the foot and then sinking softly onto the heel with a bent knee. Keep your left side forward so you end up in outside partner position. You should now be moving diagonal wall.

Woman's steps

Step1. Stand in closed dance position on your left foot with your right foot free.

Step2. Count one, two (say "slow"--two beats); rotate slightly to the left and take a step forward onto your left foot, heel first and then roll onto the ball of the foot, knee bent.

Step3. Count three (say "quick"--one beat); step to the side on the ball of your right foot.

Step4. Count four (say "quick"); bring your left foot to your right and shift your weight to the ball of your left foot. Both legs should be fairly straight, with the knees slightly flexed.

Step5. Count five, six (say "slow"); step back and slightly to the side on your right foot. Step on the ball of the foot and then sink softly onto the heel with a bent knee.

SAMBA

History

The Samba, the national dance of Brazil, made its debut in the U.S. in the early 1940's. The most important distinguishing characteristic of the Samba is its vertical bouncing action. As in the other Latin dances, ball steps are taken along with knee action and body sway. The basic rhythm is "slow-a-slow" or "one-a-two."

Basic steps

Man's Part

Step1. Begin with the closed dance frame.

Step2. Bend your right knee and step forward on your left foot on count 1.

Step3. Pause on count 2.

Step4 .Bend your left knee and step forward and to the right with your right foot on count 3.

Step5. Bring your left foot next to your right foot on count 4 and bend your right knee as you transfer your weight to your left foot.

Step6. Repeat Steps 2 through 5, this time stepping back on your right foot and to the left with your left foot.

Woman's Part

Step1. Begin with the closed dance frame.

Step2. Bend your left knee and step back on your right foot on count 1.

Step3. Pause on count 2.

Step4. Bend your right knee and step back and to the left with your left foot on count 3.

Step5. Bring your right foot next to your left on count 4 and bend your left knee as you transfer your weight to your right foot.

Step6. Repeat Steps 2 through 5, this time stepping forward on your left foot and to the right with your right foot

PASO DOBLE ("TWO STEP") (SOUTH FRANCE)

History

Originating in South France, the Paso Doble is mostly a competitive Latin style dance, but it is sometimes danced at social events in Germany, Spain and France. Similar to International Standard footwork, the footwork in Paso Doble is composed of forward steps with the heel leads. Paso Doble has less hip action than other International Latin dances. Paso Doble uses music that is played at bullfights. The man plays the role of the matador while the lady plays the role of the matador's cape, the bull or a flamenco dancer.

Basic steps

Lead Steps to the Basic

With the dancers in a rigid and closed dance frame, lead's left hand clasping the follow's right held out from the body, and his right hand at her back, her left hand held at his bicep, the dancers need to keep a rigid and close hold throughout the steps.

The lead begins facing line of dance and steps forward with the left, letting the body rotate to the center of the dance floor as the right foot steps ahead. Remaining on the balls of the feet, beats 3-8 are stepped in a chasse.

The next eight beats begin with one of the "cape" moves, as the man takes three steps in a tight, counterclockwise circle, finishing off the last beats with side steps back against the line of dance.

All of these moves should be sharp and quick, with the chest and head held up and out epitomizing "pride and dignity."

Follow Steps to the Basic

The follow basically mirrors the steps of the lead, moving backwards in the tight circle, using the motion to lend the impression of a flowing cape to the traditionally long skirts worn by the woman for the paso doble. The dance is very intensely connecting between the two, with eye contact and physical contact lending an urgent tension between the two dancers.

RUMBA (AFRICA / CUBA)

History

Not only is the Rumba the most popular Latin slow dance in America, it is also the #1 dance chosen by wedding couples. In addition, Rumba is the foundational dance of all the other Latin and American Rhythm dances. Cuban action (which makes Latin dances look Latin) is an important characteristic of this dance. The basic rhythm of the Rumba box is "slow-quick-quick." The list of Latin dances from slow to fast is: Bolero, Rumba, Cha Cha, Mambo and lastly Jive.

Rumba footwork consists of smooth toe-heel staccato action. This footwork along with Cuban motion, gives Rumba its characteristic hip moving action. The Cuban action develops naturally from alternately bending and straightening the knees. Posture in Rumba is more forward toward your partner than it is in the ballroom dances. In addition, strong Latin arm styling will give your Rumba a fantastic Latin flare.

Basic Steps

Step1: Stand up straight, take a deep breath, and face your partner. If you are a woman, hold up your right hand, and put your left hand lightly on the man's right shoulder.If you are a man, grasp the woman's hand lightly in your left hand, and put your right hand at the small of her back, above the waist.

Step2: Dance quickly. Rumba is danced in quick, light steps with movement across the dance floor and tight turns. Its basic step is in the shape of a box, done half at a time, and counted slow-quick-quick, slow-quick-quick. If you are a woman, start your basic rumba box step by picking up your right foot and moving it back only about four inches. Put your weight on your right foot. This is your first slow step.Pick up your left foot, pull it back to meet your right foot and then move it to your left about four inches. Put it down on the dance floor and shift your weight to it. Bring your right foot to meet your left foot. Those were your next quick-quick steps.

Step3: Start your basic rumba box step by picking up your left foot and moving it forward about four inches if you are the man. Put your weight on your left foot.

This is your first slow step.Pick up your right foot, and push it forward to meet your left foot and then move it to your right about four inches. Put it down on the dance floor and and shift your weight to it. Bring your left foot to meet your right foot. Those were your quick-quick steps.

Step4 : Start to complete your first box step in rumba by stepping forward about four inches with your left foot if you are the woman. This is your first slow step.Pick up your right foot, push it forward to meet your left foot and then move it to your right about four inches. Put it down on the dance floor and shift your weight to it. Bring your left foot to meet your right foot. Those were the second set of quick-quick steps to complete your rumba box.If you are a man, pick up your right foot and move it back about four inches. Put your weight on your right foot. This is your slow step to complete your basic rumba box. Pick up your left foot, pull it back to meet your right foot and then move it to your left about four inches. Put it down on the dance floor and shift your weight to it. Bring your right foot to your left foot. Those were the second set of quick-quick steps to complete your basic rumba box.

Step5: Sway those hips! Remember, each time you take a sideways step, sway your hips just like a very fast pendulum. The more you can put your weight forward on your toes, and dance in a light, choppy fashion, the easier the hip movement will be, and the more expressive the dance will be to onlookers.

14

Indian Dance & Drama: An Introduction

OVERVIEW

In the study of Natya Shastra, the most ancient and one of the world's greatest treatises on theatre, the renowned scholar, Pramod Kale interpretes Bharat Muni's idea of Drama (Natya), as:

Natya is the presentation of the essence and state of all the three worlds. . .There is no knowledge, no craft, no learning, no art, no yoga, no activity which can not find in Natya. (Kale, 1974: 2).

This concept has been the backbone of Indian life and Theatre right from the ancient times. It was so the center of all artistic activities and a popular medium of the concerts and entertainment of the elite as well as of the common masses of the country. The tradition continues even to this day. It is obvious that an Indian author, who is supposedly religious by nature, as majority of the Indians are, has a strong influence, and understanding of her culture and tradition learnt from the epics, myths, legends and folklore of his native land. Most of these writers have framed their literary work in style, themes, and presentations based on this rich traditional heritage. This tendency seems more prominent in poetry, in general, and drama, in particular.

Indians have a rich dramatic tradition dating back to pre-Vedic times. During the classical period, the language of the theatre was mostly Sanskrit. That was later replaced by the vernacular in modern times. But the Indians began writing plays in

English only in the first half of the nineteenth century after the establishment of the British rule in the country. However, it has been an often discussed topic by the students, scholars and intellectuals in the field of drama that this branch of literature in India could not flourish and enjoy the mass popularity as much as that of the vernacular dramatic literature or the Indo-Anglican poetry and novel. It is said that the dramatic output has not been on par with these branches. That may be the issue worth debating since we find very few names of repute in the entire history of Indian English drama who have a serious contribution to make. The situation looks even grimmer when the critics, as eminent as K.R. Srinivasa Iyengar, declare the Indian English theatre virtually a non-existent entity in the Indian literary horizon. The renowned critic puts it in his famous remark as:

Modern Indian dramatic writing in English is neither rich in quantity nor, on the whole, of high quality. Enterprising Indians have for nearly a century occasionally attempted drama in English - but seldom for actual stage production (Iyengar, 1995: 226).

Similarly, the research in this branch also appears inadequate as compared to the Indian English poetry and novel. Furthermore, not much critical attention has been paid to study the cultural, historical, mythical, legendary, and folklore themes employed by the Indian English dramatists, so far. Some well known and a few lesser-known Indian playwrights have explored this heritage for their dramatic subjects to bring to light the contemporary problems faced by the common man and kept the Indian theatre alive and vibrant. Rabindranath Tagore, Sri Aurobindo, Girish Karnad, T.P. Kailasam, Asif Currimbhoy, Badal Sircar and Uma Parameswaran are the pioneers in this field.

They have probed this rich cultural heritage of the Indian civilization to highlight some or the other contemporary issue of the modern day Indians. It is often said that the culture, tradition, history, myths, legends, folklore, literature, art and other performing arts of a country do have some relevance to the country's social, philosophical, intellectual and political make-up and her progress even in modern days. Their exploration, the study of their sources, the classification of the myths, their thematic use in dramas to highlight the contemporary social and individual problems and their present day significance for the people of the country, have not so far been done thoroughly. Present research work is a simple attempt to focus on these issues.

Enormous research is going on in the field of myths, legends, and folklore all over the world ever since the publication of British anthropologist, Sir James Frazer's The

Golden Bough in the early nineteenth century. India is the source and also the storehouse of numerous myths since antiquity. In fact, as Laxmi Lal says: "The Indian is myth-born and myth fed" (Lal Laxmi xi). She further points out:

Myth, legend and folklore have also been a prime cultural and educational tool in India. Our fine and performing arts, whether of street, village, court or temple, throughout the country draw heavily upon them. They form a common resource pool for this vast nation with its maddening diversity. They gather this diversity and lead it to some sort of unity. As far as India goes, sufficient unto eternity is the myth thereof. Our story-hoard is truly inexhaustible. Illiteracy in India has not been quite the disaster it might have been because the village story-teller and all our arts, our rituals and our festivals have spread wide the wisdom encapsulated in our myths. (Lal xi).

Thus, the general outlook of the Indians and their thoughts, have always been dominated by these myths, legends, folklore, history, and epics. It is a land of idolatry, iconography, hero worship, diverse culture, and religions, a host of festivals, numerous rituals, and superstitions, numerous castes, creed, and languages. Because of the very strong cultural bond, religious hold and superstitious attitude, they create myths, legends and folklore out of virtually any unknown and strange thing, happening or of any new ritual they come across.

Due to their tolerant and submissive nature, innate mortal fear, religious awe, cultural compulsions, superstitious mentality, beliefs in supernatural, impact of social and familial taboos and also due to the caste, creed, regional, and sex discriminations most of the Indians feel insecure in their day to day lives. And these very things make them uneasy and psychologically dependent on unreal fantasies for mental support. Out of these religious, social and mental needs evolve certain myths, folktales and rituals which most of the Indians follow involuntarily in their day to day lives. Because of the innate story-telling nature, they feel the urge to narrate them to others like newly framed stories.

In such a situation, anything extraordinarily done in their society becomes a myth or a new folktale and any doer of above than ordinary exploits becomes legendary, heroic and historical. Many Indian English dramatists have deftly exploited such myths, legends, folklore, historical personalities and unusual events found in the Indian society to present, symbolically, the contemporary social predicament of the modern man. The present research thematically analyses these myths, legends and folklore used by these dramatists in their plays to highlight the contemporary issues or problems faced by the common Indians. It is thought that these issues evolve out of the personal, social and religious needs of the individual and his society. Myths, legends and folklore of a culture, too, are born out of such needs. So the study of their religious views, their social approaches to the beliefs of religion and their psychology gains significance in such kind of research.

Therefore, the present research concentrates on these myths, legends and folklore from psychological point of view of the dramatized characters found in the English plays by T.P. Kailasm, Asif Currimbhoy, Badal Sircar and Uma Parameswaran, in general, and Rabindranath Tagore, Sri Aurobindo and Girish Karnad, in particular. The textual, historical, sociological, and archetypal approaches as per the need of the individual themes of the plays have also been taken into consideration for the thematic analysis of their dramas in this thesis.

This research work is planned in six chapters. In the first chapter entitled "Indian Drama: An Introduction", the study traces the origin and the history of Indian theatre since ancient times in order to explore the influence of ancient dramatic traditions and the thematic use of myths, legends and folklore on the contemporary playwrights. In addition, these technical terms and their influence on the Indian Literature are discussed in detail.

The second chapter entitled, "Indian English Drama: The Epics Revisited", highlights the thematic use of the myths and legends from the two Indian epics by the world-renowned Indian English dramatists. These critically acclaimed playwrights, e.g., T.P. Kailasam, Asif Currimbhoy, Badal Sircar and Uma Parameswaran, who have used in their dramas the myths and legends specifically from the epics and whose plays are thought to be the landmarks in the development of the Indian English theatre, have been thematically studied in this chapter. From the third chapter onwards, the research work concentrates specifically on the renowned dramas in English by Tagore, Aurobindo and Karnad.

The entire dramatic literature of these playwrights carries high resonance of nativistic strains. Their commitment to socio-cultural, religious and political aspects of Indian society has provided remarkable impetus to other playwrights writing in English and in other languages also. They form the bulk of English dramatic writings in India today. In addition, most of their plays are based on the mythical themes. This research so focuses its study on these three literary giants individually in third, fourth and fifth chapter, respectively, to explore their thematic use of myths, legends and folklore in their plays. These chapters are entitled as - "Rabindranath Tagore: the Myth Maker", "Sri Aurobindo: the Mystic Legend", and "Girish Karnad: the Folk Artist".

The research then concludes with the sixth chapter entitled, "Conclusion", followed by the "Classified Bibliography" of the works cited and refered in the thesis.

INDIAN THEATRE - A MYTHICAL PAST

Drama is a performing art. As Marjorie Boulton, the renowned drama scholar, in her book, The Anatomy of Drama, comments: "A play is not really a piece of literature for reading. A true play is three dimensional; it is literature that walks and talks before our eyes" (Boulton 3). Besides other necessities, it requires primarily a script, actors and a stage before an audience to play the scenes. It is more pleasing to the human senses to watch live the performance of the actors on the stage than to read or hear their words.

That's why, compared with other forms of literature, viz., poetry and fiction, it is more difficult to produce. It is this difficult art which infatuated the Indians since time immemorial that resulted in a world class theatre on par with the theatres of the world. This theatre in India has a history of about five thousand years. It is one of the oldest art forms as old as the Indian music and dance. The Indians all over are known as highly religious, passionate, melodramatic and expressive. They have a long history of expressing their religious sentiments and social discontents through drama mode. In this regard, the renowned critic, C.D. Narasimhaiah's quote, in one of his edited journals, The Literary Criterion, is quite appropriate to this age-old theatre when he says ". . . in a country where religion has been the breath of our nostrils, it is love of play that gave a start to the Theatre" (Narasimhaiah, 1993: 2).

This start of the theatre had its roots in the oral narrations and public recitations of the Indian epics, the Ramayana and Mahabharata. These performances were always religious in content. Such narrations were then followed by the flowering of Classical Sanskrit theatre of the ancient and medieval times. This theatre actually influenced the modern Indian drama in all languages including English. Hence, it would not be inappropriate to shed further light on the Classical Sanskrit theatre even when this research focuses only on the Indian plays available in English.

The theatre in India, as conjectured by many scholars and critics, started in ancient times as a narrative form centuries before the rules of the Natya Shastra were established. There are several theories in scholarly discussions today that point out to this antiquity of the Indian Theatre, of when and how the plays were supposed to have been first written and staged in India. Here are a few opinions from some of the Indian scholars who have associated the beginnings of the Indian dramatic scenario with that of the country's religion, the rituals and also of the myths and legends, gods and goddesses, devils and demons, and above all, of the ancient Indian scriptures - the Vedas.

The eminent Indian English playwright of the present generation, Girish Karnad, referring to the Natya Shastra throws light upon such a beginning of the Indian theatre in his famous World Theatre Day Message delivered through International Theatre Institute of the UNESCO, Paris, on March 27, 2002, and also in the post script notes of his play, The Fire and the Rain (1998, 70-75). In this message, he says:

The Natyasastra is one of the world's earliest treatises on theatre. It dates back to at least the third century B.C. and its first chapter tells the story of the Birth of Drama. It was a time when the world was sunk in moral turpitude. People had become slaves to irrational passions. A new means had to be found ("pleasing to the eyes and ears as well as edifying") which could uplift humanity. So Brahma, the Creator, combined elements from the four Vedas (sacred texts) to form a fifth text, the Veda of Performance. But since the gods are not capable of the discipline of drama, the new Veda was passed on to Bharata, a human being. And Bharata, with the help of his hundred sons, and some celestial dancers sent by Brahma, staged the first play. The gods enthusiastically contributed to the enhancement of the expressive possibilities of the new art. The play Bharata presented dealt with the history of the conflict between the gods and the demons, and celebrated the ultimate victory of the gods. The production delighted the gods and the humans. But the demons in the audience were deeply offended. They therefore used their supernatural powers and disrupted the performance by paralyzing the speech, movements and memory of the actors. The gods in turn attacked the demons and killed many of them. Mayhem ensued. So Brahma, the Creator, approached the demons and spoke to them. Drama, he explained, is the representation of the state of the three worlds. It incorporates the ethical goals of life - the spiritual, the secular and the sensuous--its joys and sorrows. There is no wisdom, no art, no emotion which is not found in it. He then asked Bharata to proceed with the performance. We are not told if the second performance was any more of a success. (Karnad.).

Thus, the renowned Indian English playwright gives his own mythical version of how the Indian drama was initiated in its early stages. We have to note that he cited the religio-mythical interpretation of the origin of the Indian drama in ancient times. It is a known fact that an Indian - whether an artist or a layman - is a thoroughly religious and culturally bound person. There always is a strong influence of the traditional Hindu culture on his mind which forces him and his actions to think in terms of religion and carve myth out of virtually anything that he comes across. Karnad here renders his true upbringing as a religious Indian by quoting the aforementioned religio-mythical account of the beginning of the history of the Indian drama. May be that is the reason almost all of his plays are based on religio-mythical themes.

Similarly, the noted Indian Theatre Scholar, E. P. Horrwitz, theorizes about the origin of Indian Drama in the following manner:

In the beginning was the Veda, and divine races peopled the earth . . . The five organs of sense were evolved in order that gods and mortals might quench their thirst for worldly pleasures. Indra, delegated by the other gods, approached the throne of the Godhead, and said: "O Brahma, we wish to feast our eyes and ears on a dramatic spectacle; deign to create the merry play for our enjoyment." And the Creator nodded graciously, and fell into a profound meditation. And out of the Divine Thought sprang the NATYA VEDA, that is, the Veda of the Theatre. Such was the Will of the Lord who made the fifth Veda, drawing the quintessence of the drama out of the four Vedas--dance from the Rig, song from the Sâma, mimicry from Yajur, and passion from Atharva. Brahma then summoned Vishwakarma, celestial architect, that he might build a stage in Indra's heaven. The sage Bharata was appointed as theatrical manager and as conductor of the heavenly performances. (Horrwitz 19-31).

Such is supposed to be the mythical account of the origin of the Indian theatre. Even a Western scholar of drama thinks in terms of the religious influence on the Indian culture in his critical estimate of the Indian dramatic scene. Naturally, an inborn Indian thinker or writer would utilize his cultural upbringing through his dramatic creations or critical introspections and produce dramas based on the myths, legends, folklore and historical events of the country. That has resulted in a rich harvest of Indian plays in all languages influenced by this culture. Many are based on mythical responses of the country.

Furthermore, the renowned theatre scholar, M. L. Varadpande, in his thoroughly researched book, Traditions of Indian Theatre, sheds light in scientific manner over the origin of the Theatre in India. In this book, he reflects:

The antiquity of the Indian Theatrical arts is not merely a matter of conjecture but a logical deduction from available data. We get its first glimpses in the form of dancing figures drawn on the walls of prehistoric caves by the early habitants of the ancient land. The primordial dance- drama with ritualistic overtones - performed to ensure success in a hunt or a war - is still a part of indigenous tribal culture. The great Indus civilization was not without its share of dramatic entertainment. The existence of terracotta animal and human figurines with detachable limbs controlled by strings is indicative of puppet plays. And there are masks and dancing statuettes unearthed by the archeologist's spade along with a seal with a harp engraved on it. (Varadpande 3-6).

Thus, all these conjectures and hypothesises give us an idea that the Indian Theatre has a long history of millenia. It so started in ancient times with the recitation of the religious tales at homes or in the places of public worships. On the occasions of certain religious festivities and rituals, these tales were sung to the accompaniment of music and dances. These elements later got incorporated in the theatrical performances on stage. Thus, singing and dancing, too, along with the religious themes became integral elements of the Indian theatre. That could be the reason for the songs and dance sequences found in many an Indian play even today. Similarly, the epics, the Ramayana and the Mahabharata, have played a great role in shaping the Indian theatre. The public recitations of these epics on raised platforms in those days paved the way for the later dramatic activities of the country, as pointed out earlier. Therefore, these epics can be considered as first plays that originated in India in ancient times. They have provided the inspiration to the earliest Indian dramatists of the country which continues even today. The noted theatre critic Suresh Awasthi's comments in this regard are quite appropriate when he says:

The post-Vedic literary period marks an important phase in the making of Indian drama. The epics Ramayana and Mahabharata with their dialogues oriented poetic structures, the tradition of recitation by a whole class of reciters, clearly suggest their vital role in the making and development of drama. The epics not ony have enriched Indian performance tradition, they have given the country a distinctive performative culture. (Awasthi 1).

This epic oriented narrative form later gradually took shape and evolved into well structured plays which were, besides the epics, also based on non-epic and social themes. Language of these performances initially was Sanskrit, the language of the elite in those days. Soon the playwrights began to explore more people oriented themes. About this time two thousand and two hundred years ago, the classical Sanskrit theatre was probably established. The first nine centuries of the Christian era was the time from its beginning when this theatre actually flourished. In those days, these dramas were mostly written and performed for the pleasures of the royals, the elites and upper classes of the society and were played in their palaces, courts and even in the houses of the rich. They were out of reach of the common people. Gradually, this monopoly of the elites came to an end with the social and religious reforms in the Indian society by the likes of Budha and Mahavira, and the plays also began to appear in Pali and other vernacular tongues for the entertainment of the general populace. Soon the theatre became a form of entertainment for the common masses, too. Moreover, no new plays in Sanskrit were written nor was there any dramatic genius worth mentioning appeared after about ninth century of the first millenium. Gradually, the Sanskrit Classical tradition faded and gave way later to many more performance oriented, regional narrative forms popularly termed as 'LokNatya' or 'the Peoples' Theatre'. Suresh Awasthi so reflects:

After the breakdown of Sanskrit classical tradition in North India in the 10th century, there was a reflowering of the performance tradition in South India. It was first manifested in Kutiyattam of Kerala, the only surviving performing tradition of Sanskrit drama. (73).

As these forms gradually became popular, the Sanskrit classical traditions declined; but not before yeilding a world class dramatic literature for all the ages to amuse. A host of outstanding dramatists who enriched this tradition emerged to entertain the generations of theatre lovers in the Classical Age. Most famous among them were Bhasa, Kalidasa, Bhavabhuti, and Shudraka, along with the lesser known Bhatta Narayana, Vishakhadutta and Harsha. Their plays were primarily based on the epics, puranas, popular myths, legends and folklore of the time. The classical Sanskrit scholar, Richard P. Goldman, in his research paper entitled, "Myth As Literature in Ancient India: The Saga of Sukracarya And the Demons (MatsyaPurana, 47)", cites in this regard as such: . . . an overwhelming number of literary works in Sanskrit have taken their imagery, characters, and, above all, themes, from epic and Puranic mythology. . . Like their counterparts in Classical Greece and modern Ireland, the poets and dramatists of Ancient India took their inspiration frequently from the epic-mythical traditions of their countries. Thus, it was the mythic figure, whether epic prince, celestial nymph, or the Supreme Lord of the universe, that was considered the fittest subject of poetry and drama. (Goldman.).

Bhasa (2nd century B.C.), "a wizard of words" (Venkatachalam 95), wrote plays that were heavily inspired by the epics, history and well-known legends of his days. His Sanskrit plays, Pratima Natakam, Madhyam Vyayoga, Swapnavasavadatta, Charudatta, etc. are popular even today. One of Sri Aurobindo's plays in English, Vasavadatta, is inspired by Bhasa's Swapnavasavadatta.

However, Kalidasa (1st century B.C.) is arguably ancient India's greatest Sanskrit poet and dramatist. Three famous romantic plays written by him are - Malvikagnimitra, Vikramurvasiya, and Abhigyanshakuntalam. The last was based on a myth from the Mahabharata and is the most famous one. Even today it is performed in many languages in India and abroad. It was the first Sanskrit play translated into English and German by Sir William Jones in 1789. Likewise, Shudraka's Mrichhakatikam is also a popular romance based on ancient history and folktale which captivates the modern Indian audience as it did centuries ago. Another medieval dramatist, Bhavabhuti (7th century A.D.), is said to have written Malati-Madhava, Mahaviracharita and Uttar Ramacharita. Among these three, the last two cover between them, the entire epic of Ramayana. Thus, even in ancient and classical times we find the popular myths, legends and folklore of the period being dramatized by the Indian dramatists. The tradition continues, though to a lesser extent, even today in almost every Indian language including English.

This classical Sanskrit theatre, however, was heavily influenced by the technical rules for the dramatic performances prescribed by the Natya Shastra which is believed to be the earliest dramatic treastise of the world. It is considered as the grammar or the holy book of Indian theatre. The authorship of this book is not yet assertained conclusively. However, in popular opinion, it is supposed to have been composed by Bharat Muni. Its time span has also been placed inconclusively between third century B.C. and A.D. eighth century. It, however, is quite certain that this book and the dramatic treatises it contains have a very strong impact on the composition and staging of the plays in the country ever since the Classical time. This book, in fact, has shaped the Indian theatre as is found today. In almost every respect it follows the rules and regulations laid down by the thirty six chapters of the Natya Shastra. The book not only sheds light on the dramatic art, but also "reveals the state and stage of development in Indian mythology" (Vatsyayana 14) which influenced the Indian theatre since its inception. Since then, the narratives and the dialogues of the plays were insterspersed with dance and music as is instructed in this book. So they became an integral part of the Indian theatre ever since. This tradition also found its way in the popular Indian cinema in modern times.

All the classical dramas and later the modern vernacular plays, usually started with elaborate rituals as advocated by the Natya Shastra. These rituals were mostly religious in their content. Some pre-play ceremonies or 'purva-ranga' of music and dance were performed during such rituals before the start of the actual action of the drama. The 'sutradhar' (drama anchor) then entered with his two assistants and offered puja (prayer and offerings) to the presiding deities of the theatre - Lord Nataraja or Lord Ganesha - to ensure the success of the play. After this, the sutradhar summoned the leading actors and opened the play with a prologue. The play then usually centred on the mythical tale or the romance of the leading protagonists supported by 'vidushaka' (clown). This clown was a noble, good-hearted character but a deliberate fool and a trusted friend of the hero. He was the darling of the theatre going public in those days. He brought amusement and comic relief to the audience almost in the manner of Shakespearean clown. Following the decline of the Sanskrit dramatic tradition around tenth century, these classical conventions of the opening prayer, the song, the sutradhar and the vidushaka were also adopted by the 'LokNatya' (the 'Peoples Theatre') thus showing the influence of the age-old classical conventions even on the modern folk forms. Many a dramatists in English or in vernacular still follow these classical techniques of playwrighting. Hence, even today, influence of the dramatic techniques as advised by the Natya Shastra, is found in the modern Indian plays. After the 15th century, however, the Indian drama activity almost ceased due to foreign invasions. But the tradition continued, and continues to this day, through the 'Loknatya' found in every state of the country from 17th century onwards.

This movement of Loknatya soon spread to all corners of India. Various regions of the country innovated new styles of performance and forms of drama of their own. These are found in the dramatic presentation of Bhand Pather of Kashmir; Wari Liba of Manipur; Ojhapali of Assam; Pala of Orissa; Pal, Gan and Jatra of Bengal; Swang of Haryana and Punjab; Khyal and Gavari of Rajasthan; Ramlila and Nautanki of North India; Pandavani and Maach of Madhya Pradesh; Akhyan and Bhavai of Gujrat; Nachya, Khele, Tamasha and Lawani of Maharashtra; Burrakatha of Andhra Pradesh, Kathakali of Kerala, Yakshagana of Karnataka, Terukuttu of Tamil Nadu; the Puppet shows, etc. These drama forms were performed on temporary platforms in the templeyards on certain festivities or village rituals. All these performaces were and are still heavily influenced by the epics as well as the local myths, legends, and folklore of the corresponding regions. The modern Indian theatre owes its existence to this Lok Natya movement which is still alive and vibrant today in some parts of the country despite the more popular forms of entertainment through t.v. and cinema.

Indian Theatre - The Contemporary Presence

After the exit of the classical theatre, the medieval history of India was devoid of any serious drama activity. Though the dramatic traditions continued through the Lok Natya, no serious stage-play worth to mention was written or performed during this period. Modern theatre activities in India actually began in the mid nineteenth century only after the British consolidated its rule in the country. Along with new scientific inventions, advance warfare and their own system of administration, they also brought the English theatrical traditions to India. The British so opened a theatre named 'Play-House' in Calcutta in 1756. It is said to be the first English theatre in India.

In 1777, 'Calcutta Theatre' was initiated by the British behind the Writers' Building in Calcutta. Shakespear's Hamlet, Richard III, etc. and some other English farcical plays were staged in these theatres. The translated version of Sakuntala by Sir William Jones was also staged in 1789, in the Calcutta Theatre. One Mrs. Bristo, an English drama lover, also established a private theatre in Chourangi in 1789. She produced a play, Poor Soldiers on its stage, and also participated in it as a leading character. It was the first instance of women staging and acting in a play in public theatres in India. Lateron, a Russian musician Lebdef established the Bengal Theatre in Calcutta. He staged a few Bengali plays in English translation such as Disguise and Love is the Best Doctor in 1795 and 1796. The Hindi drama scholar, Dr. Agyat, reports in his book Bharatiya Rangamanch Ka Vivechanatmak Itihas (Hindi) that "Some local Bengali women were reported to have participated as actresses in these plays for the first time in the history of Indian theatre" (Agyat 114).

Further, in the Western region of the country, 'Bombay Theatre' was opened in 1770 at Horniman Circle, out of public contributions. In 1848, 'Royal Theatre' came into existence in the Bombay region. It was established for the Parsi players by the leading public figure of those days, namely, Jagannath Shankar Seth. Slowly, other theatres began to emerge in the western, sourthern as well as in the eastern part of the country to give boost to the Indian dramatic resurgence. Very soon, the Bombay region in the west, Calcutta in the east, and Madras in the south, became the hubbub of the dramatic activities in India. In 1831, Prasankumar Thakur established Hindi Rangmanch in Bombay. In 1843, on the request of the Sangli King, the Marathi playwright Vishnudas Bhave produced Seeta Swayamwar based on the Seeta myth from the Ramayana. In 1880, Annasaheb Kirloskar staged Abhignan Shakuntal by Kalidasa in Marathi. By 1850, the modern theatre activity also began in Bengal, Karnataka and Kerala. From 1858 onwards Gujarati and Urdu plays were staged in many theatres in Mumbai and Gujarat. The Parsis then started their own drama company. Their plays were popularly known as 'Company Natak'. This theatre, besides the innovative use of language, also paid much attention to stage decor and stage specialties. They toured various parts of the country with their drama troups and thus had a lion's share in rejuvenation and popularization of the Indian theatre in modern times. This 'Company Natak' influenced many a dramatist in later times, prominent one among them is Girish Karnad. Their dramas were quite famous in the theatre halls of Karachi, Calcutta and Mumbai. Thus, from 1850 to 1940 there was a great resurgence of theatre in different parts of the country. These theatre groups so had a significant contribution for the development of the Indian Theatre in pre-Independence days. These hundred years can rightly be called the Golden Age of the Indian Theatre in any language.

All these dramatic movements in pre-Independence days concentrated on social problems as well as the ideology of the freedom movement on the stage making it a very powerful medium that made a great impact on the life of the common man. After the country's Independence from the British in 1947, the Professional and Non-Professional Theatre or Amateur Theatre came into existence in the Indian theatrical horizon. Some of the theatre personalities from these groups, such as Badal Sircar, Satyajit Ray, Girish Karnad, Vijay Tendulkar, Habib Tanvir, Mohan Rakesh, etc., brought new ideas, new techniques and new zeal from Europe and America and started producing plays of rare marit in regional languages as well as in English. Thus, the Indian drama in post Independence phase, slowly but surely, began its march towards its past glory by infusing the Western as well as the Indian elements in their plays. The same has continued till date.

Indian English Drama

The Indian theatre so has a rich dramatic tradition in the regional languages. However, it required the dawn of the nineteenth century to begin the dramatic creativity in English by the Indians. With the advent of the British Empire, the English as a language started to take roots in the Indian soil; however, it took almost another century before it could be firmly rooted in the Indian ethos. Until then, the creativity in the Indian English literature, including drama, was quite sporadic. Indians first began composing poems and bits and pieces of prose in English. Later, the English dramatic creativity started to rise in the Indian horizon, slowly, tentatively and in an experimental manner.

The first Indian play written entirely in English was Krishna Mohan Bannerji's The Persecuted or Dramatic Scenes Illustrative of the Present State of Hindoo Society in Calcutta (1831). Soon, Michaele Madhusudan Dutt translated his own Bengali plays into English. His plays are Ratnavali (1858), Sarmista (1859), and Is This Called Civilization? (1871). There was another attempt in English made by Ram Kinoo Dutt through Manipura Tragedy (1893) in those days. However, these plays have little significance, quantitatively or qualitatively, as far as the development of the Indian English Theatre is concerned. The introduction of the play-writing in English by the Indians was, thus, as previously mentioned, "neither rich in quantity nor, on the whole, of hight quality (Iyengar 226). They were initially tentative in dramatizing their creative urge. Even today, they do not seem completely at ease with the playwrighting in English owing to the language hurdle and lack of public support. As a result, we do not see the crop of Indian English plays in abundance in comparision with the vernacular theatre in the country. Still about 300 plays are found in English. Among them, more than fifty are entirely based on the myths, legends and folklore of the country.

Moreover, after the initial lackluster attempts by the Indians to write plays in English, there came a very good coterie of writers who contributed significantly at least to the development of Indian English dramatic literature. Many of them are great playwrights in terms of their dramatic output, in terms of quantity, dramatic quality, their fame in the literary world and their individual contribution in the development of the Indian English drama. Some of them have probed the rich cultural heritage of the country for the thematic use of myths, legends, folklore and historical traditions in their plays. Among these playwrights, Rabindranath Tagore, Sri Aurobindo, T.P.Kailasam, Harindranath Chattopadhyay, A.S.P. Ayyar, Bharati Sarabhai, etc are the chosen few who flowered on the Indian theatrical scene brilliantly in Pre-Independence days. They are followed after Independence by the dramatists of outstanding merit such as Asif Currimbhoy, Bharati Sarabhai, Badal Sircar, Vijay Tendulkar, Habib Tanvir, Girish Karnad, Uma Parameswaran, Mahesh Dattani, Manjula Padmanabhan, etc. All these playwrights are fine craftsmen of their dramatic art. They have tried with the best of their abilities to enrich Indian English drama and to make the English theatre popular. The quantity and quality of their dramatic output are quite praiseworthy. They are now known as pillars of the modern Indian English dramatic world.

Pre - Independence dramatic scenario in Indian English literature is thus the starting phase in the development of the Indian English drama. The Indian dramatists and their plays written during this phase were getting some notice by the outside world. The Post - Independence Indian theatre, however, began to make a noteworthy impact on the critics all around. After the exit of the Englishmen from the political power of the country, the English language and the creativity in that tongue began asserting their influence with more and more charismatic playwrights enriching the

Indian English Theatre. That has forced the drama critics to pay their serious attention towards this neglected area of Indian literature. We find several Indian dramatists of stature creating works in English of no mean a quality than that of the poetry or fiction. Asif Currimbhoy, Gurucharan Das, Partap Sharma, Girish Karnad, Mahesh Dattani, Vijay Tendulkar, Badal Sircar, Habib Tanvir, Manjula Padmanabhan, Uma Parameswaran to say the least, enriched this branch and helped to provide due recognition to the Indian English Theatre in modern times. We also find some changes in this theatre after Independence in thematic pattern, dialogue, technique and, the use of English. Besides, there is resurgence in the use of myths, legends, folklore and history of the country with the rise of these contemporary playwrights. This research work so finds such myths, legends and folklore in the Indian plays available in English - either original, translated or transcreated - in order to search for their origin, types, their contemporary significance and their allegorical dramatization. So, a study of these terms also becomes important to interprete their thematic use by the dramatists. Hence, this chapter further attempt to explain the terminology associated with myths, legends, and folklore.

A Study of Myths

The belief in religion and myths is universal. It is found in many cultures world over. The origin of myths is, however, debatable. Opinions of the scholars in this field are all varied. Ashutosh Bhattacharya, a well-known name in the study of the myths and folklore of Bengal, cites the primitive beliefs in creation as the possible source of origin for the myths. He points out:

> The fact of creation of the universe had puzzled the primitive brain. In an age in which there is no scientific explanation for the mysteries of creation, the human mind tried to solve them in its own unscientific way. (Bhattacharya Asutosh 18).

The result is a fictional account of the individual's imagination which turns such a belief into myths in due course of time. For Northrop Frye, the world-renowned critic, myth is formed out of the 'archetypes' of such a human belief. In his celebrated work, "The Archetypes of Literature", he further throws light on this phenomenon. He reflects:

> In the solar cycle of the day, the seasonal cycle of the year, and the organic cycle of human life, there is a single pattern of significance, out of which myth constructs a central narrative around a figure who is partly the sun, partly vegetative fertility and partly a god or archetypal human being. (Frye, 1972: 429).

Therefore, the mythical world belongs to the world of the divine and human, the world of illusion and reality. The study of this mythical world got impetus in the modern world only after the publication of the renowned anthropologist, Sir James Frazer's fascinating account of myths and magic of different cultures in his celebrated work, The Golden Bough. He believes that myth is a primitive habit of mind. In his opinion, it is almost an addiction of the ancient people to magic which lead to the evolution of ancient religion and myths. In the Preface to the abridged edition (1922) of this book, referring to a primitive belief of an armed priest of the Golden Bow (a sacred tree) to circumambulate the tree continuously for fear of his own death in the hands of a rival priest, Frazer remarks:

I am so far from regarding the reverence for trees as of supreme importance for the evolution of religion that I consider it to have been altogether subordinate to other factors, and in particular to the fear of the human dead, which, on the whole, I believe to have been probably the most powerful force in the making of primitive religion. (Frazer.).

Thus, in Frazer's opinion, myths are formed due to the innate fear of death which led to the primitive religion of man. The fear of religion is not far removed from the primitive beliefs of such powerful but negative influence of death. In fear of their lives, people were led to resort to the religion for psychological support. The myths, therefore, originate in such religious beliefs of man. Because of that, they have been associated with divinity and god's creations. Northrope Frye, endorses this opinion. He remarks:

By a myth . . . I mean primarily a certain type of story. It is a story in which some of the chief characters are gods or other beings larger in power than humanity. Very seldom it is located in history: its action takes place in a world above or prior to ordinary time, in illotempore, in Mircea Ediade's phrase. (Fry, 1974: 163-64).

Myths are, therefore, sacred and always involve a supernatural force or a deity in their content. A noted Indian historian, Nagendra Kr. Singh in his book, Vedic Mythology, expresses similar views. He says that "the basis of these myths is the primitive attitude of mind which regards all nature as an aggregate of animated entities." (1997: 11). Further, in another book, Indian Legends, he explains:

Mythology, in general, may be described as a historical and scientific study of myths and legends; the whole body of divine, heroic and cosmogonic legends comes under its purview . . . Myth in common parlance savours of what is untrue, unreal, all the same it has a hold on man's imagination. There is a certain amount of rational element in it, as, for instance, in the myths relating to the Dawn and the Sun. Sometimes, the irrational element, as in the story of the Creator himself committing incest, renders a myth repugnant. Plato would reject such untrustworthy stories of gods from his ideal State! (Singh, 1997: 11).

Thus, in popular and scholarly opinion, myths are about gods or semi-divine heroes. Myths about the gods are as numerous as the cultures that produce them. These myths, so, are generated by the cultural needs of the people. They authorize the cultural institutions of a tribe, a city or a nation by connecting them with universal truths. That way, "myths are embedded in cultures and can be interpreted in relation to the social structure of a given point of time" (Das, 2005: 85). All cultures, including the Indian, have developed over time their own myths, consisting of narratives of their history, their religions, and their heroes. They are passed from one generation to the next through oral narrations.

However, the word myth connotes several meanings. "Freud's belief that myths are sex-ridden and Jung's assertion that myths are racial archetypes prove the significance of myth in the modern world" (Dixit, 2003: 87). So a myth highlights different aspects of the world around us in various colours. As the Classical scholar, Robert T. Goldman, points out: ". . . it is by no means always clear what a myth is trying to say - in a literal sense" (Goldman.). For the online encyclopaedia, Wikipedia, myth in Greek means 'mythos' (wikipaedia) which "originally meant 'speech' or 'discouse' but which later came to mean 'fable' or 'legend'" (Doyle.). It represents "the retelling of stories that a particular culture believes to be true and that use supernatural events or characters to explain the nature of the universe and humanity" (ibid.). However, not every narrative is a myth unless it is deeply rooted in tradition. The Classics' Scholar, Tyler Lansford, in his web article, Mythology, opines that myth is "a narrative that through many retellings has become an accepted tradition in a society" (Lansford).

In common usage, however, myth means a fictional story which many believe to be based on fact. It is a product of the past and mostly is considered by the modern scientific world as unscientific, superstitious and ritualistic in form. Traditionally it takes birth in the individual's imagination out of his religious beliefs, his fears of the death and the unknown or unsolved mysteries of the cosmic world around him. It also conveys his passions, his sentiments, and his hopes for better future. Through continuous use, it is then rooted in the collective consciousness of the society of which he himself is a part. Nagendra Kr. Singh so elaborates:

From myth spring the epic romance and tragedy. Myth, therefore, touches the deepest desires of man - his fears, his hopes, his passions, his sentiments as it validates the social order, justifies the existing social scheme and ranges from expressions of sheer artistry to legalism. (Singh, 1997: 11).

Although myths are often considered to be accounts of events that have not happened, many historians consider that myths can also be accounts of actual events that have become highly imbued with symbolic meaning, or that have been transformed, shifted in time or place, or even reversed. Webster's New World College Dictionary so points out:

Myth is a traditional story of unknown authorship, ostensibly with a historical basis, but serving usually to explain some phenomenon of nature, the origin of men, or the customs, institutions, religious rites, etc. of a people: myths usually involve the exploits of gods and heroes. (Webster's New World College Dictionary, 2007: 954).

The world literature is full of such tales. These stories express the viewpoints and beliefs of the country, time period, culture and or religion which gave birth to them. One can speak of a Jewish mythology, a Christian mythology, a Hindu mythology or an Islamic mythology, in which one describes the mythic elements within these faiths. Exploits of Greek and Roman gods such as Prometheus, Achilles, Zeus, Hercules, Oedipus, Perseus, Andromeda, Romulus, Remos, stories associated with Moses, Jesus, miracles of saints and prophets all over the world, religious dynamism of Hindu gods like Vishnu, Shiva, Laxmi, Parvati, Durga, Rama, Krishna, etc., fall in the category of myths. These myths express the views of a particular sect or religion and also point out how the religious heroes' exploits benefited the common man. Indian culture is full of such stories from the religion or from the unknown riddles of the past. She has in fact the largest collection of such tales in the world and is considered all over as the storehouse of myths.

Classification of Myths

Myths can be categorized in different types according to the practices by which they are primarily considered by the scholars of mythology and used by the authors for their creative outputs. Some myths however fit in more than one category. Scholars and various encyclopedia all across the globe classify these myths as - Ritual Myths, Origin Myths, Cult Myths, Prestige Myths, Eschatological myths, Creation Myths, Culture Myths, Philosophical Myths, Political Myths, Social Myths, Gender Myths, etc. Some of them are also used by the Indian English dramatists for their themes. These types are further explained below:

Ritual Myths: These myths explain the performance of certain religious practices or patterns in the temples or centers of worship. They are associated with certain primitive ceremonies based on religious beliefs to calm the wrath of gods or to appease them for certain wants. Sacrificial rituals in ancient times involving natural objects and animals in expectations of rains, crops, fortune or begetting of children etc., fall in this category of myths. Rabindranath Tagore has deftly made use of such myths to throw light upon the religious hypocrisy of priests of his days in some of his plays.

Origin Myths: These myths describe the beginnings of customs, names or objects in ancient times.

Cult Myths: These are often seen as explanations for elaborate festivals that magnify the power of the deity. India is a land of festivals. The Indian dramatists hence have used these myths also to critically evaluate the age-old beliefs of cult myths in contemporary times.

Prestige Myths: These are usually associated with a divinely chosen hero, city, or people and their miraculous exploits. Tales associated with Hindu gods and goddesses fall in this category. Sometimes, these tales are also known as 'legends'.

Eschatological Myths: These are stories which describe catastrophic ends to the present world order of the writers. These extend beyond any potential historical scope, and thus can only be described in mythic terms. Such myths relate to or deal with the ultimate destiny of mankind and the world. Apocalyptic literature such as The Revelation of St. John the Divine is an example of a set of eschatological myths. Some myths found in vedic literature and puranas also exemplify eschatological myths.

Culture Myths: Culture Myths are associated with a particular cultural belief where the divinely gifted hero delivers unimaginable things to the needy by performing miraculous deeds. The Greek myth associated with Prometheus, Perseus, etc, and the Hindu myths of Lord Rama, Krishna, Arjuna, etc. fall in the category of Culture Myths. Occasionally, such heroes did these things by cheating or trickery for which they were also punished by the gods. Myth of Prometheus and Karna's learning of Brahma Vidya, the highest art of warfare, from Parashurama by cheating, are examples of such type of myths. This mythical type is a favourite subject for some of the Indian dramatists. T.P. Kailasm has used them extensively in his Kannada and some of the English plays.

Creation Myths: Another notable type of myth is the creation myth, which describes how that culture believes the universe or the objects of the nature such as the planets, fire, rain, seasons, animals and also the birth of man and gods, were created. They are also known as Nature Myths or Cosmic Myths. These myths provide an explanation of the origin of the universe in all its complexity. They are an important part of most mythological systems. These myths often invoke primal gods and animals, titanic struggles between opposing forces or the death and or dismemberment of these gods or animals as the means whereby the universe and its components were created.

Philosophical Myths: Myths dealing with the human cycle of birth, death and rebirth fall into this category. Indians have strong faith in this type of system. Therefore, some of the Indian dramatists have made use of the myths associated with the birth or rebirth of an individual for their dramatic themes.

Political Myths: These myths try to interpret the rights, duties and responsibilities of the king and his subjects. Indian dramatists, especially Tagore, have also used them in their plays extensively to critically evaluate the system of monarchy and its effects on the common masses.

Social Myths: The myths originated from certain social customs, tradition, taboos, prohibitions, etc. are the social myths. Sometimes, they yield to certain fantastic beliefs which can also be called as folktales. Such myths are also dramatized by the Indian playwrights to highlight and criticise the inhuman practices of religion and caste distinctions prevalent in the society. Sri Aurobindo, Tagore and Karnad have dramatized such myths to bring to light the harmful effects they are producing over the Indians in modern times.

Gender Myths: These myths refer to the gender discriminations in a society. They point out to the supremacy of men over women or subjugation of women by the men. Such types of myths are deeply rooted in the male dominated cultures like India and Africa. Sexuality and female chastity are paramount in such cultures because of which women are relegated to the secondary position in their family and society and are subject to suppressions. The Indian myth of 'Agni-Pariksha' by Sita from the Ramayana point out to this type of myth. Girish Karnad has deftly made use of this concept in his renowned play - Naga-Mandala.

All these types of myths have been used by the authors all over the world for their literary creativity. They carry many layers of meaning. Different authors interprete a myth in different ways. Sometimes, a myth can turn into a legend or a legend into a folktale. They have been actually created by human beings for many reasons over thousands of years. Since then, they have become a superb product of humanity collectively and a rich resource for the enjoyment of all mankind.

A Study of Legends

The terms legend, folktale and fables are sometimes used interchangeably with myth. Technically, however, these are not the same. It is rather difficult to distinguish them. Mostly, a legend originates in history. It is a fantastic tale of a heroic person who actually existed in the past but whose exploits are not the authentic records of history. Unlike the folktales, which take place in a make-believe world, legends seem plausible and tell about events which could have taken place in the past. Some people believe in them while others are skeptical. Therefore, legends exist between fact and faith, illusion and reality. They are told in such a manner that it acquires a ring of truth. They, however, provide examples of the virtues of honoured personalities from the history of a nation. Usually, the subject of the legend is a saint, a king, a hero, a famous person, or a war. Nagendra Kr. Singh further elaborates the meaning in his book, Indian Legends, as:

A legend is meant a story which describes an ancient event in which the characters are form, or akin to, mankind and in which the emotions and the experiences, such as those of human beings are described. (Singh, 1997:12).

Similarly, Asutosh Bhattacharya finds the origin of these legends in the history of a particular culture kept alive through oral literature. He thinks that ". . . due to extravagant imagination applied to them by the rural composers the historical elements ultimately became secondary and at times not discernible at all" (Bhattacharya 132). Arthurian legends, Robinhood legends, legends of the Buddha and his disciples, legends of Alexander the Great, legends of Shivaji the Great, etc., are some of the examples of legends which have been kept alive by the folk literature all across the globe.

A Study of Folklore

Foklore is a branch of oral literature with unknown authorship. These are developed out of the practical experiences and superstitions of common folks of a particular culture, subculture or a group. Lack of proper scientific knowledge or intellectual ignorance of the scientific ideas of certain occurrences in nature and unintelligible events of the society lead these people to imagine unimaginable fictitious accounts which they narrate to others with an innate urge to unload the mystery of those occurrences. They are then spread in the society through oral tradition. Over the years, with some changes, these ficitious narrations get deeply rooted in the collective consciousness of the culture and forms part of folklore. Webster's New World Dictionary points out that they are "the unwritten traditional beliefs, legends, sayings, customs etc. of a culture." While folklore can contain religious or mythic elements, it equally concerns itself sometimes with the mundane traditions of everyday life. Such tales are then transmitted from generation to generation through oral forms of literature such as folktale, folk-drama, folk-song, ballads, fairy tales, rhymes and riddles, folk-music, folk-art, folk-magic, dances, proverbs, jokes, etc. All these folk types then become parts of the local folklore.

There is no other part of the literature which contains so many strange ideas and wonderful jests than the folklore. Sometimes, its world is replete with sexuality. The renowned critic, Hans Bertens, comments: ". . . some theorists, following michaele Foucault's lead, even see sexuality as the central principle of social organizations" (Bertens, 2003: 218). Since folklore originates from the society, it is but natural to see the sexual apprehensions of these folks in their narrations also. The world-renowned folklorist, Balwant Gargi, in relation to the sexual aspects in folk-theatre, comments:

THE FOLK theater is impolite, rude, vulgar. It shocks prudes. The secular forms - Tamasha, Nautanki and Naqal - dominating the northern and western parts of India are replete with sexual jokes. It is considered improper for women to watch these plays. In the city of Poona, many professors and intellectuals, champions of culture, refuse to see a folk play because of its "vulgarity". (Gargi.).

It is this aspect of folklore that also finds way in some of Indian plays. The psychological problems associated with such sexuality, especially of the women folk, have been dealt with by Girish Karnad in his play Naga Mandala which is based on two Kannada folktales. Not only the folk narrators but also the playwrights follow such themes in their plays to present the shattered psychological world of Indian women in modern times.

Fable, Folktale, Fairie Tale and Folk-drama, so, belongs to the genre of folklore. A fable is a fictitious narration intended to enforce a useful truth, especially one in which animals or inanimate objects speak and act like human beings. Unlike a folktale, it has a moral that is woven into the story and often explicitly formulated at the end. Traditional stories of Aesop, tales from the Hitopadesha, Panchatantra, etc. are well-known fables well preserved in oral traditions over the years.

Similarly, a folktale is circulated by word of mouth among the common folk with a message that tells the particulars of an act or occurrence or course of events. The noted critic Prema Srinivasan, in her article, "Sudhin Ghose and the Revitalization of Indian Folklore" published in C.D. Narsimhaiah edited Makers of Indian English Literature, calls such tales as the "television of printless society" and remarks that they were "created originally for the amusement of the whole community" (Srinivasan, 2000: 158). She further quotes A.K. Ramanujan from his Folk Tales From India, who "calls the folk tale a poetic text that carries some of its cultural contexts within it" (159). Ramanujan further calls it a 'traveling metaphor' that finds a new meaning with each new telling. "Northrop Frye argues that the simplest manifestations of myths are to be found in folktales" (Das 85). They are, in reality, pure fiction which has no particular location in either time or space. However, despite elements of fantasy, a folktale is actually a symbolic way of presenting the different means by which human beings cope with the world and their problems. The sociologist, Indra Deva, in the essay "The Cultural Level of Unlettered Folk", elaborates:

> The richly developed tradition of folk literature is highly differentiated and relates particular genres to appropriate seasons, social groups, occasions like marriage and birth, rituals, and types of work which they accompany. (Deva 1997: 97).

In this sense, folktales, and also the folk-plays, concern people, either royalty or common folk or animals, who speak and act like people. Stories about the supernatural and magic form the important set of folktales. They tell about specific beings such as giants, dragons, monsters, demons, witches, magicians and humans with powerful and supernatural capabilities. They have a style of their own. They tell a single story without any plot or subplots. It has a standard opening formula - the most common being " 'Once upon a time', 'once there was a king and a queen' or 'There was once a time when all things could speak' ", etc. They also have a standard ending often bringing the audience or the reader back to the real world. They also contain a limited list of stock characters such as a king or a queen, a wise man, a crooked one, etc. One thousand one tales of Arabian Nights, Adventures of Robin Hood, Anderson's tales, tales from the Panchatantra, Jatakas, Kathasaritsagara, etc belong to the genre of folktales which are still popular in the modern world.

Literary Uses

God is a perennial source of inspiration for the artists and writers all over the world since time immemorial. Naturally, mythology has influenced performing arts, literature and theatre everywhere from earliest times. There is a bulk of oral and written literature based on the myths, legends and folklore found in every culture. Apart from cultures in which myth-making is bound up with ritual, myths have provided a wealth of material for the writer and artist since the beginning of recorded history. This relationship of myths with literature is as significant as it is multi-dimensional and complex. Writers all across the globe tend to draw their themes from these readily available sources. The divine characters employed by Valmiki, Vyasa, Homer and Ovid in their epics, became the common property of succeeding generations of poets and dramatists all over. Ovid's Metamorphoses narrates a mythical story of how Zeus fathered Perseus by approaching Danae in a shower of gold. Similar is the myth of Karna and Kunti in Vyasa's Mahabharata where the Sun god impregnated Kunti to father the legendary Karna. Lateron, Greek and Indian poets and playwrights drew upon this traditional body of myths quite effectively to create such human characters in classical times as Agamemnon and Clytemnestra, in Oresteia of Aeschylus, Antigone and Electra of Sophocles and Euripides respectively, and Pururavas and Urvasie in Vikramorvashia of Kalidasa, etc. Milton's Paradise Lost and Sri Aurobindo's Savitri in later times are prime examples of the literary influence of ancient body of myths and legends.

The mythology also provided themes for some of the world's greatest literary giants. Goethe constantly used the classical myths in his drama and poetry. Petrarch and Boccacio, too, made use of classical mythology in their Latin and Italian poems. This mythology also provided legends to the literary giants of the likes of Marlow and Shakespeare, for their poems Hero and Leander and Venus and Adonis, respectively. Similarly, the legend of Troilus and Criseyda find its way in the works of Chaucer and Shakespeare. James Joyce in Ulysses, Thomas Mann in his novel The Transposed Heads, T.S. Eliot and W.B. Yeats in poetry, Shakespear, G.B. Shaw, Anoulh, Eugine O Neill in plays have extensively used the ancient myths, legends and folklore in modern times. Similarly, in India, an overwhelming number of literary works have taken their imagery, characters, and themes from epic and Puranic mythology. Richard Goldman, the scholar of Sanskrit Classics, elaborates this influence on Classical Sanskrit drama, which equally applies to the modern drama as well. He points out:

Like their counterpart in Classical Greece and modern Ireland, the poets and dramatists of Ancient India took their inspiration frequently from the epic-mythical traditions of their countries. Thus, it was the mythic figure, whether epic prince, celestial nymph, or the Supreme Lord of the universe, that was considered the fittest subject of poetry and drama. (Goldman.).

He further explains:

In essence, it is a complex of a number of mythical elements which date back to the Vedic period and various elements of sectarian Hindu myth. The basic situation is the ongoing struggle for rulership of the universe between the Devas, the gods of the Vedic pantheon, and the Asuras (Daityas, Danavas), the demons of Vedic and classical myth. (ibid.).

It is this mythical world which also appears in the plays of Classical Sanskrit dramatists, viz., Bhasa, Bhavabhuti, and Kalidasa and later in the modern playwrights such as Rabindranath Tagore, Sri Aurobindo, T.P. Kailasam, Badal Sircar, Habib Tanvir, Girish Karnad, etc. Their plays, viz., The Purpose, Sacrifice, Chitra, Perseus the Deliverer, Vasavdatta, Evam Indrajit, Charandas Chor, Ghasiram Kotwal, Hayavadana, Naga Mandala, etc. are heavily laden with known and unknown myths, legends and folklore, that shaped the Indian dramatic scenario to a delightful entity.

Bibliography

Abhinaya-Candrika and Odissidance: *Sushma Kulshreshtha and A.C. Sarangi, Eastern Book Linkers,* Delhi 2001

Adavus and Sancharis in Bharatanatyam: *Vidya Bhavani Suresh, Skanda Pub.,* Chennai, 2002

Ang Kavya : Nomenclature for Hand Movements and Feet Positions in Kathak: *Pt. Birju Maharaj, Har-Anand,* New Delhi, 2002

Ashish Khokar's Attendance : The Dance Annual of India: *Shanta Serbjeet Singh, Ekah-Printways,* New Delhi, 2003-04

Bhaava Niroopanna/Kanak Rele: *Nalanda Dance Research Centre,* Mumbai, 1996

Bharatanatyam: *Ashish Mohan Khokar, Rupa & Co.,* New Delhi, 2002

Bharata Natyam : Du Temple a La Scene: *Raghunath Manet, Tala Sruti,* Pondicherry, 1999

Bharatanatyam : How to...: *Jayalakshmi Eshwar., B.R. Pub.,* Delhi, 2002

Chidambaram Home of Nataraja: *Vivek Nanda with George Michell,* New Delhi, 2004

Dance Dialects of India: *Ragini Devi, Motilal Banarsidass,* Delhi, 2002

Dhananjayan on Indian Classical Dance: *V.P. Dhananjayan, B.R. Rhythms,* Delhi, 2004

Kathak Sagar: *Bharti Gupta, Radha Pub.,* New Delhi, 2004

Nangiar Koothu : The Classical Dance-Theatre of the Nangiar-s: *Nirmala Paniker, Natana Kairali,* Trichur, 1992

Rukmini Devi Arundale : Birth Centenary Volume: *Shakuntala Ramani, Kalakshetra Foundation,* Chennai, 2003

Rukmini Devi : Bharata Natya: *Kalakshetra Pub.,* Chennai, 2003

The Science of Bharata Natyam: *Saroja Vaidyanathan, Kanishka,* Delhi, 2000

Staging Resistance Plays by Women in Translation: *Tutun Mukherjee, Oxford University Press,* New Delhi, 2005

Index

I

K

M

N

O

P

R

S

T

U

W

Y

□□□